Adult Survivors of Sexual Abuse

This book is dedicated to Peter Dimock and Jim Struve.

"Imagine waiting thirty years
before finding these two brothers."

Adult Survivors of Sexual Abuse

Treatment Innovations

Mic Hunter
EDITOR

SAGE Publications
International Educational and Professional Publisher
Thousand Oaks   London   New Delhi

For information address:

 SAGE Publications, Inc.
2455 Teller Road
Thousand Oaks, California 91320

SAGE Publications Ltd.
6 Bonhill Street
London EC2A 4PU
United Kingdom

SAGE Publications India Pvt. Ltd.
M-32 Market
Greater Kailash I
New Delhi 110 048 India

Printed in the United States of America

Library of Congress Cataloging-in-Publication Data

Main entry under title:

Adult survivors of sexual abuse: Treatment innovations / edited by
    Mic Hunter.
        p. cm.
    Includes bibliographical references and index.
    ISBN 0-8039-7192-3 (hbk. : acid-free paper). —ISBN 0-8039-7193-1
(pbk. : acid-free paper)
    1. Adult child sexual abuse victims—Rehabilitation.
    2. Psychosexual disorders—Treatment. I. Hunter, Mic.
RC569.5.A28A34   1995
616.85'836906—dc20   94-49383

This book is printed on acid-free paper.

95 96 97 98 99 10 9 8 7 6 5 4 3 2 1

Sage Production Editor: Tricia K. Bennett

Contents

Foreword

There is a growing interest in literature on sexual abuse, to the point that new journals have been created that focus exclusively on topics related to sexual abuse. Yet we still have much to learn about the causes, effects, and treatment of sexual abuse.

As a result of the publication of *Abused Boys: The Neglected Victims of Sexual Abuse,* I have been invited to speak at numerous conferences and workshops. The most rewarding aspect of these experiences has been the men and women that I have met. The contributors to this book are among those who have been most helpful in advancing my understanding of the effects and treatment of sexual abuse. Their thinking has been so useful to me that I wanted to ensure that their thoughts were made available to other therapists. It was this desire that motivated me to invite them to become involved in this project. All of them are clinicians and know the experience of sitting in an office facing another human who has been severely abused. *Child sexual abuse* is not an abstract concept to them, but an all-too-familiar phrase that still causes a visceral response. In their quest to reduce human suffering, they have developed practical and effective methods of treatment. You will find much of value in what they have written. I am honored to have my efforts appear with their work.

The book begins with a chapter by Mark Schwartz, Lori Galperin, and William Masters. They lay the foundation for the remainder of the book by providing a theory for understanding the effects of child sexual abuse using an extreme stress response model. Effective and efficient treatment ought to be based on a sound theoretical foundation so that the therapist has a mental road map to provide guidance through the often-confusing terrain of psychopathology and psychotherapy. Schwartz, Galperin, and Masters provide such a model. They are able to take the complex, overwhelming problem of dealing with trauma and describe it in a manner that the practicing psychotherapist will find practical. You will find that the remainder of the chapters build on this foundation and expand on the ways it can be applied in the clinical setting.

The book is divided into two main parts: helping adult survivors with sexual problems and helping adult survivors with special needs. Jeff Brown begins Part One, *Helping Adult Survivors With Sexual Problems*, with his chapter on interventions for treating couples whose sexual relationship has been damaged by a history of sexual abuse in the childhood of one of the partners. Brown wrote the chapter in such a manner that the material is useful regardless of the makeup of the couple seeking treatment. Those clinicians who work with same-sex couples as well as heterosexual couples will find the information valuable.

The second and third chapters focus on working with clients who exhibit compulsive sexual behavior. Schwartz, Galperin, and Masters again join forces to author a chapter on treatment with this population. As with their earlier chapter, they furnish a theoretical basis that clearly supports their therapeutic recommendations. Their work is followed by my chapter, in which I provide a method for making use of a client's compulsive sexual behavior pattern to determine if unresolved childhood sexual abuse is creating the need for the adult behavior pattern. You may be surprised when you notice how both of these chapters make use of very similar thinking to understand compulsive behaviors. In 1992, after I presented my thoughts on this topic at a conference in New Orleans, I was delighted to learn that Schwartz, Galperin, and Masters also had come to strikingly similar conclusions based on their own clinical experience. It is clear that our thoughts have continued to follow a parallel course.

Part Two, *Helping Adult Survivors With Special Needs*, begins with Robert Mayer's chapter on the struggles he has experienced while attempting to help clients with complex disordered personalities. In addition to providing treatment recommendations, his writing reveals the personal impact that working with these individuals can have on a therapist. Dr. Mayer's description reminds the reader that in some cases, the therapeutic process may be nearly as upsetting for the therapist as for the client. I find it most refreshing that Dr. Mayer is willing to describe his failures as well as his successes.

I began my career as a professional helper in 1980 as a chemical dependency counselor. Nothing in my training had prepared me for coping with the overwhelming number of my clients who reported that they had been sexually abused as children. My desire for information and skills to help these people is what motivated me to return to graduate school for additional training. Unfortunately, coursework in the treatment of sexual abuse was nonexistent in any of the programs that were available at the time. Sadly, conditions have not improved significantly. Even recent research (Alpert & Paulson, 1990; Minnesota Higher Education Coordinating Board, 1993) notes the scarceness of graduate-level sexual abuse training. Chemical dependency counselors still yearn for practical information on the treatment of sexually abused persons who are struggling to recover from alcohol and other drug addictions. I wish Caryl Trotter's chapter on the stages of recovery and relapse prevention had been available when I faced all of those newly sober men and women who were recalling their childhood abuse experiences and struggling to avoid using drugs as a way to cope with their pain. She presents a model that ties together assessment and intervention. She is able to bridge the gap that often exists between those who treat the effects of chemical dependency and those who treat the effects of sexual abuse.

The chapter on psychotherapy with couples is written, appropriately enough, by a wife-and-husband team. Betty Button and Allen Dietz focus on providing couples therapy for adults who experienced childhood sexual abuse. They bring both their professional and personal experience to an area of treatment that has received very little attention in the literature.

Larry Morris brings the wisdom of his decades of clinical experience to the final chapter of the volume. He focuses his efforts on the importance of using a multidimensional approach when treating men who were sexually abused as children. Dr. Morris was the Chair of the Third National Conference on Male Sexual Abuse Survivors and has dedicated much of his professional life as a psychologist to seeing that damaged boys and men receive ethical and effective treatment. Because he has been hinting at retiring in the near future, I wanted to ensure that he was given a chance to update us on his thoughts since the release of

Males at Risk (Bolton, Morris, & MacEachron, 1989) before he spends every day hiking the Grand Canyon.

I am glad that people such as these authors exist and are kind enough to share their knowledge. I know that, just as I did, you will find these chapters useful and practical.

Mic Hunter
St. Paul, Minnesota

Sexual Trauma Within the Context of Traumatic and Inescapable Stress, Neglect, and Poisonous Pedagogy

Mark F. Schwartz

Lori D. Galperin

William H. Masters

■ Posttraumatic Stress

The *Diagnostic Statistical Manual-III (DSM-III)* defines posttraumatic stress disorder (PTSD) as the result of a "recognizable stressor that would evoke significant symptoms of distress in almost anyone" (American Psychiatric Association, 1987, p. 236). The implication of this terminology is that the *natural* response to such trauma is PTSD—that the response is not an "illness" and that any person experiencing an event of that magnitude is likely to be similarly affected. Thus, rather than stigmatizing trauma victims by assigning to them a mental disorder, it might be more reasonable to categorize the adaptive and maladaptive survival strategies, describe such individuals as "survivors," and then

1

label the "pathological intensifications" (Horowitz, 1986) of such strategies as a mental disorder.

Because a child's natural defenses include dissociation—even amnesia—the cycling of numbing and intrusion responses that predictably occur following posttraumatic stress (Horowitz, 1986) may continue to cycle indefinitely. The numbing portion of the cycle involves a person feeling like an object, treating others like objects, and responding objectively without the use of emotions to guide actions and without the capacity for genuine caring and compassion for self or others. Therefore, the numbing results in restrictive, self-punitive responses, as well as constriction, isolation, and disconnection from others. Intrusion is the breaking through or flooding in of cognition or affect that overwhelms the individual. Typically, it is coded as anxiety, depression, or some other generalized distress, such as somatic complaints. Ritualized or compulsive behavior is often used to cope with this distress or to numb out further, which adds to the individual's disability. Specifically, when the intrusion phase begins, compulsive behavior may function as a vehicle for the re-creation of numbness. When the numbing becomes intolerable (i.e., when the person feels so removed, inhuman, or unreal that all connection to self, others, and physical reality feels lost), compulsive behavior or rituals are then used to reestablish feeling.

It is likely that without external guidance and support from caregivers, the result of early trauma will be pathological intensification or mental disorder. Thus the impact of trauma can be measured only by assessing both event and context (i.e., the presence or absence of nurturing and support from the caregivers). With sufficient support, the trauma may be "finished," "worked through," or resolved without any resulting pathological intensifications.

■ Disorders of Extreme Stress (DES)

Whenever a person experiences severe and chronic stress that is inescapable for prolonged periods, the resulting syndrome is predictably different from that of a posttraumatic stress, which consists of an overwhelming acute event that has a termination point. There is also a vast literature reviewed by van der Kolk (1989) that suggests that the physiologic concomitants of chronic, inescapable stress are different from those for acute stress. For many children who experience PTSD, there is a backdrop of stress in the day-to-day atmosphere of abuse, neglect, and danger to which some children are subjected both in and out of their homes. Whenever children are afraid to walk inside their homes because of chaotic, unprovoked, and inconsistent rage and hostility randomly projected onto family members, the environment can be considered similar to inescapable stress (DES). For such children, witnessing molestation, seeing one parent beaten or raped by the other parent, being locked in hot cars on summer days, or almost being drowned in bathtubs culminates in a pervasive sense of unpredictability, danger, and terror. Whenever such episodic posttraumatic stress occurs in the context of this pervasive, overwhelming, chronic stress, the long-term effects will be much more devastating.

Judith Herman (1992) and Bessel van der Kolk (1993) have recently reviewed the existing literature and suggested that the distorted survival strategies that result from inescapable stress in humans include, predictably, depression and anxiety; somatic symptoms; dissociative symptoms; compulsive reenactment; susceptibility to revictimization; intimacy and relationship disorders; and some personality adaptation in the borderline, narcissistic, antisocial, or schizoid realm.

> *Children who are chronically traumatized by their caretakers may have experiences similar to those of torture victims.*

Children who are chronically traumatized by caretakers in an environment of endemic family stress may have experiences similar to those of torture victims, which include the creation of dependency, intimidation, disorientation, and isolation (Suedfeld, 1990). Children are by definition dependent on caretakers. Abusive parents further engender torturous dependency by withholding basic care and opportunity. When children are forced to submit and obey as the price for being allowed cleanliness, food, clothing, access to friends, or just momentary respite from abuse, they are made into slaves. Their fates become entirely contingent on the whims of the captors/parents, and their realities reshape to fit the rules of the game. The name of the game is the subjugation of vulnerable, trusting, and ultimately desperate children by adults who are often powerless everywhere else in the world.

If children believe that they are in mortal danger and that the threat is embodied by the people on whom they are most reliant, the result is a feeling of such profound powerlessness that any will to continue is totally eradicated. Therefore, resilient children bounce back through an instinctive reframing of their environments that restores hope: They conclude that they are bad and have caused their own suffering, that their caregivers truly love them, and that if they can only try harder or be better, everything will change. To wit: They are not without love and need only perfecting to be truly deserving.

The shame and isolation of "the secret" often compounds and reinforces these dynamics. When the secret is sexual abuse, children often have been told an array of confusing lies: "I love you best of all," "This is our little secret," "If your mother knew, she wouldn't love you—she would know you're a bad little girl," and so on. These confusional techniques occur together with the disorientation of overwhelming, incomprehensible stimulation, which is often accompanied by excruciating physical pain. The mood of the torturer changes radically from one moment to the next: A kiss on the cheek follows a pillow over the face that nearly ends life. The isolating shame and secrecy further reinforce dependency on the torturer: "You're my special one," "If anyone else knew, they would hate you, but you'll always have me."

The longer the abuse continues, the more bound to the abusers the children feel and the more removed they become from other potential connections. The longer the abuse continues with no intervention, the more certain children become that they are not worth saving. Our culture is one in which adults are deemed more aware and knowledgeable than children. Mothers in particular seem to know things magically that children think are unknown. Likewise, the God of Western culture is considered to be all-knowing—even Santa Claus has inside information and knows if you've been bad or good. Amid all of these mythologies and belief systems, how can children imagine that no one notices? When intact, a parent's position is in some measure a buffer or insulator between the child and the dangers of the world. A child being abused by his or her father can have one of two beliefs about his or her mother: "She knows but I'm not worth saving" or "She doesn't know and I have absolutely no one capable of protecting me." Again, it becomes more acceptable to feel bad and unworthy than at the mercy of all the world's dangers. The net effect of the required adaptations to this array of implicit double binds is comparable, in essence, to those arising from intentional brainwashing. The process is the same: Bonds are severed, disorientation is engendered by deprivation or overstimulation, confusion is engendered by double messages and contradictions without resolution, and dependency on the torturer for cessation of the suffering is implicit.

This result may be intended or merely a by-product of domestic cycles of abuse and neglect, but the damage is of at least comparable and perhaps greater magnitude in domestic circumstances because the children's/prisoners' ego formation is still unfolding and parents' access to the children is total. Virulency of trauma is increased by factors such as premeditation, maliciousness, and the possibility of recurrence. For natural disaster and kidnap victims, as well as POWs, there is the hope that one day the experience will end. There may be the remembrance of a time of normalcy or happiness. However, for the child victim of domestic violence, this is reality as far as the eye can see—both backward and forward. For child victims, even when the abuse stops, the cycle often does not because the chronic, learned helplessness still renders them targets for further victimization throughout life. Their capacity to say "no" seems to be permanently injured. Initially, there are cycles of protest, despair, and apathy (Bowlby, 1969) until apathy finally becomes a relatively constant state and the individual succumbs.

> *For child victims, chronic, learned helplessness often renders them targets for further victimization throughout life.*

■ Neglect

Alice Miller (1983, 1986) has written about the hidden cruelties of our philosophy and practice of child rearing as a society—what she calls poisonous pedagogy. Underlying such philosophies is a belief that children are impulsive, out-of-control creatures who require discipline to rein them in and civilize them. Instead of recognizing their acting-out behavior as the result of not feeling loved, attended to, and nurtured, parents assume that the behavior is a result of "badness." Therefore, they feel entitled to punish, deprive, neglect, scream at, or threaten to or actually abandon such "bad" children. In so doing, they believe that they are acting in the best interests of the children. Children learn not to question such disciplinary tactics for fear that worse will follow. When the children respond with anger to being treated unfairly, they are often punished more and told by the angry and sometimes out-of-control parents (ironically) that anger is not permitted (i.e., "Don't you talk back to me, young lady" or "If you cry, I'll give you something to cry about")—a compelling indication that no emotional response is permissible.

Therefore, children learn to suppress their natural responses to abuse, which creates a broadening of psychopathology. Paradoxically, health care workers can coconspire with families when acting-out children are scapegoated and taken to professionals to get "treated" or to be made "well."

It is only against the backdrop of poisonous pedagogy that the devastating impact of sexual and physical abuse, both acute and chronic, can be fully comprehended. To fully assess the extent of injury and the necessary and sufficient components of rehabilitation for the victims, we must consider the acute PTSD; the chronic, extreme stress that constitutes the context of the trauma and the neglect; and societal response. Children are totally dependent on adults for life itself, and society's attitude commonly has been one of ownership, that is, that parents have the right to bring up their children any way they wish. Within this pedagogical context, children assume that sexual abuse, for example, is a form of punishment, something they deserve for being bad—something being done "for their own good" by adults who know what's best.

In addition to the indigenous poisonous pedagogy, there is in our culture's conceptualization of child rearing a very poor articulation of what all children require to thrive. The result is that parents, children, professionals, and state agencies cannot define neglect adequately. Neglect is the absence of what all children need to thrive, but of what does that consist? When children are neglected, they feel unlovable. Typically, it does not occur to them to think that their caregivers are imperfect, incompetent, incapable of loving, or, at the worst, sadistic. To define a standard of comparison, one might simply ask: What is the impact on a child of having two parents, each of whom is tremendously selfish and self-absorbed, each of whom puts his or her needs above those of everyone else, 100% of the time? What is the damage, even though no overt abuse occurred? In some ways, neglect may be more pernicious than abuse, but because the two often occur together, it becomes quite difficult to determine which is most injurious or exactly where the damage of one ends and the other begins.

All children need respect, consistency, attention, support, role models, praise, protection, loving touch, assurance, and play as much as they need food and shelter. Children need opportunities to learn and make mistakes without pressure or punishment. They need to be accepted as unique, not considered replicas of their parents or older siblings, and they should be encouraged in self-expression even when their opinions are different from those of their parents and teachers. They need to be let in on the secret that adults are imperfect, and that sometimes children are right and caretakers are not. They need to be provided with developmentally appropriate challenges and choices so that they develop the ability to evaluate, learn, and, most of all, trust themselves. Finally, as children mature neuromuscularly, they must gradually separate from caregivers and establish a sense of autonomy to operate effectively in a constantly changing environment.

Too often, the aims of child rearing are discipline and submission rather than guidance and appropriate limits. The tactics used are reflective of the underlying goal and rely heavily on shame induction (Bad boy! Bad girl!); threats of abandonment and the withdrawal of love; obedience, conformity, and never questioning authority; and the suppression of what is natural, spontaneous, and unique. If socialized properly, children are supposed to collude with ease and never say "the emperor has no clothes!" Hence they must disqualify their own sensory experiences and not see or be aware of everyday discrepancies and injustices.

In a modern technological society, the problems become compounded. In 20th-century Western culture children get material possessions, but have few opportunities to develop their creativity. Emphasis is placed on meeting needs externally rather than developing internal capacities. Values become imposed or imbibed from the outside rather than cultivated from within. Often, there is the hypocrisy of "do as I say, not as I do," and achievement and attainment are worshipped as the new twin gods of modern existence. Children quickly learn that achievement equals desirability, and self-image becomes linked to what they have, do, and can get, rather than any durable sense of intrinsic worth.

As they get older, they lack the ability for introspection or simple enjoyment and instead feel increasingly driven to attain and acquire more and more in order to escape the feeling of inner emptiness. There is confusion as to what exactly is important and when it becomes enough, and all play becomes impossible unless it is linked to achievement. Because so many children today grow up with deficits of this type, there are high levels of endemic societal distress that, being so widespread, go unlabeled as dysfunctional. Children who lack basic internal resources are even less equipped to contend with the additional and extreme demands that acute and/or chronic stress generate. They have nowhere to turn, either externally or internally.

The sexually traumatized individual, particularly the victim of incest, is typically dealing with posttraumatic stress, DES, neglect, and poisonous pedagogy simultaneously. For this reason, therapy rarely can be focused only on the multiple rapes. Instead, individuals must eventually recognize both what they deserved to get but did not and what they got that they did not deserve, and grieve these multiple losses within the context of a nurturing therapeutic relationship. Then they need to be given the opportunity and guidance to be able to learn new habits and skills that are different from those derived within the original abusive, neglectful environment.

■ Encapsulation Syndromes

Even if children are counseled soon after being raped, they are often unable to disclose or remember the details verbally. They can reenact the abuse with dolls or recreate the details through drawings, but there seems to be impairment in cognitive verbal articulation. This phenomenon is reflective of dissociation, which is the separation or nonintegration of trauma-related emotions, thoughts, sensations, or behaviors (Braun, 1988). *DSM-III* defines dissociation as "a disturbance or alteration in the normally integrative function of identity, memory or consciousness" (American Psychiatric Association, 1987, p. 253). For abused children, dissociation is an automatic survival strategy. It enables children to deflect traumatic experiences into a separate consciousness, making daily functioning possible. Thus a child who is raped by his or her father before going to school in the morning is still able to go to school, participate in class, and interact with peers 2 hours later. Through dissociation, the child is able to believe that "it didn't happen," "it didn't happen to me," or "it happened to someone else." The cost of such rigid compartmentalization is that the child's development is "fixated" or impaired with each traumatic experience. Each experience provides a new block of unintegrated material and a further break in the continuity of experience and consciousness. Summit (1983) describes the child as encapsulated within a bubble and feeling dirty, bad, damaged, or defective. Although the individual continues to age developmentally and acquire new skills and life experiences, this part of the self does not seem to age. New experiences do not penetrate the semipermeable membrane, leaving the individual with the original core beliefs of defectiveness unaltered and, therefore, regardless of achievements, feeling like an imposter. It is as though the adult has developed a functional persona as an overlay, but the core "defective child" remains unintegrated. To many adults, the lack of integration may be experienced as an absence or a void—the "empty unfillable hole in their abdomen"—that they attempt to assuage with addictive consuming.

By dissociating, the individual is prevented from registering the pain that would shatter functioning, but is likewise prevented from expression of the strong feelings and grieving necessary for completion of the stress response cycle. This unexpressed emotion that the encapsulated bubble contains periodically intrudes as rage, which is either acted out or directed inward. Deprived of any memories of the traumatic events in which these feelings originate, and with a distorted perception caused by the parents' destructive parenting behavior, the child, and ultimately the adult, is left feeling defective, bad, shamed, and isolated, which affects how he or she relates to others. Dissociated aspects of trauma also may leak back into consciousness, causing cycles of intrusion and numbing that result in feelings of terror, powerlessness, and rage.

> *Dissociated aspects of trauma may leak back into consciousness, causing cycles of intrusion and numbing.*

Flashbacks to more specific elements of the original trauma or conflict may also occur. Emerging in this out-of-context manner, they typically cause the individual to feel "crazy" or hopelessly out of control of his or her mind and body. Identity, esteem, body image, sense of personal power, effectiveness, trust, and intimacy are so damaged that personal relationships become unstable and tumultuous. These traits have traditionally been labeled as "borderline," but would be better characterized as "accommodation syndromes," to emphasize that individuals' perceptions are reasonable within the context of their trauma-engendered accommodations to the perceived developmental events.

■ Repetitions

Horowitz (1986), who has studied the adaptations to severe stressors in childhood and adulthood, has suggested that the common, "natural" result of severe trauma is repetition, which consists of flashbacks, intrusions, and reenactment until there is completion or mastery of the original, overwhelming stress. Such mastery requires that individuals relive their experiences, revising the age-specific cognitive confusion and releasing the intense emotions. If the stress response cycle is not successfully completed, individuals may reenact disguised repetitions with accompanying numbing and intrusions throughout their lives. (For example, some battered children and battered monkey infants grow up to batter their children; see Table 1.1 for more examples.) As has already been noted, the most potent coping strategy for childhood trauma is dissociation, and the dissociative process by definition interferes with completion of, mastery of, or working through the trauma. The result is that most victims of childhood trauma are left to repeat in disguised form, ad infinitum, the events that are too terrifying to remember.

Table 1.1 lists clinical examples of reenactment. These compulsive reenactments—often revolving around themes of self-punishment, self-cutting, hypersexuality, workaholism, binge or purge eating, or thematically repetitive, destructive relational attachments—become ritualized expressions of unresolved trauma. The habitual behaviors serve as a regulatory mechanism and thereby contain "unmetabolized" trauma as previously described, mediating the cycle of intrusion to cause numbing, and the cycle of numbing to create the capacity to feel. Compounding the problem, these reenactments may also become part of addictive cycles due to the "high" from endorphin release triggered by the flashback of the original trauma (van der Kolk, 1989). Likewise, the pleasure and stress release of the habituated act further perpetuates the habit. Thus the factors that maintain destructive behavior may become independent of the factors that originally caused them. These reenactments also can become a distraction from the emptiness and isolation that have resulted from trauma and dissociation, giving the individual the illusion of connectedness, power, and control, as well as brief, illusory relief from chronic loneliness and dysphoria. In this context, compulsions serve as clues, or windows, to the original abuse in and out of the family, and they maintain survival in what feels like a situation of potential annihilation. More and more it becomes clear that an essential component in alleviating compulsion is identifying its original source and understanding both its original and continuing functions.

When mental health professionals confront destructive acting out without knowledge of its origins, they may, paradoxically, increase the level of shame generated from individuals' inability to change a pattern of behavior they have honestly and mightily struggled to control.

TABLE 1.1 Clinical Examples of Reenactment of Trauma

1. Marrying a "second" alcoholic or someone else who is rejecting.
2. Physically abusing one's own child after one has been abused.
3. Finding oneself in a dangerous situation, such as outside a porno shop in a car alone.
4. Finding oneself getting romantically involved with a priest again or with someone who is married.
5. A woman marrying a man who molests her daughter and then remembering her own incestuous relationship with her own father.
6. Finding work in the emergency room of an inner-city hospital and repeating the chronic and severe chaotic terror in one's childhood.
7. Having chronic affairs with strangers, combined with sexual inhibitions with one's own husband or wife.
8. Repeating the rape by one's father or brother through compulsive "tricks" with strangers.
9. Needing to be beaten or humiliated while having sexual interactions.
10. Using traumatic sexual fantasies to be aroused or to enable orgasm with a loving partner.

Changing the individuals' behavior and self-perceptions can be useful even in the absence of knowledge of the past in some cases. However, the rigid belief that one is always responsible for one's actions can be, in some instances, extremely inaccurate and potentially destructive. Unconscious reenactments, based on distorted survival strategies, sometimes result in destructive behavior beyond conscious control. Self-responsibility is possible in such cases following effective psychotherapy that optimally allows the individual to recognize the original function of the symptom and to achieve resolution of the original trauma that had been fueling the prior unconscious enactments.

■ Physiologic Parallels

The tendency to form repetitive behavior patterns as a result of trauma is more than psychological. Van der Kolk (1989) has reviewed an accumulation of animal and human research indicating that traumatic stress results in changes in the brain and autonomic nervous system that may mediate and exacerbate a variety of cognitive and behavioral symptoms.

With deregulation of the autonomic nervous system, trauma survivors are incapable of enacting the fight-or-flight response as part of Selye's (1956) General Alarm System, which leaves them vulnerable to dangerous situations. In addition, they seem to have chronic excessive sympathetic activity, which explains why they often respond to non-emergency situations as if there were a crisis, and indeed sometimes seem to be "crisis generating." Such research helps explain why medications that block adrenaline, such as clonidine or propranolol, seem to be effective in calming the trauma victim. Van der Kolk (1989) also draws a parallel between trauma victims and the rhesus monkeys who were stressed experimentally in early life. Such monkeys later respond violently to amphetamines and chronically drink more alcohol, suggesting a neurobiological link between early trauma and vulnerability to addiction.

Van der Kolk (1989) also has reviewed changes in the central nervous system—in the hyperarousal system—due to chronic alteration in the central neurotransmitter systems. Using the paradigm of response to inescapable shock in animals, he notes that catecholamine depletion is the result of traumatic stress in both humans and animals. This also leads to rational pharmacologic solutions to the use of pharmacologic agents that alter norepinephrine metabolism, such as tricyclics and MAO inhibitors in selected trauma victims. The noradrenergic tracks emanating from the locus coeruleus to the hippocampus and amygdala also play a role in facilitating memory retrieval, which may implicate this system in flashbacks and nightmares of individuals with a history of posttraumatic stress.

Finally, prolonged stress causes analgesia in mice and rats, and similar effects clinically in some trauma victims. This response can be inhibited by the opiate receptor blocker naloxone. This suggests that the analgesic effect of trauma occurring clinically with many veterans and sexual abuse survivors is certainly opiate-mediated. Prolonged stress activities anesthetize receptors in the brain in a manner similar to injection of exogenous opiates such as morphine (Christie & Chester, 1990). Therefore, the self-cutting and other anesthesia frequently demonstrated in survivors can be blocked with opioid antagonists (Braun, personal communication, 1992, and in our own clinical experience) and show cross-tolerance with morphine. It is likely that after exposure to severe stress, reexposure to traumatic situations in humans can evoke an endogenous opioid response, producing the same effect as a narcotic. Thus it may be possible that such individuals may develop physiologic masochism and may actually become addicted to stress to relieve depression and pain.

■ Trauma Coding

Trauma coding refers to the control that trauma maintains over survivors, shaping their lives as victims. Primary drives such as the need for nurturance, affection, and genital eroticism are paired with severe abuse and torture, leading to strong and complex double binds that make it difficult to let go of the trauma. Some survivors believe that acknowledging that their caregivers hurt them means that they have to hate their caregivers and dismiss all positive childhood memories as distortion. Some survivors need to hold on to their hate because it keeps them bonded tightly to their abusers. Working through the trauma requires that individuals eventually break the trauma coding and free themselves from the rage and hatred that bind them to the people who hurt them in order to be free to create lives that are not organized around the abuse and abusers. On the other hand, many trauma survivors need to hold on to illusions that someone, usually the nonperpetrating parents, really loved them. Otherwise, they become overwhelmed with affect and cognitions that suggest that their lives have been all bad, that they are alone, that any good moments were lies, and that they might as well die. For this reason, they initially attempt to rigidly defend the nonmolesting parents as though the parents were the children and they the responsible adults on the scene. Acknowledging the losses and illusions replete within childhoods filled with neglect and abuse may be more difficult than processing the overt trauma by a given perpetrator.

> *Acknowledging the losses and illusions replete within childhoods filled with neglect and abuse may be more difficult than processing the overt trauma.*

Table 1.2 lists the components of breaking the trauma coding. Breaking the coding requires accurate, nondistorted memory of childhood and accurate attribution of responsibility for abuse and neglect to those responsible. Adults reexamine and revise their childhood perceptions of the abuse. The core beliefs that derived rationally from the childhood

TABLE 1.2 Breaking the Trauma Coding: Reempowerment

Breaking the trauma bond requires:
1. Accurate memory of childhood traumas.
2. Not distorting the events.
3. Placing responsibility for abuse and neglect on those responsible.
4. Using the adult's reasoning capacity to reexamine and revise the child's perceptions.
5. Examining the core belief systems that were established on the basis of the childhood events and making them reality-based with regard to the new perceptions.
6. Expressing the emotions never expressed as a child.
7. Expressing the adult emotions of sadness and anger directed at the perpetrators.
8. Working through the strong emotions to a point where one does not want either revenge or parental acceptance.
9. Reestablishing a relationship with one's inner child, on the basis of survivorship and compassion.
10. Establishing and redefining relationships with adults that are not reactive or similar to early relationships.
11. Establishing boundaries with others in a nonvictim stance, which is based on mutual respect, compassion, and egalitarianism.
12. Learning tools for healthy expression of intimacy, sensuality, and sexuality.

experiences are then reexamined. Finally, the affects that were inhibited or suppressed as children are encouraged and facilitated as a focused process. The result is that adults work through their experiences sufficiently to allow themselves to need neither parental acceptance nor revenge. Only then are the skills for adult relationships able to be developed and at last unburdened by transference emanating from past relationships.

A female survivor once described several repetitions, including having had her tubes tied at the age of 18 for fear of one day molesting her own child.

As a child I would lock myself in the bathroom and play with dolls the way I had been touched. One would be in bed, the other would fondle him or her. I couldn't understand why I did that or where it came from. I was ashamed of this awareness, but couldn't help acting it out. I thought the shame belonged inside me, that the awareness was created solely from me.

During my teenage years, I turned to boys to duplicate some of those feelings—of being cared for or loved. I knew I was fooling myself. I felt the emptiness I was left with after my liaisons with boys, but it was all I had. I was desperate to feel loved. My need for affections was so great, I couldn't say no to many people and I rarely did.

Do you want to know why I had my tubes tied at age 18? Because whenever I thought of myself around my child, a mental image would always appear. The image was clear, and I believed in its certainty. I saw myself not being able to control the thing that lived in me from you. I saw myself fondling sexually my own infant!

This illustration poignantly conveys the profound fear in adults of internalizing their persecutors and becoming perpetrators themselves. It is frightening to trauma survivors to hear themselves saying the same abusive phrases said to them, to feel themselves capable of the same neglect or abuse that rendered their own childhood a living hell. Some survivors do eventually victimize themselves and/or others in a manner similar to that of their perpetrators. Many survivors' worst nightmare is that part of the pattern of revictimization and of trauma coding culminates in their abusing or neglecting their own children. Kempe, Silverman, Steele, Droegenuelle, and Silver (1962) noted several decades ago that 100% of batterers were battered in childhood. This repetition is difficult to comprehend without understanding the unconscious reenactment resulting from trauma coding. Some trauma victims also reenact these perpetrations in their sexual fantasies, cementing the erotic, violent connection. Some actually reenact the perpetrations outwardly and become victimizers of themselves or others. The result of such shame-producing repetitions is the double-bind belief that they cannot be angry at their aggressors because they are equally bad and have also hurt others. It is imperative that the revictimization process end, that the victims make amends, and that they learn compassion and self-forgiveness.

■ Introjection

All children learn by modeling adults, particularly their parents. Abused children are being told continually that their parents' affection is conditioned on their performance, which is never sufficient. This creates perfectionistic, self-critical inner voices that berate and criticize children's actions; these are the voices of the abusive parents, which have been introjected. Typically, there has been minimal reinforcement for good performance, much less any "unconditional positive regard," and therefore the self-nurturing and self-appreciating internal messages are nonexistent. When others attempt to provide the latter, there seems to be no internal system to accept such accolades, and therefore individuals tend to avoid or to not hear such strokes, and to sabotage their achievements.

This can be a feature of or coexist with an even more insidious phenomenon—identification with the aggressor. The abused child can identify with either the aggressive, powerful perpetrator or the weak, passive, but usually equally angry partner. Living in a home with continual passive and active rage, the child is like a sponge, absorbing the high levels of resentment. The child will tend to identify with the powerful aggressor, as if to say, "I'll become like him or her so no one can ever hurt me again." In addition, the child tends to rebel against internalization of the weak parent, who is despised for not protecting the child. The result is the development of thoughts and behaviors similar to the perpetrator, whom the child supposedly hates. One survivor, who was molested in infancy by her father, writes the following to her mother:

> And there is a big part of you in me now. I'm struggling to get rid of it, it is a lot like exorcising a demon—except that the you in me is like an implosion of blackness more than an explosion of rage. Oh yes, when your personality surfaces in me, I become punitive, paranoid, critical and blaming. All I feel is hate and fear. But when that passes, I'm left with black hole, devoid of feeling. I'm empty, an emptiness that is palpable and painful. It's a blackness I can't describe. It is as if my knowledge and duplication of your horror is robbing me of who I really am. I, the real person, the person who's been lost for so long is missing. And sometimes it feels that if I can't rescue her soon from that void, she'll be lost forever.

In this quote, she is able to articulate powerfully the core of her self-hatred. She despises her mother and despises herself for internalizing and absorbing aspects of her mother.

■ Discussion and Clinical Implications

The depression, anxiety, compulsive reenactment, susceptibility to revictimization, dissociation, somatization, relational and intimacy distress, and personality development that result from sexual trauma in the context of inescapable stress is reasonable given the magnitude of the stressor and the developmental parameters. We believe these symptoms and syndromes are best treated using abreactive and cathartic forms of psychotherapy.

In abreaction, the events are recalled with detail, as if they are happening again. The corrective experience occurs by combining the adult's resources with the child's terror and fear in a safe, controlled setting with a therapist. This time, there is mastery and completion of the overwhelming traumatic cycle. An essential feature of this experience is cognitive restructuring, which allows revision of the original accommodated beliefs, ideas, and associations. Emotions engendered by the events are released, allowing a discharge and completing the cycle. Following the reliving and revising of the traumatic experiences, individuals typically require long-term psychotherapy to learn new skills and to continue the revision of belief systems that will ultimately enable them to have relationships and to establish self-efficacy in dealing with life's challenges without further reenactment from trauma coding.

PART ONE

Helping Adult Survivors With Sexual Problems

Treating Sexual Dysfunction in Survivors of Sexual Abuse and Assault

Jeff Brown

It is only in the past few years that clinicians and researchers in the area of sexual abuse have begun to seriously consider the possible repercussions to adult survivors' sexual functioning. Many professionals previously believed that sexual matters would take care of themselves if clients had sufficiently worked through their abuse histories.

Among the plethora of popular materials regarding sexual abuse, only a few authors (Hunter, 1992; Maltz, 1991; Maltz & Holman, 1987) have provided abuse survivors with information about healing the sexual aspects of abuse. With notable exceptions, the majority of the professional literature either ignores or makes vague or fragmentary reference to these issues. Virtually no substantive information is available regarding male or nonheterosexual individuals.

The majority of female survivors of childhood sexual abuse are reported to have experienced long-term sexual repercussions. Jehu (1990) reported that 94% of his sample had some form of sexual dysfunction. Briere and Runtz (1990) reported a "statistically significant unique relationship between sexual abuse and dysfunctional sexual behavior" (p. 360) among their sample of 277 female undergraduate students. Courtois (1988) reported that 70% of her sample of female incest survivors reported moderate to severe effects, whereas 30% reported no or limited sexual effects.

Regarding adult female survivors of sexual assault, Becker, Skinner, Abel, and Cichon (1986) reported that 58.6% of their sample of survivors (versus only 17.2% of a nonsurvivor control group) had a variety of sexual problems. In Mackey et al.'s (1991) sample, the majority of the women (some of whom had also experienced previous childhood sexual abuse or sexual assault) experienced a range of sexual and/or intimacy difficulties.

In spite of these findings, the majority of the research in this area is sufficiently flawed so that the professional can make only guarded hypotheses regarding treatment approaches or research directions. As in much of the rest of the psychological literature, problems with source and size of samples, lack of adequate definitions, and the overreliance on retrospective research are common:

- Becker, Skinner, et al. (1986) note that the use of samples provided from a crisis center may differ with individuals from other sources, such as delayed treatment seekers (Stewart et al., 1987). Finkelhor (1980) notes that conclusions drawn from late adolescent or early adulthood samples may be influenced by factors related to establishment of adult sexual behavior.
- Use of broad-based phrases to measure dysfunctional sexual behavior, such as "I like to dress in 'sexy' clothes" (Briere & Runtz, 1990, p. 363); vague and subjective descriptions, such as "promiscuity" (Fromuth, 1986, p. 11); and inaccurate or misleading diagnostic categories (use of themes of "obligatory sex, decreased desire or avoidance of sexual intimacy and adverse feeling states" to define "desire dysfunction" [Mackey et al., 1991, p. 98]) make it nearly impossible to determine what is actually being measured.
- The nearly singular application of retrospective research in the area of sexual abuse results in conclusions that are readily influenced by the adaptation of what has been recalled by the survivor (Briere & Runtz, 1992, p. 197).

Therapists and researchers also would be well advised to guard against inaccurate inferences regarding cause and effect (Briere & Runtz, 1992). The impact of sexual abuse, including sexual functioning, can be easily confused with family background and dysfunction (Fromuth, 1986); age of adults and consequent developmental stage (Finkelhor, 1980);

patient status or help-seeking behavior (Becker et al., 1992; Fromuth, 1986); immediate short-term effects versus delayed long-standing effects (Becker, Skinner, et al., 1986); prior trauma or secondary trauma (Cunningham, Pearce, & Pearce, 1988; Mackey et al., 1991); and a history of physical abuse (Cunningham et al., 1988; Dimock, 1988). In addition, it should not be assumed that all sexual abuse or assault survivors have been negatively affected. Courtois and Watts (1982) found that 60% were "more satisfied than dissatisfied" (p. 85) during sex. In his research of sibling sexual contacts, Finkelhor (1980) found high levels of sexual self-esteem among some individuals in the group studied.

■ Assessing General and Sexual Functioning Concerns

In general, clinicians can use sexual history guidelines such as those provided by Becker and Skinner (1984) to obtain most of the information they will need. Jehu's (1990, pp. 327-342) thorough-going "interview protocol" and Westerlund's (1992) incest questionnaire provide additional survivor-specific guidelines.

Assessing Childhood Abuse Elements

The research to date suggests that a number of factors may contribute to later sexual functioning difficulties. As a part of the assessment, the clinician should consider

Type of activity. "A number of studies concur that molestation involving more intimate contact is more traumatic than less intimate contact" (Browne & Finkelhor, 1986, p. 73).

Age of onset. Browne and Finkelhor (1986) conclude that the relationship between age of onset and degree of trauma is unclear. Courtois and Watts (1982) conclude that earlier onset results in more trauma. But Cunningham et al. (1988) found a higher incidence of gynecological problems in females who were older than age 12 at onset.

Frequency of abuse, involvement in intercourse, physical abuse, and revealing the abuse. All of these are equated with more gynecological problems (Cunningham et al., 1988).

Source of abuse. More trauma is reported if the father is the perpetrator (Browne & Finkelhor, 1986). If sibling abuse is involved, the age difference, the victim's age at onset, whether force was used, and engagement in exploitive sexual behavior all appear to result in greater trauma (Finkelhor, 1980).

General sexual functioning. Studies have referenced a variety of difficulties with general sexual functioning among survivors. A number of dysphoric feelings during sexual activity, including guilt; shame; confusion between affection and sex, and between partner and offender (Westerlund, 1992); concern about sexual orientation (Dimock, 1988); and disgust at partner's body (McGuire & Wagner, 1978) are reported.

When faced with a particular case that does not adequately adhere to actual diagnostic criteria (American Psychiatric Association, 1987), a clinician can use available research to assess client sexual functioning and form working hypotheses regarding the following problems.

Sexual desire disorders. A number of researchers report a significant incidence of sexual desire disorders among survivors of childhood sexual abuse. McGuire and Wagner (1978) noted that many women in their sample had "minimal sexual appetite" (p. 12). Jehu (1990) found that 56% of his sample "complained of impaired sexual motivation" (p. 221). Westerlund (1992) reported that 14% of his sample experienced no sexual desire, another 16% had reported a desire disorder at some point in their history, and 53% reported some interference in sexual desire. Conversely, Fromuth (1986) found no correlation between a history of abuse and frequency of intercourse or level of sexual desire. Some clinicians (Dimock, 1988; Olson, 1990) have noted a correlation between sexual addiction and a history of childhood sexual abuse in males.

Arousal stage disorders. A variety of anxiety and phobic responses are apparently common for female survivors during the arousal phase. Dissociative states often serve to inhibit active arousal; the survivor may describe herself as "numbing out" during sexual activity (Gil, 1988; Glanz & Himber, 1992; Maltz, 1988, 1991; McGuire & Wagner, 1978; Westerlund, 1992). In Westerlund's (1992) study, 26% reported actual absence of sexual arousal, whereas 84% reported some interference (26% consciously inhibited their arousal). Forty-nine percent of Jehu's (1990) sample reported impaired arousal. Two studies reported that a significant number of women in their samples reported pain with intromission. Jehu (1990) found that 27% complained of dyspareunia and 7% reported vaginismus, and Westerlund (1992) found that 23%

reported dyspareunia and 28% reported vaginismus. Both of these are higher incidences than previously suspected (Jehu, 1990, p. 223).

Orgasmic stage disorders. The research data on the orgasmic capacity of survivors are mixed. Fromuth (1986) and Westerlund (1992) reported minimal impact, whereas Jehu (1990, p. 222) found that 45% of his sample had "impaired orgasm," and Gil (1988) concluded that this class of dysfunctions was the most common in both male and female survivors.

Assessing Adult-Onset Sexual Assault Elements

In their review of the literature, Gilbert and Cunningham (1986) conclude that

no predictive value [regarding level of trauma] has been found for such factors as (a) whether the rape was reported, (b) the survivor's vulnerability to claims that she was responsible, (c) the survivor's belief that she lives or works with supportive others, (d) the survivor's level of sexual activity before the rape, (e) level of victimization, [or] (f) perception of self as a rape victim. (p. 72)

However, the following factors may be aspects to consider as part of the assessment.

Source of the abuse. A study by Mackey et al. (1991) concluded that the greatest disruption in most of the areas of sexual functioning that they measured occurred when the perpetrator was a health care professional.

History of previous sexual abuse. Sexually assaulted females with no previous history of sexual abuse or assault were significantly more sexually impaired and reported arousal dysfunctions most frequently when compared with other sexually assaulted females with a previous history of sexual abuse or assault (Browne & Finkelhor, 1986; Mackey et al., 1991). In addition, those with a previous history of childhood abuse were more likely as adults to be sexually assaulted by their husbands (Browne & Finkelhor, 1986).

General sexual functioning. In addition to a variety of specific functioning difficulties noted below, there are some references in the literature to general factors in sexual functioning among survivors of sexual assault. Mackey et al. (1991) determined that the greatest effect (regardless of whether or not the respondent had experienced previous childhood sexual abuse or adult assault) was on "the sexual relationship with a partner in general" (p. 97). Another significant area noted was communication difficulties (Mackey et al., 1991). In their longitudinal study of 81 adult rape survivors, Burgess and Holmstrom (1979) noted that 35% reported avoidance of certain acts and 50% reported worries regarding their partners' reactions.

Desire stage disorders. Regarding functioning difficulties that may be classified as desire dysfunctions (American Psychiatric Association, 1987), Becker, Skinner, et al.'s (1986) study found this area to be the most frequently reported problem (55.9% versus 5.9% of a matched nonassault group). Problems with fear of sex (59.9% versus 23.5%) were reported by this same group. Mackey et al. (1991) observed that 20% to 38% of their sample reported desire-related problems that included "obligatory sex, avoidance of sexual intimacy, and adverse feeling states" (pp. 98-99). Burgess and Holmstrom's (1979) sample most frequently reported a drop in sexual frequency (71%) followed by decreased activity (33%), no change (19.5%), and increased activity (9.5%), particularly in the first 6 months following the assault(s). No rationale for these changes was reported in this study.

Arousal stage disorders. These were reported at a rate of 50.7% for Becker, Skinner, et al.'s (1986) sample. Flashbacks during sexual activity are apparently among the most common problems reported (Burgess & Holmstrom, 1979, report 50%; Mackey et al., 1991, report 19% to 40%). Anxiety may be a cofactor for some individuals. Mackey et al. (1991) found anxiety particularly high among assault survivors who had also been sexually abused as children. Two studies also examined the incidence of problems with intromission. Burgess and Holmstrom (1979) found that nearly 25% of their sample of 63 women reported pain or discomfort with intercourse; they were unclear whether any of the women experienced actual dyspareunia or vaginismus. Becker, Skinner, et al. (1986) found that 10.7% of their sample reported dyspareunia and 2.0% reported vaginismus.

Orgasm stage disorders. The data regarding orgasmic dysfunction are limited and somewhat confusing. Although Burgess and Holmstrom (1979) reported that 41% of their sample "reported having difficulty either experiencing any sexual feelings or being orgasmic during sex" (p. 654), Becker et al. (1986) reported no significant difference between their assault group and control group, and Mackey et al. (1991) reported orgasmic difficulty only among those who had also been sexually abused as children.

■ Intervention

Theoretical Bases of Intervention

Finkelhor and Browne's (1985) developmental conceptualization of "traumatic sexualization" in childhood sexual abuse can provide a theoretical framework for understanding how sexual abuse may contribute to later sexual functioning difficulties. They theorize that elements such as repeated reward for developmentally inappropriate sexual behavior, fetishism of anatomy, evocation of a sexual response in a child, use of enticement (versus force), and providing "misconception and confusions about sexual behavior" serve to develop "unusual emotional associations" with sexuality, inappropriate behavioral repertoires, and confused sexual self-concepts (p. 531).

Others (Becker & Skinner, 1984; Jehu, 1990) have conceptualized a link via classical conditioning between the sexual assault/abuse and the negative reactions that follow. Later generalization of a negative response to other nonabusive sexual situations often follows as conditioned responses (dissociation) follow conditioned stimuli (noises, smells, and sights previously associated with the abuse/assault). This model provides an explanation for the "trigger reactions" that survivors often report, even to nonsexual stimuli such as certain places, time of day, dress, and so on.

Sex therapists and those who work in the area are often struck by the myriad of mistaken but understandable notions and behaviors related to sexuality that adult survivors commonly evidence. Jehu (1990) proposes the applicability of a cognitive model to help understand the connection between abuse/assault and later behaviors. The essential principle here is that survivors develop certain "dysfunctional assumptions and rules" (Jehu, 1990, p. 243) as a result of their trauma that continue to drive their intimate and sexual behaviors in the present.

As is often the case, the actual connections between later sexual functioning and abuse are probably multicausal. The variety of differences in sexual repercussions between male and female survivors, sexual assault survivors and child abuse survivors, and even individuals of the same gender and similar experience, for example, are too numerous and complex to be explained by single-factor theories. In their attempt to consider multiple factors, Maltz and Holman (1987) highlight family dynamics, coping styles of individual survivors, and other negative and positive relationship experiences as examples of contributing elements to the survivor's sexual/intimate adaptation.

Therapeutic Considerations

Timing

The majority of the material in the field appears to follow a traditional emphasis on the need for primary abuse intervention before proceeding with a specific sexual focus. Although they stress the need for flexibility, Maltz and Holman (1987) conclude that "Most survivors are ready to address sexuality concerns only after having spent much time working on incest in general" (pp. 118-119). Individual and/or group work that concentrates on building the therapeutic relationship, improving self-esteem, working through emotional content, controlling self-destructive behaviors, and building support is considered preliminary to improving body image and addressing sexual responsiveness (Maltz & Holman, 1987; Talmadge & Wallace, 1991).

Individual and/or group work is considered preliminary to improving body image and addressing sexual responsiveness.

Increasingly, this notion is being challenged (Becker, Skinner, et al., 1986; Glanz & Himber, 1992; McCarthy, 1990). McCarthy (1990) concludes that "if the sexual problem is treated with 'benign neglect' while the therapeutic focus is on the rape trauma, the sexual dysfunction is likely to become chronic and more severe. Overlays of resentment, blaming, and avoidance will develop and make treatment more difficult" (p. 144). In their discussion of interventions with female survivors of sexual assault, Becker, Skinner, et al. (1986) argue that deemphasis on the sexual component may serve to "delegitimize" the sexual problems

(p. 47). From this point of view, intervention emphasizes working with the impact of the past trauma on the present and future, integrating the trauma into ongoing treatment (McCarthy, 1990), including the partner in the process early on (Talmadge & Wallace, 1991), and redefining the goal as "having sex not having good sex" (Glantz & Himber, 1992, p. 149).

Over the past few years, I have been provided with numerous examples of problematic outcomes of traditional models of abuse recovery intervention similar to the model espoused by Maltz and Holman (1987). Sexual patterns seem to become more intractable, especially in situations in which survivors' therapy has taken several years, and the sexual elements in their relationships have been reduced to no or limited sexual contact. In their attempts to empower the survivors to set boundaries and clarify needs, some therapists may have overemphasized the "just say no" stance. Consequently, survivor clients have been taught inadvertently to fear and/or reject any elements of sexuality in themselves or their partners. In many of these same situations, the respective partners have developed their own intractable patterns that include resentment and anger, fear about any expression of affection or sexuality toward their partners, confusion about their sexual adequacy, and reluctance to assert their needs.

My colleague Ruth Markowitz (personal communication, July 16, 1993) has proposed a reconceptualization of the timing of intervention as a process metaphorically paralleling the "start-stop" technique used in managing premature ejaculation. Using this metaphor, the therapist encourages the couple to consistently seek intimate and sexual interactions to the point of discomfort, explore alternative expressions whenever possible, and "restart" the process later in situations in which temporarily stopping is indicated.

Modalities

Couples therapy. Couples therapy is seen by some as the treatment of choice for sexual repercussion issues (Maltz, 1988; McCarthy, 1990). Maltz (1988) relies on the precedent of Masters and Johnson, who have stressed the importance of shifting the focus onto the relationship rather than the individual when sexual concerns are being treated. An additional argument is that both individuals are involved, and that, in fact, the nonabused partner is a secondary victim (Maltz, 1988).

Maltz (1988) proposes a four-stage couple's intervention model. The initial phase, "identification of the problem," focuses on assessment of the relationship between the sexual abuse and current sexual functioning concerns (Maltz, 1988, pp. 150-151). Phase two, "working together," explores the abuse in an attempt to develop perspective and clarify feelings toward the offender(s) (Maltz, 1988, pp. 155-157). "Changing old patterns," the third phase, emphasizes building new foundations for the couple's sexual expression (Maltz, 1988, pp. 157-161). The final stage uses various techniques to "create positive sexual experiences" (Maltz, 1988, pp. 161-166). A more complete description, which details a nine-session format, is elaborated in Maltz and Holman (1987).

Others have emphasized blended individual and conjoint approaches (Jehu, 1990). Glanz and Himber (1992) recommend both individual and couples sex therapy approaches, but express concern that these be provided by separate therapists so that transference issues are managed better.

Group therapy. Short-term group approaches with survivors have also been attempted. A 10-session group for partnered and nonpartnered victims of sexual abuse parallels the P-LI-SS-IT model originally developed by Anon that has been proposed by Becker and her colleagues (Becker, 1989; Becker, Skinner, et al., 1986). These sessions progress from providing education to using various homework exercises to develop greater sexual comfort and acceptance.

I have used a two- or three-session psychoeducational focus with combined groups of gay, lesbian, bisexual, and heterosexual couples with apparent success. Areas emphasized include developing skills in sexual communication, discussing the abuse and related triggers, exploring the impact of abuse on sexual cognitions and behaviors, enhancing the couples' sexual repertoire and concepts of sexuality, and learning tools for intervening with dissociation and flashbacks. Sharing common issues appears to help couples reduce feelings of shame, differentness, and isolation. The use of a psychoeducational focus provides a nonthreatening introduction and a foundation of information for repercussion-oriented conjoint therapy.

Techniques

Although a variety of techniques have been proposed and used by practitioners, the "state of the art" is characterized by trial and error, use with modification of previously developed therapy approaches, and limited measurement of outcome.

Anxiety reduction. Several techniques have been used in attempting to reduce individual anxiety and negative/phobic responses to sexual stimuli. Jehu (1990) recommends the selective use of "coping skills training" techniques such as relaxation training, "guided self-dialogue," "imagery rehearsal," and cognitive restructuring to help survivor clients "cope directly with immediate stresses" (pp. 250-263). The use of systematic desensitization principles has been proposed by Westerlund (1992) and Stewart et al. (1987) and is similar to Jehu's (1990) "imagery rehearsal." In situations involving the repercussions of abuse, clients develop a hierarchy of sexual activities from most to least comfortable, learn various relaxation skills, and eventually pair both in imagery. Actual behavioral rehearsal often follows.

Cognitive interventions. The use of various cognitive interventions is also a frequently mentioned technique. Becker, Skinner, et al. (1986) concluded that this form of intervention was the most efficacious because survivors' misperceptions of sexual stimuli was the most significant feature. Maltz (1988) reframes the intervention focus to one of "creating a new meaning for sex" (p. 160). Redefining sexuality will require that survivors and their partners explore meanings that were developed out of each of their experiences. For many survivors, sex is

> *For many survivors, sex is often equated with loss of control, powerlessness, anger, rage, shame, secrecy, betrayal, and denial of personal reality.*

often equated with loss of control, powerlessness, anger, rage, shame, secrecy, betrayal, and denial of personal reality. McCarthy (1990) recommends using behavioral exercises that challenge previously formed beliefs about sexuality. He stresses that "cognitions regarding 'deserving' to be a sexual person, pleasure-orientation to sexuality, and sexuality as reinforcing the intimacy bond are especially therapeutic" (p. 145). Westerlund (1992) instructs survivors to use various self-affirmations related to body image and sexuality. Engaging the partners via verbalization of positive sexual statements is encouraged in Westerlund's interventions with couples. Similarly, I have found it helpful to discuss and compare with couples their various learnings about sexuality and how they can assist each other in correcting nonaffirming beliefs. Use of cognitive restructuring is believed by some to be more effective if it follows anxiety reduction interventions (Jehu, 1990).

General sexuality related interventions. In addition to actual sexual functioning difficulties, various related sexual issues are common for the adult or childhood abuse survivor. Lack of information or presence of misinformation often complicates the situation, as do poor sexual communication skills. Related issues regarding body image and shame about sexuality are frequently noted in the literature. In the case of childhood sexual abuse, the survivor is additionally robbed of normative sexual experiences and consequently may be unable to fully participate in adult sexual play.

One of the earliest interventions for an individual or couple involves broadening meanings of sexuality, sensuality, and related intimacy. The overemphasis on genital and orgasmic aspects of sexuality, as is common in Western cultures, is a frequent starting point of intervention. This is particularly essential with couples struggling with sexual repercussion issues because a broadened repertoire of intimate expression will form a foundation of safety, respect, comfort, enjoyment, and mutuality. As discussed previously, defocusing from genital/orgasmic aspects can also promote incorporation of earlier developmental sexual experiences that the survivor may not have previously experienced. Assisting the couple or individual to redefine healthy sexuality from an educational and experiential base is essential (Maltz & Holman, 1987).

In many cases, redefining sexuality will require the clinician to assist the couple or individual in building adequate sexual communication skills. Communicating about sexuality may break earlier injunctions of secrecy and evoke feelings of shame. In addition, certain phrases or words, or even any talk about sexuality, may be equated by the survivor with the abusive experiences. Yet it is possible that certain nonverbal cues or actions also may be associated with abuse. Ruth Markowitz and I have used a number of communication exercises to build comfort and competence. These have included activities such as learning to identify comfortable and uncomfortable sexual words, discussing sexual likes and dislikes, sharing the abuse story, practicing sexual negotiation skills, and making nonverbal sexual communications explicit.

Sexual dysfunction techniques. A number of therapists have proposed using standard or modified sexual dysfunction techniques and procedures. Many of these therapists rely on the initial use of various relaxation techniques individually and as a couple to build a foundation of comfort and reduced apprehension (Westerlund, 1992). When used with couples, these techniques can also provide a low-risk, nonsexual basis of intimacy and touch that can be paired later with more formal sexuality exercises.

Many of the authors in the literature surveyed recommend the use of "presensate" couples' exercises (Maltz, 1988, pp. 163-164). Glanz and Himber (1992) advise that "the point of departure should be far more removed from intercourse than in normal sensate focus exercises" (p. 149). The use of activities such as hand holding, foot massage, hair shampooing, and bathing/showering are recommended as exercises that rebuild sensual/sexual touch (Maltz, 1988). Markowitz (personal communication, July 16, 1993) often encourages couples to return to earlier activities of sexual development, such as looking into each other's eyes, hand holding, petting with clothes on, and so on prior to "adult" sexual behaviors for the same reasons. In some cases, it has been my experience that only "no touch" activities are initially possible. Following the use of presensate exercises that can last several months (Maltz, 1988), modified sensate-focus sexual therapy is regarded as the treatment of choice (Glanz & Himber, 1992; Talmadge & Wallace, 1991; Westerlund, 1992). This may include solitary exercises such as the use of dilators, Kegel exercises, fantasy enhancement, self-massage, body exploration, self-pleasuring, and visual self-examination (Becker, 1989; Jehu, 1990; Maltz, 1988; Maltz & Holman, 1987; Westerlund, 1992), as well as many nongenital/genital exercises with the individual and his or her partner. Westerlund (1992) recommends the following modifications to sexual therapy:

1. Expanding the number of sessions before using sensate focus techniques
2. Anticipating heightened feelings that may be connected with the abuse history
3. Building in safety aspects such as survivor control of sexual activity and role of giver
4. Monitoring and intervening if associations with the perpetrator and his or her partner occur

Jehu (1990) adds the following:

5. Empowering the survivor to be in control of mutual activities and their duration

6. Monitoring the situation to avoid recreating the abuse

In addition, I have found the following helpful:

7. Recommending that the couple discontinue sexual activities temporarily if the survivor feels childlike or "small"

8. Encouraging the couple to explicitly discriminate between affectionate touch and sexual touch

9. Suggesting that both partners regularly reaffirm that they want sexual healing as well as acknowledge doubt if it exists

10. Holding the couple accountable for consistent and clear limits that must be renegotiated before modification

11. Supporting partner limit setting in addition to survivor limit setting

Special Issues in Working
With Survivors and Their Partners

Engaging the couple. Engaging both the survivor and his or her partner can be very difficult. In my experience, one or both of the individuals often will look for signs that the therapist is aligning with the partner. Any statements or reactions that may be perceived as minimizing the impact on the survivor's partner, for example, may be perceived as showing "survivor bias." Conversely, a survivor once left a session in which she was being encouraged to offer nonsexual alternatives to sexual activity with her partner because she felt the therapist was blaming her for the sexual difficulties in the relationship.

Developing shared responsibility. As an additional aspect of engaging the couple, issues related to definition of the problem and assignment of responsibility are often a significant aspect of early intervention. Because one individual often presents with a sexual symptom, one or both of the members of the couple may view this person as the identified patient; the therapist's task is to facilitate a reframing of this "symptom" as a shared problem in which both play a part (Talmadge & Wallace, 1991). As discussed earlier, it is often helpful to reframe the situation of the nonsymptomatic partner as being that of a secondary victim (Maltz, 1988). The majority of those who have written about their therapeutic interventions in this area have stressed the need to eliminate sex that involves obligation or deference (Jehu, 1990; Maltz, 1988; Talmadge & Wallace, 1991). Because the majority of survivors were abused in situations that involved elements of lack of control and lack of respect for their needs and feelings, it is important that a couple's current sexual expressions not replicate these traumatic dynamics. When these dynamics are repeated, the nonabused partner can unwittingly play the role of perpetrator with the abused partner becoming the helpless recipient.

> *It is important that a couple's current sexual expressions not replicate traumatic dynamics from their abuse.*

In situations in which little or no sexual involvement has occurred for an extended period of time, issues of guilt and anger/rage for both individuals are common. For the survivor, the guilt over being unable to be expressive sexually, the related fear of abandonment, and anger and rage over the partner's expectations are frequently recurring feelings. For the nonabused partner, the guilt over previous incidents of sexual activity, as well as current sexual desires, interacts with feelings of anger and rage over rejection and identification as the perpetrator. These feelings often recycle as the couple engages in presensate and modified sensate-focus activities.

Triggers, flashbacks, and dissociation. As reported earlier, the occurrence of flashbacks and the related use of dissociation, often triggered during sexual interactions with a partner, are common among survivors. Westerlund (1992) recommends training the survivor in "image stopping" and "image altering techniques" to reduce the frequency of the intrusive material. Glanz and Himber (1992) present dissociation to the survivor as "something to be expected" and encourage the survivor to decide when he or she "comes back" whether or not to continue sexual activity.

Interventions with couples tend to follow the recommendations of Talmadge and Wallace (1991), who apparently advise that the survivor and partner "incorporate" the flashbacks and dissociation that follows into the sexual exercises rather than "encourage her to keep it at bay." Initial intervention with a couple frequently involves exploration of the abuse incidents and coping strategies in some detail in order to identify possible trigger stimuli clearly. Consequently, the frequency of flash-backs can be reduced through avoidance of certain smells, sounds, situations, and so on. A variety of "grounding" techniques have been developed by various researchers and clinicians for individuals and couples to use during the flashback/dissociation. Encouraging the survivor to keep his or her eyes open to "know who is with her/[him]," to use self-reassurance (Talmadge & Wallace, 1991, p. 179), to remind oneself of differences in past and present (Maltz, 1988), to talk with the partner to let him or her know what is happening, and to state wants and needs at the moment of flashback (Westerlund, 1992) are among the suggested techniques. Partners can use verbalizations to help their partners be aware of their current reality, reaffirm that they are not the abusers (Talmadge & Wallace, 1991), support emotional discharge (Maltz, 1988), and stop sexual involvement.

The clinician must also help the survivor and partner develop strate-gies for determining how to proceed once the flashback/dissociation incidents have occurred. In some cases, it may be necessary for the couple to discontinue any further sexual interaction at the time. Unfor-tunately, the occurrence of flashback-dissociation-discontinuance can become problematic in itself and become a defensive strategy for the survivor or couple to avoid further intimate involvement. Encouraging the couple to resume their activity, substitute other sexual expressions, or schedule a later time for resumption can help prevent this problem (Talmadge & Wallace, 1991).

"Nontraditional" people and patterns. The literature is virtually silent about interventions with gay, lesbian, or bisexual couples; male survi-vors; or partnerships with two abused individuals. Many of the tech-niques and modalities appear to be applicable, but clinicians will have to rely on their impressions, trial and error, client reports, and informa-tion not specific to the sexual repercussions of abuse.

In general, clinicians can expect to find that gay and lesbian clients engage in a broader repertoire of sexual activities than do heterosexual individuals, hold a wider range of values regarding sexual monogamy, and possibly experience different types of sexual functioning difficul-ties (Nichols, 1989). The impact of HIV on gay and bisexual men's sexual expression and the apparent higher rate of sexual abuse among lesbians (Becker, 1989) are specific factors that should be taken into account. In my experience, male couples will often hide any indication of sexual interaction problems out of shame, threat to their sense of competency and masculinity, or overidentification with the sexual versus other aspects of the relationship. Because sadism and masochism practices appear to be more common among gay men and lesbians, it may not be unusual for some of these couples to engage consciously or unconsciously in practices that involve "role play" of situations that parallel abuse experiences. At a minimum, these couples should be encouraged to explore possible parallels to the abuse and experiment with alternatives.

Little information about sexual repercussions in male survivors (heterosexual, homosexual, or bisexual) is available. Issues related to the male sex role that connect sexual behavior and history to competence, power, masculinity, and intimacy are often contradicted in abuse that involves helplessness, powerlessness, force, passivity, and shame. This confusion may be replicated in sexual interaction patterns with a partner. Among the most apparent to me are issues of power and control. Given the cultural identification of power and masculinity, male survivors have been observed attempting to hide feelings of powerlessness, holding to rigid sex role expressions in lovemaking or using aggression in sexual behavior to compensate. I have noted similarities between female and male survivors regarding experiences of flashbacks and dissociation during sexual play; difficulties pairing intimacy and sexuality; and lowered sexual desire, especially in committed or long-term relationships.

In situations in which both coupled individuals are survivors of abuse, the clinician can expect complex interactions between each individual's history and patterning. As a consequence, pacing and progress are slowed and the use of each person's strengths needs to be maximized.

Partner concerns. A number of self-help books for partners of abuse survivors have surfaced over the past few years. Many of these appear to do a reasonably good job of educating partners (particularly if they are heterosexual males) about the issues and needs of survivors. The emphasis often appears to be related to how to assist or support partners. In their book *Incest and Sexuality*, Maltz and Holman (1987) detail the primary characteristics that their sample of adult female survivors of abuse identified as important aspects of support from their partners. These include, in order of most significant to least significant, ability to respond to emotions, letting partners know that the relationship is more important than sex, sharing nonsexual touch, responding with gentleness, supporting partners' sexual refusals, talking about feelings, and displaying sensitivity. For the nonabused partner, these expectations can feel one-sided and serve to build resentments, particularly if the length of the recovery period is protracted.

Anger and rage often serve to camouflage a partner's feelings of abandonment, helplessness, neglect, guilt, and sexual inadequacy (Westerlund, 1992). Unresolved personal issues, such as dysfunctional coping patterns, sexuality, role and patterning in the family of origin, or intimacy dysfunctions, can be elicited in the presence of these feelings, expectations, and ongoing stressors. To complicate matters, male partners in particular are often reluctant to share these feelings with others, seek support or assistance, or let the survivors know how the situation is affecting them (see Hunter, 1990; Thomas, 1989).

Viewing this situation systemically, both the partner and the survivor are often engaged in a "parallel process" involving interactions between needs, current stage of accommodation to the abuse material, emotional content, use of support, and interactions with other systems (family, court, therapists, etc.). At various points, the survivor may feel neglected or ignored, identify the partner with the abuser(s), react more as a child than an adult, become demanding for needs fulfillment, or withdraw into the safety of self or others. The partner may also feel neglected or ignored, become overly involved in advocating and taking care of the survivor, seek outside sexual involvements, or become demanding or withdrawn. These same dynamics can be expressed or acted out as the couple engages in some form of intimate connection (sexual or otherwise). Dynamics involving mutuality, power and control, support, and various affection and intimacy needs are often unknowingly expressed in the couple's sexual/intimate interactions as each person's current feelings interact with the other's. In cases in which both individuals have been abused, these dynamics are multiplied.

In intervening with a partner or a couple, the therapist is well advised to consider the dynamics discussed in the preceding paragraph. The complexity of these various aspects usually requires the clinician to intervene more broadly than with sexuality interventions alone. The therapist needs to mirror empathy for each individual, and subtle and not-so-subtle projections need to be confronted explicitly as do various dynamics in the system. Sexuality or touch-related exercises can be geared to challenge these dynamics as well as enhance physical intimacy.

Relapse prevention. The concept of relapse prevention will be familiar to clinicians who have worked with clients who have addictive or compulsive disorders. Recently, McCarthy (1993) suggested using this concept with sex therapy. For individuals and couples focusing on sexual repercussion issues, relapse is more often the rule than the exception. Consequently, the concept of "inoculating" (McCarthy, 1993) the couple in order to help them develop strategies to handle future difficulties is a particularly helpful strategy. Specific strategies and techniques include follow-up sessions with the therapist for 2 years; engaging in ongoing, nondemanding pleasuring sessions regularly; generalizing and expanding sexual repertoires; and developing coping techniques for negative or "failed" sexual experiences (McCarthy, 1993).

> *For individuals and couples focusing on sexual repercussion issues, relapse is more often the rule than the exception.*

Therapist issues. Therapists can expect a multitude of questions and concerns from those who seek therapy regarding the sexual repercussions of abuse. In addition, Talmadge and Wallace (1991) describe this clientele as "rigidly defended and less forgiving of treatment errors" (p. 180). In her research with 43 women who were childhood abuse survivors, Westerlund (1992) found that many who acknowledged sexual repercussions were unwilling or reluctant to seek help from a therapist who specialized in sexual issues. Predominant in the responses were concerns about the therapist; respondents noted trust of motivation of the therapist and expectations that sex therapy would be coercive as influencing their reluctance.

When these clients finally do seek appropriate treatment, therapists must be prepared to explicitly discuss roles, gender, boundaries, power issues, rules and expectations, goals, and alliance concerns. This early and forthright approach will help establish a foundation of openness rather than secrecy, clarity rather than ambiguity, and empowerment rather than passivity.

Issues of power and control are perhaps among the most common client-therapist struggles when intervening in sexual issues with survivors and their partners. If possible, it is wise for the clinician to avoid creating or framing issues that create power struggles. Minimizing the doctor/patient dichotomy where appropriate and validating resistance (Talmadge & Wallace, 1991), avoiding a coercive stance and empowering the couple to set the pace and degree of activity (Westerlund, 1992), and intervening in transferences that project power dynamics (such as therapist as offender, mother, etc.) are important strategically in this effort.

Complex boundary issues are often a part of the therapist's concerns. These are already numerous when working with the survivor alone; when working with a couple, these are multiplied. In many cases, the couple will have never discussed sexuality concerns with each other or anyone else. The therapist easily can be seen as invasive, insensitive, or even abusive if certain trigger words are inadvertently used. (I am reminded of an incident in which the word *penis* was used in an education session for couples with repercussion concerns; one couple was deeply offended and did not return for subsequent sessions.)

■ Conclusion

As research continues in the area of sexual abuse, treatment of the sexual repercussions of abuse is beginning to emerge as a key issue that historically has been misunderstood or disregarded.

Pioneering research by Maltz, Becker, McGuire and Wagner, Fromuth, and others over the past 10 years or so has enabled others to advance knowledge in this area. The challenge to researchers and therapists is to continue to build on this knowledge base to develop increasingly advanced and specific methodologies. Therapists and clients alike can now draw on materials and techniques that renew hope for healing and the possibility of enjoyable adult sexual expression.

Healing

"Only the wounded can heal"
At least only the compassionate
Can know what healing is about
How deeply, deeply healing is needed.
After being wounded again and again
And fiercely pierced
And walking in utter loneliness
Through dark nights and bright days
For ever so long
One learns
Enough
To know in one's heart
What healing is not.
Healing has to do with union and reunion
Reconnection
Re-creation
And becoming whole.
Risking the exquisite and horrible
Vulnerability of intimacy
And intimacy of vulnerability
Healing is walking with another
On life's journey
Being together
Through suffering, change, and growth.
Healing is the depth connection
Representing
God in each of us
Deep within ourselves
And through the vast universe
Always available
For us
Just as are some people,
If only we will come
Out of hiding.

Author Unknown

3

Dissociation and Treatment of Compulsive Reenactment of Trauma
Sexual Compulsivity

Mark F. Schwartz

Lori D. Galperin

William H. Masters

In order to cope with overwhelming stress, children have a miraculous capacity to dissociate and avoid assimilating the full impact of a traumatic event. This dissociation can consist of simply not registering a sensory event and/or becoming sufficiently numb so as not to see, feel, hear, know, or consolidate an experience into memory. Trauma survivors often describe out-of-body experiences in which they watched from the ceiling the experience of being raped, and then depersonalized it (i.e., it didn't happen to me, it happened to the "body" or to the "sex organs"). Multiple Personality Disorder (MPD) may develop with extreme dissociation. Alter personalities or personality fragments unfold that communicate to the host personality, "I experienced that event because you could never have survived it."

In such cases, the person dissociates by a part of the self splitting off and becoming separate, insulating the person through amnesic barriers.

In many cases of trauma, the amnesic barriers are not complete, and fragments of personality exist encapsulated, less rigidly, yet still frozen in time and accessible only through trance work. Such fragments may speak in a child's voice and still manifest the child's fears (e.g., fear that the perpetrator can still do harm, or that a parent will dispense punishment for telling, even though the client is now an adult). Unlike with MPD patients, however, there is no complete personality with a separate developmental history or impermeable amnesic barriers, so these patients are diagnosed with atypical dissociative disorder (Braun, 1986). Fragmentation of personality can permit double-bind beliefs to coexist. Survivors can both know and not know that they were sexually abused, simultaneously feel as though they love as well as hate their parents, and firmly believe that the abuse both was and was not their fault. Because memory can be stored within these personality fragments, the phenomenon reflects what has been described as state-dependent learning. In state-dependent learning, contextual stimuli can directly activate stored memories so that the individual automatically experiences a "flashback," or the feelings, thoughts, sensations, or cognitions of the frightened child. Various events, triggers, drugs, or therapeutic experiences can disinhibit and thereby reactivate memories.

The result of this dissociative process is that an individual feels unintegrated. He or she may feel like an imposter: The person everyone knows is not consistent with his or her impulsive urges, behaviors, or self-knowledge. Individuals may forget many years of their lives and function moment to moment without the benefit of previous models or experience. They experience constriction and isolation from others, as well as the "empty hole" in their stomachs that is unfillable. They often describe feeling like objects or robots, functioning well

> *Individuals may forget many years of their lives and function moment to moment without the benefit of previous models or experience.*

with jobs and job descriptions, but feeling inept and childlike in social roles. They often will continue to dissociate or "space out" automatically as adults without control in various situations as a way of defending against shame or the intrusion of old memories.

Addiction is often a tool both to numb out when beginning to think and feel and to experience highs that allow people to know they are still alive and human when feelings of depersonalization, numbness, emptiness, and physical and emotional analgesia pervade. In addition, alexithymia results in the inability to use dissociated emotions to signal constructive action. Thus a female trauma survivor can walk into a dangerous neighborhood at 3 a.m., drunk, and not be fearful, thereby setting herself up for revictimization. Likewise, she can choose a misogynist male similar to her perpetrator as a partner because she defines what she accepts and expects based on the past. Because cognition is dissociated, she does not learn from negative experiences. Finally, her body can actually become analgesic due to the numerous changes in the central nervous system concomitant with trauma (van der Kolk, 1989). She may therefore inflict bodily harm by bingeing, purging, starving, cutting, head banging, nail pulling, hair pulling, prostituting, or poisoning her body with drugs in order to obtain "release," cope with distress, escape inner emptiness, or just feel something through the fog of the dissociative numbing. Destructive eating and/or forced sex can create a sense of safety or affection for the individual with a dissociative disorder. Such behavior can also give the person the experience of perceived control when feeling powerless. Even being out of control is paradoxically experienced as a sense of control (i.e., "This time I do it to me!").

Because constriction and isolation are the natural consequences of trauma, dissociated individuals feel pervasively disconnected and additionally unsafe when they have intrusions of affect. A sense of safety is created through ritualistic behavior, such as cleaning, caretaking, working, running, or, in binary, rigid and authoritarian thinking. Thus if socks are not folded correctly and in the right place, individuals can experience disproportionate anxiety. Those who tend to be rigid and obsessive-compulsive often move for safety into professions with many rules and much structure, such as the military.

The need for sensation-seeking and/or conflict to provide relief from inner emptiness and boredom is another common feature of chronic dissociation. Physiologically, the individual resembles an opioid addict who can register pleasure and happiness from enjoyable experiences only when also taking a drug such as cocaine. Following chronic, inescapable stress, the brain does not seem to respond to pleasurable situations normally (van der Kolk, 1989). The threshold for pleasure is elevated, and continual crises—such as those found in professions such as emergency medicine, or those generated by extreme relational conflicts—are required to temporarily escape emptiness.

■ Ego-States Therapy

Acknowledging the frozen or split-off parts of self that have resulted from dissociation, N. G. Watkins (1978) and H. Watkins (1993) have pioneered ego-states therapy, in which the therapist accesses parts of the client's self that may overlap or have semipermeable boundaries, and works with and facilitates communication among the ego states. Ego-states therapy resembles group or family therapy within a single individual.

The dissociated individual often presents in therapy with an ego state that is a false self—the imposter or good patient. Such self parts are compliant, approval-seeking, submissive, reactive, and continually scanning for acceptance and rejection. They may embody the qualities that allow the individual to function as a very competent and able administrator in work situations, but in less formatted situations, they may demonstrate little depth or capacity. Many therapists work with the false self and achieve behavioral change and compliance briefly or superficially, but the treatment is ultimately ineffective (Gay, 1993).

The "ego-state therapist" would be inclined to access other parts of self that are trauma-based, dissociated, and typically child- or adolescent-like, frozen in time. For example, once the therapist accesses "the eating-disordered self," or the "sexually compulsive self," it becomes essential to discover what happened to the person to cause the original splitting off in order to discern the trance-logical purpose of the symptom (i.e., what makes rational, reasonable sense in the context of the child's perceived experience). The semipermeable dissociative barrier—which prohibits integration and maintains the child's initial way of coping with molestation or other inescapable stress, such as head banging, not eating, or maintaining a large body size—must be bridged.

> *The mechanism through which ego states can experience the safety of feeling loved is in recreating the original form of "love."*

Similarly, chronic pain may be a signal or cry for help to the identified client from the terrified, split-off part of the self. Sexual liaisons may serve the function of recapitulating the child's original lesson that the only way to experience closeness is through sex. Often, the sole mechanism through which ego states can experience the safety of feeling loved is in recreating whatever constituted the original form of "love"—or what passed for it.

Finally, frozen rage and powerless affect have few ways of being released. The result is that sexual exploits in seduction or perpetration become the predominant form of release. Stoller (1975) has called this "triumph over tragedy" (e.g., "This time I do it to them [or me].") and the individual experiences revenge and the illusion of mastery and control over what was once beyond control. In actuality, there is no mastery or completion of the original trauma cycle, only repetitive reenactment. Trauma coding (see Chapter 1, this volume) begins this process. The addictive cycle then begins, and the individual's entire life can become dedicated to repetitive reliving of trauma in disguised form. Some individuals release rage by hurting others or violating laws and end up in prison. Some injure themselves predominantly by going to bath houses and experiencing anonymous sex many times each evening, literally reliving their original rape in a multitude of variations on the same theme. In order to control out-of-control behavior, resolve the original trauma, and deprogram the distorted survival strategies and core beliefs, it becomes necessary to facilitate abreaction, work through the original trauma, and eventually integrate the split-off parts of the self.

Abreaction With Ego States

Techniques of abreaction—which are aimed at restoring memories of the original trauma, reconnecting the feelings associated with the trauma, and revising the cognitive distortions it produced—are of primary importance to any successful treatment of dissociated, sexually compulsive clients. In abreaction, the client coordinates the adult ego state's capacities to reason in order to resolve the long-standing, trauma-generated confusion of the encapsulated child state. Abreaction encourages reassociation of the split-off cognitions, affect, and sensations, as well as a restructuring of the attributions and belief systems that arose from the destructive traumatic environment.

Abreaction consists of the intensive reliving of a traumatic experience. The experience is reassociated into consciousness and thereby made known to self and others. Vivid reliving typically involves a catharsis, a profound release of the emotions, ideas, and associations that have been encapsulated in the traumatic experience. This release completes the stress response cycle set in motion by the trauma (Horowitz, 1986; Steele & Colrain, 1990).

Effective therapeutic abreaction offers survivors the opportunity to reexperience the traumatic events of their childhoods from a new perspective, one that combines their adult and child perspectives. The child's awareness provides the adult with comprehension; the adult's ability to interpret provides the child with relief from attributions of self-blame. This combination allows for the restructuring of core beliefs, inescapable stress, destructive parenting, and consequent self-revictimizations and reenactments.

Abreaction consists of collaborative uncovering. Clients have spent a lifetime "not knowing" for fear that they would not survive the reality of their traumas, and so they typically need sufficient preparation before they can trust and feel safe in knowing the truth. There is always ambivalence: "I want to know why I have always felt so badly," and "I'm terrified that if I know I will die or get stuck back there, go crazy or kill someone."

One of the windows into traumatic memory is sexual arousal patterns. When clients' sexual arousal is paraphilic, violent, self-degrading, or reflective of rage directed at themselves, their gender, or their genital sexuality, the fantasy patterns are typically reflective of traumatic or stigmatizing events that have misdirected the unfolding of gender identity and sexual development (Money, 1986). The fantasies are typically abreacted and revivified under deep hypnotic trance. Individuals are oriented back to the past to scan for the origins of their deviation. Such accessing also allows for shame reduction because their deepest secrets are thereby made known to others and the causes of deviation understood as adaptations to early experiences, rather than innate "badness."

As stated, sexual traumatization often involves simultaneously knowing and not knowing. Most adults who suffered sexual trauma during their childhoods have partial or total amnesia regarding the abuse details, or else they minimize or distort their histories. Because their behavior is often dissociated from knowledge, sensations, and affect (Braun, 1986), they may express little or no emotion as they relate their conscious memories of abuse. In order to integrate the split-off parts of the self and dissociated traumatic material, they must "metabolize" the trauma, or break it down into smaller pieces of work, each piece building on the mastery of the last. This process of memory retrieval and reassociation relies on survivors learning to contain, or to exercise control over, the timing and pacing of abreactive work.

The client learns to respect the information that is disclosed from split-off parts of the self while also giving the message that only so much can be dealt with at once, and the best place for such disclosure is in the safety of the therapist's office. In this manner, new material is permitted to unfold in a safe, controlled, and titrated manner, allowing mastery. This mastery includes recognizing and accepting the abuse in the *past* while allowing expression and reassociation of the feelings and fears embedded in the memories, as well as correcting the distortions in thinking. Typically, this process begins with the revivification of conscious mastery memories, such as riding a bike, followed by conscious nontraumatic memory, conscious traumatic memory, and eventually nonconscious nontraumatic memory and nonconscious traumatic memory.

The primary goals of abreaction (Table 3.1) are empowerment and reclaiming control over one's life by stopping revictimization due to early trauma-coded adaptation; flashbacks; numbing and intrusion cycles; dissociation; depersonalization; somatization; compulsive behaviors; and misdirected fear, anxiety, rage, and sadness. A survivor also needs to reown the disowned parts of the self. Reintegration of one's past and the disowned parts of the self typically results in enhanced self-efficacy and self-esteem because the client no longer feels like an imposter hiding shameful secrets.

Immediately following memory retrieval, there are cycles of intrusion and numbing similar to the rape trauma syndrome following adult rape. Clients are encouraged to talk to supportive others about their memories and feelings. They are also encouraged to participate in expressive forms of psychotherapy, such as psychodrama, in order to feel strong emotions and to direct their anger in a focused, nonviolent manner toward those who hurt them. Following this release of strong emotions, they usually experience profound sadness and are encouraged to embrace the ability to grieve and to permit the sadness they feel to unfold with dignity.

The treatment of sexual compulsivity must take into account the connection between compulsive sexuality and unexpressed rage.

TABLE 3.1 Goals of Abreaction

1. Allow the client to make connections between childhood trauma and his or her up-to-now unconscious reenactment.
2. Break the secret shame by making traumatic, stigmatizing events known to others.
3. Relieve the intense affect embedded within the encapsulated traumatic event.
4. Break the spell of the trauma that has controlled life in a disguised form.
5. Free the individual from the "control" of the past trauma by allowing for restructuring of core beliefs derived from the trauma.
6. Allow for integration of one's past, present, and future, and reintegration of disowned parts of self, thereby neutralizing the "imposter" and the "hole in the stomach" of emptiness, and creating the possibility for integrity and continuity between values and behavior.
7. Permit the redirection of strong negative affect to the people who have hurt the individual rather than at the individual or nondeserving others.
8. Allow for termination of repetitive destructive relationships by enabling the development of healthy boundaries and the capacity to say "no."
9. Promote remission of the trauma-related depression, anxiety, dissociation, somatization, compulsivity, relational and sexual distress, and target symptoms.
10. Promote development of self-empowerment and self-efficacy so that the individual can attribute change, problem solving, goal attainments, and new learning to accomplishment and effort.
11. Permit resolution and working through of trauma.

■ Compulsive Sexual Behavior

A successful approach to the treatment of sexual compulsivity must take into account the connection between compulsive sexuality and unexpressed rage (see Chapter 4, this volume). Stoller's (1975) psychoanalytic formulation, which conceives of perversion as "the erotic form of hatred," is metaphoric of sexual compulsivity. The person seeks sexual release without genuinely caring about the other. The goal is to meet one's own needs regardless of whether another is harmed. Sometimes pleasure is even derived from degrading the other or the self. In such cases, rage is misdirected at oneself, one's body, one's gender, and/or one's partner. Fantasy becomes a "triumph over tragedy" by placing the unmastered trauma into the erotic theme with perceived control.

To avoid relapse, sexually compulsive clients must eventually learn to direct anger in a focused, nonviolent way at the individuals who hurt them, rather than express uncontrolled, misdirected rage. Because the modelers of strong emotions during childhood have typically been out-of-control, impulse driven, misdirected, and dangerous, clients need to be taught that anger and other strong feelings need not equal violence and to be given tools to enable safe release. "Old" anger can be resolved by giving the split-off parts of the self a voice to express strong emotions toward the perpetrator, typically using hypnosis. Cory Hammond (1978) has called this "presentification." Following a client's intense abreaction of early traumatic memory, the therapist might say:

> And as you, the adult, together with your child walk forward, you can see your perpetrator against a white wall in front of you. He's unable to hurt you now. He simply has to stand there against the wall and listen. As you look at him there and think of how he hurt you, you realize you now have the words to tell him the things you couldn't then. What is it that you want to say to him? . . . That's right, go ahead and tell him the things you couldn't back then. . . . That's it, really tell him how much he hurt you . . . tell him about the pain . . . tell him how he's continued to affect your life, your relationships. . . . Do you want to continue to give him that power over you? . . . That's right, tell him.

In this trance state, the individual is helped to have a powerful yet directed expression of strong emotions, and thereby experiences a catharsis. The adult self and child self become partners in redressing the injury. Through the adult self's support and reclamation of the child self, the way is paved for ultimate integration.

Illusion of Intimacy

Another function of sexually compulsive behavior is to provide the illusion of intimacy. Trauma results in constriction and disconnection, with belief systems revolving around low self-esteem, objectification of self and others, lack of trust, and an unwillingness to be vulnerable. There is typically discomfort with genital play and with nudity unless accompanied by dissociation into deviant fantasy. Given these obstacles and constraints, there is little potential for true intimacy. Therefore, intimacy disorder is always a core contributing factor to sexual compulsivity, and sexual compulsivity a maintaining component of intimacy disorder.

Healthy adult relationships demand two reasonably integrated individuals who are able to love and trust each other and who share their

experiences, thoughts, and feelings honestly. Following trauma resolution, the individual is able to establish the requisite self-efficacy and
self-esteem for initiating relationships. Social skills, problem-solving
skills, empathy skills, courtship skills, sexual touching skills, communication and recognition of emotion skills, and anger management skills
can then be provided in a school-like setting to help the newly integrated individual to be less terrified in close interpersonal relationships.
Couples therapy is then useful for learning how to live with another
without destructive power struggles and battles for control. For most
sexually compulsive clients, these basic skills are completely new because their early models were so lacking. Issues around gender roles
likewise require intervention because the parental modeling and sexual
abuse may have resulted in damage to individuals' comfort with their
own gender and fear or anger with the alternate gender. Stigma associated with homosexuality may further complicate this resolution.

Sexually compulsive clients are terrified of close relationships and
have developed sets of cognitions and belief systems based on their
shame-based, trauma-based families. Lying to protect their secrets and
to maintain their imposter status has been a way of life. Thus the
essential first step is called "opening the channel" (Yolenson &
Samenow, 1977). To open the channel, groups are used to make disclosure normative and to confront thinking errors, destructive belief systems (Carnes, 1982), self-deception, minimizations, denial, and ration-
alization. The group also reduces shame by rewarding disclosure of
deep feelings of inadequacy and unworthiness as well as disclosure of
self-degrading and/or perpetrating behavior.

The final component in an effective therapeutic approach to sexual
compulsion must include provisions to preclude relapse. The factors
that maintain destructive acting out are not necessarily the ones that
originate them. For example, once a person goes to a "peep show" for
the first time and experiences an intense high, relief from anxiety,
distraction from problems, sexual release, and sensations of power,
control, and connection, the behavior is likely to be used habitually to
cope. When the individual is angry, sad, lonely, or empty, he or she goes
to the peep show and attains relief. To break an addictive cycle, the
client must maintain an abstinence contract. Hospitalization, 12-step
groups, antiandrogen drug therapy, medications such as Prozac or
Anaphronil, or aversive behavioral therapy can also be used to help
establish such control. Relapse prevention (Marlatt, 1985) is then em-

ployed to help identify triggers, high-risk situations, apparently irrelevant decisions, and chains of behavior that precede a lapse. Alternative means of dealing with negative emotions, depression, and anxiety are suggested, implemented, and then reinforced. With abstinence, there will be intrusions of affect and memory. What the compulsivity served to push out of consciousness begins to emerge. If the client is able to cope effectively, the new feelings and memories can be the starting point for the necessary trauma and family-of-origin work.

■ Ego-States Therapy With Sexually Compulsive Parts of the Self

Dealing with passive rage, powerlessness, difficulties with intimacy, cognitive distortions, and addictive cycles is typically necessary, but not sufficient, for long-term control. Using ego-states therapy can be very effective, particularly with sexually compulsive clients with high dissociative scores on the Dissociative Experiences Scale (DES; Putnam, 1989), Dissociative Disorder Interview Schedule (DDIS; Ross, 1989), Structured Clinical Interview for Dissociative Disorder (SCID-D; Steinberg, 1991), and Lowenstein's Mental Status Exam (Lowenstein, 1991). Typically, hypnotic induction is used following the establishment of safety and trust in the therapeutic relationship. The client then abreacts his or her most exciting deviant sexual arousal (Glaser, personal communication, 1993) in great detail. The strong affect is then used to create an affect-bridge (Watkins, 1989) to access the events that originally contributed to the arousal pattern's formation. The client often is able to remember clearly, revivify, and ultimately resolve the specific traumatic events that culminated in the deviant sexual arousal.

For example, one client discussed a recent shameful sexual liaison that resulted in his being urinated on consensually. The feelings of degradation were reexperienced under trance and then used to bridge him back to an age-regressed state. He began to relive an incident that occurred when he was 6 years old, when three school bullies beat him up and urinated on him. At this same age, he was also used by his older brother as a sexual outlet, and peers were teasing him in other cruel ways. Repeated abreactions surrounding the trauma eventually resulted in a loss of both desire for degrading sexual enactments and urophobia. Subsequent arousal reconditioning using fantasy satiation

(Abel, Becker, & Skinner, 1990) then resulted in permanent changes in sexual arousal patterns.

The sexually compulsive ego state with pedophiles is often childlike and reenacts specific sexual abuse that has occurred in or out of the home. In most cases, however, the sexually compulsive ego state is adolescent in nature. Most perpetrators begin their activity in adolescence and deal with powerless recalcitrant passive rage by acting out sexually. By accessing this teenage part and establishing a trusting relationship and rapport, the therapist can hear the multiple sources of frustration and compassionately support and redirect the client's reactions to mistreatment from abusive adults. The adult parts of the self are typically poorly differentiated and lack moral development. The therapist, group, or therapeutic community becomes the vehicle for facilitation of values clarification and the development of an effective, powerful adult self formed on a commitment to honesty and integrity. The new adult self is eventually integrated with child and adolescent ego states.

Arousal Reconditioning

Regardless of the quality of therapy involving each of the aforementioned components of treatment, relapse is likely if the individual has low, nondeviant sexual arousal. Following treatment that has resulted in (a) the reduction of fear in close adult relationships, (b) improved social skills, (c) neutralization of rage and powerlessness from early abuse, (d) increased self-efficacy, (e) the restructuring of core beliefs and cognitive distortions, and (f) trauma resolution and integration of split-off parts of the self, the individual may experience ego-dystonic deviant sexual arousal. Fantasy satiation (Abel et al., 1990) or covert sensitization (Schwartz, 1992) then can be used to further facilitate changes in sexual arousal and fantasy patterns. Sexual therapy and sensate focus are particularly useful at this phase of therapy to neutralize specific sexual phobias and encourage healthy sexuality.

Distinct ego states that developed following multiple traumas may each have different deviant sexual arousal patterns.

In certain cases in which there has been an extensive history of abuse, distinct ego states that developed following multiple traumas may each have different deviant sexual arousal patterns. For example, one client, who had been sexually abused in a cult, verbalized the following sexual arousal patterns by different alter male and female personalities. In such a case, arousal reconditioning is introduced to each ego state separately during hypnotic therapeutic sessions.

Adolescent Bob

I like rough sex with women using drugs, sometimes letting the women be in control, sometimes me treating them like bitches and whores. I would like to have sex with mom. She's in the next room, maybe she'll walk in on me when I'm masturbating. I like big women with big breasts, obese women, whores who like it hard and do whatever I tell her to do. I like anal sex with women from behind. I like sex with two girls at the same time or another man with my wife while I'm watching. I feel I'm inadequate about my sexual self with just one testicle. I hate my self/body, everything. I'm not worth living. I like to do it 5-6 times in one night. I don't like women for very long. I like to experiment.

Judy Whore

I'm a whore and slut. I like it hard till it hurts. I like to satisfy my man. I like it in my ass real hard till it bleeds. I like for you to beat the hell out of me while you're having sex with me. I'll give you oral sex, too. I'll take on 4 to 5 men at one time. I'll do just about anything to satisfy my man. That's all I'm worth, your servant. I don't care about myself. I'm not lovable, just a whore and a slut. I like it from behind, too. Two men at one time. I'll suck your penis good and then stick it in my rectum. Do it to me hard from behind. It's the way I love it.

Janet Promiscuous Tricky

I'll take your nuts and cut them off. I hate men. I hate you. I'm like a Venus flytrap. Sweet on the outside, but deadly inside. You men are so stupid. I can get anything I want through sex. I'm a man, manipulator, conner, cunning. I love to castrate men and laugh at them afterwards. You helpless little bastards, you think through the head of your dick. Give it to me. You'll be sorry, I'll leave you wishing you had never met me. I'm your worst nightmare come true. You won't know it by my appearance, but I'll love you then I'll stab you in the back.

Johnny 8-13

I'm a woman's boy. Except I'm looking for a new mamma. Mine won't have me. I'm always trying to get a mom to let me be her son but this involves sucking her breasts and her loving me and kissing me like I'm a baby. I need all mom's attention, there's not enough to go around. I want her to make me have sex with her, and control me and I'll be her love slave. I have confused feelings about a mom—I just want one. I just want to forget about all this shame and bad feelings and retreat to my mommy, but she's not there. She's gone somewhere else.

Healthy Sexuality

Healthy sexuality requires that the individual be able to be close and vulnerable with a partner and able to focus on the partner's nude body without the need to dissociate by thinking of another partner or fantasy, numbing out, or destroying oneself. When images of trauma-coded fantasy intrude or are created to enable or enhance arousal, there remains unresolved trauma. Following further abreaction using deviant arousal as a bridge, the couple may require sex therapy to neutralize the terror, lack of knowledge, and fears of closeness and abandonment that become activated in the vulnerability of sexual intimacy. Relational therapy to teach the tools of communication, problem resolution, and active listening may also be useful because relational distress is the major contributor to relapse of compulsive behavior.

■ Conclusion

A combination of cognitive behavioral, trauma-based, and systemic models of treatment can result in greater treatment efficacy. This chapter attempts to apply the advances made in the treatment of dissociative disorders to a broadened understanding of sexual compulsivity as an unconscious reenactment of early trauma and inescapable stress. The result is a therapy that is etiologically based, time-limited, directive, empirically derived and evaluated, and humanistic.

4

Uncovering the Relationship Between a Client's Adult Compulsive Sexual Behavior and Childhood Sexual Abuse

Mic Hunter

Research has begun to confirm what clinicians have long thought about the high rate of childhood sexual abuse in adults who present with compulsive/addictive sexual behavior patterns (Carnes, 1989; Hunter, 1985). These patterns often parallel the childhood abuse and can be used to determine the type of abuse suffered and the issues that will need to be addressed in the treatment plan. Clients who do not receive treatment for early abuse are at greater risk for returning to compulsive/addictive behaviors.

AUTHOR'S NOTE: Portions of this chapter were presented in New Orleans in June 1992 at the conference "Sexual Addiction/Compulsivity and Trauma: The Interrelationship" at the invitation of Mark Schwartz, whom I wish to thank. I also wish to take this opportunity to thank Patrick Carnes for inviting me to take my practicum at the Sexual Addiction Treatment Program at the Family Renewal Center and Eli Coleman for encouraging me to present my research findings at an annual meeting of the American Association of Sex Educators, Counselors and Therapists and at several of the National Conferences on Sexual Compulsivity/Addiction.

■ Levels of Consciousness

An understanding of the workings of the levels of consciousness is important when treating persons with compulsive or addictive behavior patterns because much of the emotional material that is fueling the behavior is not conscious.

The human mind (and perhaps the mind of some other species, such as the great apes) consists of three basic levels of consciousness; the conscious, the subconscious or preconscious, and the unconscious. The conscious mind contains that on which the individual is actively focusing, such as the meaning of these words that you are currently reading. The sub- or preconscious is that which can be brought easily into awareness, such as the sensation of holding this book in your hands, but is not currently in focus because the information is not considered valuable enough to involve the conscious mind. By definition, the unconscious mind contains material that is out of one's conscious awareness yet has a profound effect on behavior. Throughout this chapter, I will be using the term *mind* rather than *brain* because I will be describing processes rather than physical structures.

Conscious behavior is the easiest type of cognition and action to modify because the material on which clients are focused is in the foreground of their awareness. Thoughts and behaviors that are repeated over time develop into patterns and then into habits. Reber (1985) defines a habit as "A pattern of activity that has, through repetition, become automatized, fixed and easily and effortlessly carried out" (p. 314). Once the tasks of everyday life are learned, they are relegated to the subconscious mind to avoid cluttering the conscious mind. These acts become so automatic that we can do them while consciously thinking of something else (e.g., driving and shifting a car). In order to learn to operate a manual transmission, the driver must be consciously aware of the actions of both feet and hands. Once the task is learned, it is successfully completed without conscious awareness unless, for some reason, the behavior is causing problems. At that time, the conscious mind will become aware of the problem and make efforts to change the behavior. For example, I borrowed a friend's automobile. Although I had never driven the particular model, I had no difficulty manually shifting it without much conscious thought. By the time I had driven through town and entered the freeway, which I had traveled numerous times in the past, my conscious mind was occupied with things other than driving until my subconscious mind attempted to shift the transmission into fifth gear. Had I been in *my* car, my conscious mind never would have become aware of this seemingly simple act. However, because I was not in my car and the transmission I was operating did not have a fifth gear, my conscious mind became suddenly aware that I had shifted into third gear at 60 miles per hour. Once my conscious mind assessed the situation and corrected my actions, I again entrusted my subconscious mind to find the way home.

Psychotherapists are constantly making comments that bring information from clients' subconscious minds into their conscious awareness (e.g., "I noticed that even though you said you are angry, you are smiling." "When you began to talk about sex, you crossed your legs and looked at the floor." "As you began to cry, you held your breath and the tears stopped."). Once clients are consciously aware of these actions, they are more able to modify them.

If the conscious mind is the foreground and the subconscious is the midground, then the unconscious mind is the background. To use a computer as an analogy: The conscious mind is what is on screen, the subconscious mind is what is on the disk that can be easily brought onto the screen, and the unconscious mind is the programming software. This programming is the source of the obsessive thoughts and compulsive behaviors that bring clients into psychotherapy.

I describe the unconscious in action to my clients with the following example: When you came into my office today and I asked you to sit down, you sat in one of the three appropriate places. You did not sit on the table or the bookcase. This is because years ago, when you were a very young child, you learned to identify furniture. At first, everything was a mystery, but eventually you learned the characteristics and functions of various types of furniture. You began to understand that although both a chair and a table have four legs that support a flat surface, a chair also has a back and sometimes arms. Once you became an expert at identifying furniture, you did not want to waste time consciously assessing each piece when you entered a room. You trusted your unconscious mind to identify quickly and effortlessly the appropriate objects on which to sit. Your understanding of this ability is important because at the same ages you were learning to identify furniture, you were also learning about power in relationships, sexuality, body functions, rules about emotional expression, and countless other topics, all of which affect how you think and behave today.

■ Behavior as a Continuum

Eli Coleman and Patrick Carnes (Hohmann, 1989; Kelberer, 1989) have had an ongoing debate about the appropriate use of the terms *compulsive* and *addictive* when discussing sexual behavior. After listening to them both at some length (Dr. Coleman was one of my instructors at the University of Minnesota and Dr. Carnes was my supervisor at a practicum site), I have decided that both of them are correct some of the time.

Reber (1985) describes a compulsion as "Behavior motivated by factors that compel a person to act against his or her own wishes" (p. 139). The *Diagnostic and Statistical Manual of Mental Disorders* (American Psychiatric Association, 1987) defines it as

> repetitive and seemingly purposeful behavior that is in response to an obsession, or performed according to certain rules or in a stereotyped fashion. The behavior is not an end in itself, but is designed to produce or prevent some future state of affairs; the activity, however, either is not connected in a realistic way with the state of affairs it is designed to produce or prevent, or may be clearly excessive. The act is performed with a sense of subjective compulsion coupled with a desire to resist it (at least initially); performing the particular act is not pleasurable, although it may afford some relief of tension. (p. 393)

Some people have argued that sexual behavior cannot be compulsive because it does not fit this definition; sexual behavior is pleasurable and is an end in itself. However, these people are likely comparing their experiences with sexual behavior and not the experiences of the sexually compulsive (e.g., the compulsive masturbator who reports that she "finally just gave into the urge to masturbate. I really didn't enjoy it, but I couldn't focus on anything else until I got it out of the way.").

The events, emotions, or thoughts that trigger the compulsive behavior and obsessive thoughts can be symbolic, that is, similar to the original trauma but different enough that the person has great difficulty seeing the connection. Because these triggers are not conscious, the behavior associated with the triggers is resistant to change.

Both compulsive and addictive behavior function as coping mechanisms—they either suppress or access memories and emotions. When assessing the addict's behavior, it is vital to keep in mind that each behavior, as well as the overall pattern of behavior, can serve either function. For example, an individual's compulsive masturbation may numb his or her loneliness and shame, whereas his or her compulsive affairs may be an attempt to access and experience joy and acceptance.

Psychological addiction can be thought of as a collection of compulsive behaviors and obsessive thoughts. Rather than merely having one compulsive behavior, the person has several and also exhibits preoccupation and a loss of control. Sexual behavior not only has become the person's primary coping mechanism, but also has begun to create difficulties for the individual. At this point, the meaning that the behavior holds for the person has become all but completely unconscious. This dynamic brings up another objection to describing sexual acts as compulsive/addictive. Because the behaviors do not appear "designed to produce or prevent some future state of affairs," it seems that they do not fit the *DSM-III-R* definition. They do not have that appearance to the outside observer or to the person performing them. This is not because the state of affairs that the person is seeking to "produce or prevent" is outside of his or her conscious awareness. By the time someone has developed a psychological addiction to an act, it has taken on a life of its own. The actions are so automatic that the addict will report that they "just happen" as if he or she played no role in the action.

■ The Effects of Ceasing the Compulsive Sexual Behavior

There are a number of questions that are useful for determining what role the compulsive sexual behavior may play in the client's life.

1. *What is the longest period of time you have abstained from this behavior?* Clients who report that they are able to resist their compulsive urges only for several hours will need a different treatment plan than those who report that they have gone for several months without taking part in compulsive rituals.

2. *What reasons did you have for abstaining (e.g., to prove you could, because you were having problems)? What did you learn about yourself as a result of this period of abstaining?*

3. *What happened when you stopped, reduced the frequency of, or modified the compulsive behavior?* If a behavior emotionally numbs the client, he

Conscious→Patterns→Habits→Obsessions & Compulsive Behavior→
Addictive Behavior

Figure 4.1. Behavior and Thoughts as a Continuum

or she will report becoming anxious, shameful, depressed, and so on. If a behavior is used to create emotional responses, clients will report becoming distant, lonely, cut off from themselves or their bodies, and so on. Those who have another addictive pattern often report that the other behavior (overeating, drug taking, gambling, etc.) increases when the sexual behavior is reduced.

4. *What would you be thinking of if you were not preoccupied/obsessing about these behaviors?* Of course, this will be a difficult question for the client to answer because obsessive thoughts seem automatic—subconsciously triggered in most cases. Although clients may not be able to answer this question the first time it is asked, they are likely to ask themselves the same question the next time they begin to obsess. For example, one client became aware that every time she started to think about her father, she suddenly found herself obsessing about sexual matters. She had not been aware of this connection until she was asked the above question.

5. *What would you lose if you completely stopped this behavior?* The answers to this question frequently demonstrate how all-encompassing the compulsive behavior has become and what a central role, both positive and negative, it plays in the person's life: "I can't imagine not doing it. I wouldn't have any reason to live. Life would be bleak," or "At last I would be free. I could face myself and others."

■ Sexual Abuse as an Underlying Cause of Compulsive and Addictive Sexual Behavior

Research has found that a large percentage of those who identify themselves as sexually compulsive or addictive also report experiencing childhood sexual abuse. In a survey of members of the mutual-help organization Sex Addiction Anonymous, Hunter (1985) found that 37% of the members knew they had been sexually victimized during childhood. Carnes's (1989) research on patients at an inpatient treatment program for addictive sexual behavior found that 81% knew that they had been sexually abused as children. There are those whose sexual

> *Clinicians may become overly committed to uncovering the repressed memories and lose track of the important treatment goals.*

behavior is compulsive/addictive and yet they are unable to identify any abusive sexual events in childhood. It has been my clinical experience that these persons were usually severely neglected as children, having been left alone frequently for long periods. They are often compulsive masturbators and/or compulsive with pornography. Clinicians who are convinced that everyone who exhibits compulsive sexual behavior has

been sexually abused as a child may become overly committed to uncovering the repressed memories that they are sure must exist, and thus lose track of the important treatment goals.

In recent years, more and more clients have contacted psychotherapists already identifying a history of childhood sexual abuse, but most presenting complaints are related to the adulthood consequences of the abuse. Providing a protocol for an assessment of sexual abuse is beyond the scope of this chapter. However, it is important to know if a client has any desire in knowing if he or she was sexually abused. Three questions that I have found useful to ask clients are the following:

1. *What is* your *definition of sexual abuse?* An individual's definition frequently will preclude anything that he or she experienced. That was the case for the client who told me she had not been sexually abused, but also told me that she used to "suck on my grandfather's penis." When asked her definition of sexual abuse, she replied, "That is when someone has intercourse with you when they are mad at you." According to her definition, it would have been inappropriate for her to describe herself as a sexual abuse victim.

2. *If you had been sexually abused, would you want to know?* If a person does not want to know that he or she was sexually abused, there may be a very good reason to remain unaware of any knowledge of the abuse. Awareness of childhood abuse may overwhelm the person's defenses and make his or her current problems worse.

3. *Why or why not?* Valuable information can be gathered by inquiring the reasons the person wishes to know or not know about a history of abuse. For example, one client stated that he did not think he had been sexually abused, but added that if he had been, he would want to know about it because it might help explain the reason he could not stop his pattern of compulsive masturbation, even though he attended several mutual-help meetings per week and had been in psychotherapy for several years. In this case, it is wise to inquire: What is the longest period of time he can avoid masturbating? What takes place during the time he is not masturbating? How does he feel? What thoughts or dreams is he aware of during these periods? What happens when he returns to masturbating?

Clients who say that they do not want to know if there is sexual abuse in their backgrounds are making it clear to the therapist that this topic is too threatening to address at this time. The client just discussed, who stated he was not interested in knowing if he had been sexually abused, responded, when asked his reasoning behind this decision: "Well, I wouldn't be able to spend any time with my father then." He did not appear to grasp the significance of his response, which I noted but did not pursue until much later in the therapeutic relationship, at which time he recalled having been anally assaulted by his father. To force or coerce a client who states that he or she does not want conscious awareness of sexual trauma to recall such an event is a re-creation of the original abuse: an authority figure, behind closed doors, insisting that something painful be done against one's will, in secret.

Merely because one sexually abusive experience has been identified does not mean that it is the root of all the compulsive behaviors. Each compulsive sexual behavior may have a different origin, different offenders, and a different purpose. The purpose of a compulsive behavior may be to shut down a response or to create a response. Examples of shutting down include becoming emotionally or physically numb or creating a dissociative state. Instances of creating responses include reenacting an abuse experience, obtaining physical sensations, or ending a dissociative state.

Once an individual has reached the point of addictive sexual behavior, sensations and emotions become sexualized. In the words of Terry Kellogg (personal communication, 1982), "To a sex addict, sex is the answer; what's the question?" For example, during a session, a sexually compulsive client suddenly had a frightened look on his face. When asked what was troubling him, he reported that he had "suddenly gotten horny." When asked what physical sensations he was experiencing that he was labeling as horniness, he stated that he had a "tightness in the crotch and a pressure on his penis." After being encouraged to go to the restroom and drain his full bladder, he reported that the horniness had disappeared. Similar sexually compulsive persons interpret their emotional responses as signals to be sexual. When lonely, they seek sex rather than companionship. When hurt or sad, they seek sex instead of comforting. Fear and shame are frequently misinterpreted as sexual responses.

Numerous compulsive sexual behaviors involve fear, voyeurism, exhibitionism, extramarital affairs, anonymous sex, and masochism. To illustrate, one client reported that when he had trouble sleeping, he would go under a certain bridge in town, remove his clothes, and wait for someone else to do the same, at which time they would have sex. The site of this bridge was well known for this type of activity, as well as for frequent murders. When asked to describe the physical and emotional responses he experienced while under the bridge, he reported that he had "a rapid heart rate, sweaty palms, fast shallow breathing, and overall tight muscles." He viewed these as an indication of sexual excitement. When asked if it was possible that these responses were in fact clues of fear because he was naked and unarmed in a dark, dangerous place, he denied such a possibility until he attempted to return to the bridge. That time he experienced the same body reactions as terror, rather than sexual excitement, and was able to avoid remaining at the site. On subsequent nights when he was unable to sleep, he telephoned members of his support group who had agreed to accept calls from him regardless of the time of day.

Shame is the most common emotion that is sexualized by compulsively sexual people. This is due to the powerful pairing of shame and sex during the experience of sexual abuse as a child. When the victimized person becomes a sexually active adolescent or adult, he or she will frequently report feeling shameful even during appropriate sexual interactions. A total of 87% of the members of the mutual-help group Adult Children of Sexual Dysfunction who responded to a questionnaire (Hunter, 1992) reported that the statement "As an adult, I experience confusion, discomfort or terror in the face of sexuality" definitely applied to them. When given the statement "As an adult I experience fear or shame when I act in healthy sexual ways," 75% reported that it "definitely applies to me." Shame is a common response in those who have experienced sexual trauma. In the sexually compulsive individual, shame has become so associated with sex that experiencing shame triggers the compulsive sexual urge. Taking part in the compulsive sexual act creates momentary relief from the shame, but then causes an even greater shame response (see Figure 4.2).

> *In the sexually compulsive individual, shame has become so associated with sex that experiencing shame triggers the compulsive sexual urge.*

■ State-Dependent Learning

The idea that an adult behavior has its root in childhood experience is certainly not new. One might say that it is the very cornerstone of most of psychology and psychotherapy for the past 100 years. The pattern of repeating experiences, even though self-harming, has been labeled using numerous terms:

Repetition compulsion—"a common form of compulsion in which there is an irrational and rather irresistible desire to repeat some behavior" (Reber, 1985, p. 639)

Counterphobic character—"a person who regularly engages in and derives pleasure from behaviors and activities that 'normally' would be regarded as dangerous and anxiety-provoking" (Reber, 1985, p. 164)

Traumatophilia or *traumatophilic diathesis*—"individuals who somehow seem to put themselves repeatedly into situations in which something goes seriously wrong, resulting in injury to themselves or others" (Reber, 1985, p. 789)

The model that best fits with my clinical experience is that of state-dependent learning. Information related to previous experiences is more likely to be recalled when one is exposed to a setting that is similar to the one in which the original experience took place. For example, one is more likely to recall a coworker's name when seeing him or her in the

Sexual abuse leads to→
Sexualized shame, which leads to→
Compulsive sexual behavior, which leads to→
Additional shame, which leads to→
Further compulsive sexual behavior→Ad infinitum→

Figure 4.2. The Relationship of Sexual Abuse, Shame, and Compulsive Sexual Behavior

environment in which he or she is commonly seen, the workplace, than when encountering him or her in an unfamiliar site, such as on a street in another town. When people are exposed to trauma, they go into an altered state of consciousness. Their mood and brain function is different from their usual day-to-day mood and brain functioning. Exposure to stimuli that represent the trauma can trigger memories of the trauma. That which triggers recall of the previously learned material can be intrapsychic as well as external. Places, thoughts, images, sounds, emotions, or sensations all may cause the individual to reexperience emotions, sensations, or thoughts that were first experienced during childhood sexual abuse. In the language of *DSM-III-R* (American Psychiatric Association, 1987), these are "recurrent and intrusive distressing recollections of the event" and "sudden acting or feeling as if the traumatic event were reoccurring (includes a sense of reliving the experience, illusions, hallucinations, and dissociative [flashback] episodes, even those that occur on awakening or when intoxicated)" (p. 250). When in such a state, individuals' behavior is determined by what they think is taking place rather than what may actually be taking place. Therefore, they may behave in inappropriate ways, such as repeating a self-harming pattern.

The concept of state-dependent learning is clinically useful in three ways. First, it provides the therapist with a model to explain clients' behavior patterns that otherwise seem nonsensical. Second, it provides the client with an explanation for repetitive, self-defeating behavior patterns other than the one they have been using (e.g., "I'm crazy"). Third, accessing the state of mind that the client is in during compulsive sexual acts makes the process of decoding the meaning of the act easier.

When working with a person whose compulsive sexual behavior almost always includes the use of mood-altering substances, it is important to determine if a concurrent drug addiction also exists or if the substance used is a part of the state-dependent learning. Frequently, adults will make available alcohol and other drugs to children prior to beginning sexual contact. The ingestion of mood-altering substances as an adult then recreates the state during which the childhood sexual abuse took place, and enables the person to remember many of these memories.

Because state-dependent learning is idiosyncratic, the psychotherapist is unlikely to be able to decode the meaning of the client's behavior. More progress will be obtained when the client determines the meaning of the behavior.

■ Clues to the Age at Which the Abuse Took Place

In order to narrow the age range when assessing for the possibility of sexual abuse, ask the client to determine at what age the sexual behaviors became compulsive. This may be the age at which the client was in such emotional pain that he or she needed to become emotionally numb to cope. When taking a family history, an alert therapist may notice signs of spontaneous age regression, such as a change in tone, voice, or body posture, or the use of language that is more appropriate for a child. At such moments it is useful to ask, "What age do you have a sense of being right now?" In most cases, that client will be able to identify an earlier age within 1 or 2 years. At that point, the therapist should ask, "What was happening at that age?" Frequently, this is the age at which the client was abused. Once an age range has been established, the therapist will have an idea of the developmental issues facing the client. For example, if one uses Erickson's (1950) psychosexual model, a client who was abused between the ages of birth and 1 year (Freud's oral stage) will likely have issues with basic trust and mistrust. Therefore, a major portion of the therapy will need to be devoted to providing an environment in which safety can be experienced and trust can be learned.

■ Clues to the Goals of the Sexual Behavior and the Issues of the Abuse

One method of helping a client to identify the goals of the compulsive sexual behavior and the issues related to the sexual abuse is to ask for a description, either spoken or written, of the client's ideal sexual fantasy or the fantasy most often used during masturbation. When listening to or reading the client's fantasy, it is the task of the therapist to become aware of themes within the fantasy. For example, is there a theme of being powerful? Perhaps the client experiences a lack of power in his or her current life. If so, then one of the treatment goals would relate to the client obtaining a sense of being powerful in a safe manner. Does the fantasy contain someone being overpowered? In such a case, the therapist may want to ask the client, "Was there ever a time in your life when someone overpowered you?" The therapist may also ask the client to free-associate about particular aspects of the fantasy or to, in the language of Gestalt therapy, "become" certain objects within the fantasy and speak as them. For example:

Therapist: When you masturbate, what do you most often think about?
Client: Women and sex, of course.
Therapist: Any particular woman?
Client: Women I have seen on the street.
Therapist: What is their most common body build, hair color, style of dress? Describe them to me, if you would.
Client: They are pretty, well-built.
Therapist: What happens in the fantasy?
Client: Well, I am alone with her someplace . . .
Therapist: What kind of place?
Client: Usually it is her bedroom. And we have sex.
Therapist: What is the process? How does it come about that you have sex?
Client: Well, actually I just grab her and pull off her clothes.
Therapist: What is she wearing?
Client: A blouse or shirt or dress. Could be anything.
Therapist: Is there any aspect of the dress that is important?
Client: What do you mean, important?
Therapist: Is there any aspect of the fantasy that tends to remain the same over time that, if changed, would make it less exciting?
Client: I guess the best parts are that she resists at first but then she ends up enjoying it.
Therapist: Anything else?
Client: And she has to have on white underwear.
Therapist: What does white underwear mean to you?
Client: I don't know what you are asking.
Therapist: How would the fantasy be if she was wearing black underwear?
Client: It wouldn't be the same. Only sluts wear black underwear.
Therapist: What kind of women wear white underwear?
Client: Good girls.

What is developing is the theme of overpowering an innocent "good girl" who eventually likes what is happening to her. Further discussions over several sessions led to the recalling of a female baby-sitter who was sexual with him when he was a young boy. His fantasy mirrored his actual experience in that it involved a more powerful person being sexual with an innocent who was frightened but eventually came to enjoy the physical sensations (which, of course, does not make the act less abusive on the part of the woman).

A second example involves a man whose masturbation was sometimes compulsive, but at other times seemed to cause him no difficulties. He reported that one difference between his compulsive masturbation and the other times he masturbated was how he stimulated himself. When he was compulsively masturbating, he would rub against the sheet of his bed. He recalled that although he started masturbating as a boy, masturbation did not become compulsive until his adolescent years. After being asked what was taking place during those years, he identified that this was the time when his father remarried. As he continued to describe the events of those years, he disclosed for the first time that when his father was away from the house, his stepmother used to come into his bedroom at night and fondle his penis. The client was afraid that if his father found out what was taking place, he would be forced to leave the house. He began to lay face down and pretend to be asleep when his stepmother came into his room. His penis would become erect when he felt her sitting on his bed, but he would continue to pretend to be asleep. Eventually she would leave and he would masturbate by rubbing against the sheets face down. He learned to associate fear, sexual arousal, and being face down on a bed. As an adult, when he was afraid due to financial, employment, or relationship problems, he would get an overwhelming urge to masturbate in this manner. Although he had never repressed the memory of his stepmother's actions, never before had he identified the connection with fear.

If the client is too uncomfortable discussing a detailed sexual fantasy, the client can be encouraged to keep a journal.

If the client—or therapist—is too uncomfortable discussing a detailed sexual fantasy, the client can be encouraged to keep a journal listing the sights, smells, sounds, and times of day or year that trigger obsessive thoughts and compulsive behaviors. Again, the task of the therapist is to help the client identify patterns and themes that may be clues to the goals of the sexual behavior and the childhood trauma. For example, one client identified that he always acted out sexually the week of major holidays. When he began to discuss his memories of various holiday rituals that took place in his childhood home, he recalled that his uncle came to visit his family at these times. As he described the events in more detail, he became sexually aroused. When asked what he would be feeling if he were not sexually aroused, he eventually identified feeling afraid and ashamed. Prevented from acting on his sexual urges by being in the therapy session, he was able to continue experiencing the emotions to a level he had not in the past. He began to recall that his uncle would sleep in the same room with him. As he talked, he began to report pain in his rectum but did not understand the origin of the pain. As he focused on the physical sensations, he began to recall his uncle having anal sex with him. This awareness came about without the use of formal hypnotherapy and no suggestions from the therapist other than, "And what are you aware of now?"

■ Decoding the Possible Meaning of Specific Sexual Behaviors

The following material is based on my clinical experience and is not intended to be generalized to nonclinical populations. In addition, because my observations are limited to my client population, which consists primarily of Caucasian, college-educated, middle-class, adult males and females from the Midwest, I encourage the reader to show caution when addressing these behaviors with other types of clients.

Voyeurism

When working with a client who reports being voyeuristic, always assess for exhibitionism as well. It is vital that the topic be addressed several times throughout the therapeutic relationship because clients may acknowledge one behavior, the one they wish to stop, but deny the others that they still want to continue.

Voyeurism is usually only thought in terms of sight. For example, Reber (1985) defined voyeurism as a paraphilia characterized by a pattern of sexual behavior in which one's preferred means of sexual arousal is the clandestine *observing* [italics added] of others when they are disrobing, nude or actually engaged in sexual activity. (p. 825)

Likewise the *DSM-III-R* (American Psychiatric Association, 1987) focuses on the visual:

The essential feature of this disorder is recurrent, intense, sexual urges and sexually arousing fantasies, of at least six months' duration, involving the act of *observing* [italics added] unsuspecting people, usually strangers, who are either naked, in the process of disrobing, or engaged in sexual activity. (p. 289)

However, numerous cases involve what I will term *auditory* voyeurism. These individuals experience recurrent and intense sexual arousal to the sound of persons masturbating, having sexual intercourse, and talking about sexual behavior. They often go to great efforts to seek relief, including using drinking glasses pressed against walls in hotels to amplify the sounds coming from the next room or purchasing medical stethoscopes or parabolic microphones. They may even tape-record these amplified sounds for later use during masturbation. Just as with visual voyeurism, auditory voyeurs prefer that the individuals being overheard are unaware. Persons who voluntarily permit themselves to be heard do not provide the desired effect.

One frequently finds that the client with voyeurism of either type came from a family with poor boundaries. There was little or no privacy and open nudity was common. The children witnessed adults involved in sexual activity, either because the adults did not attempt to conceal their behavior by closing doors or because the adults actually may have encouraged the children to watch as sexual behavior took place. In addition, these families often had an intrusiveness combined with hostility. The adults consistently barged into rooms while the children bathed, used the toilet, or dressed. Any protest, no matter how politely stated, was laughed off or met with anger. Many clients will reluctantly acknowledge that they believe their parents, particularly mothers, would purposely wait until they were masturbating before entering their bedrooms without knocking on the door. In some cases, the parent would talk with the adolescent as if nothing unusual was taking place. One client described his experience with his mother:

She would ignore me until I went to my room and then walk in unan-
nounced to ask me what I wanted for supper. She would stand there and
stare at my erect penis while she chatted. If I was sitting on the bed with
my back to the door, she would walk around the bed so she could get a
good view of me.

The theme underlying voyeurism is inappropriately seeing or hearing sexual acts. Therefore, the client may not have been sexually abused
by being touched or penetrated but may have witnessed others being
sexual or sexually abused. Again, the meaning of the compulsive sexual
behavior can be identified by asking what the client hopes to gain by
the behavior. For example, one voyeuristic client reported that he
always wished that when he was window peeping, that the man he was
spying on would see him hiding in the bushes, invite him in, and
befriend him. Rather than being purely about sex, the client's acts were
related to being lonely.

Exhibitionism

The actual *DSM-III-R* (American Psychiatric Association, 1987) diagnostic criteria of exhibitionism is not gender specific, but because of the
sexism in American society, when most people think of an exhibitionist,
the image of a man in a raincoat "flashing" comes to mind. The *DSM-
III-R* contains the sentence "The condition apparently occurs *only* [ital-
ics added] in males, and the victims are almost entirely female (children
or adult)" (p. 282). A woman who exposes her body to strangers for
sexual arousal is not usually thought of as exhibitionist. The diagnostic
criteria, which include the phrase "recurrent and intense sexual urges
and sexually arousing fantasies involving the exposure of one's genitals
to an unsuspecting *stranger*" (p. 282, italics added), ignore the household exhibitionism of which clinicians who work with sexual abuse
clients often hear (e.g., the stepmother who comes into her teenage
stepson's bedroom in a see-through nightgown that exposes her breasts
when she leans over and kisses him, or the father who comes into the
family room when his teenage daughter has several of her friends
visiting and sits with his legs spread and the tip of his penis showing
out of the leg of his shorts).

People who are exhibitionistic often had intrusive parents. This is
particularly true if there is a theme of anger in the exposing. In the
words of the *DSM-III-R*, "In some cases, the desire to surprise or shock

the observer is consciously perceived or close to conscious awareness" (p. 282). A client frequently will expose when angry and engage in voyeurism when lonely. This is important for the client to understand so that appropriate actions can be taken to avoid taking part in the sexually inappropriate acts. When anger is the underlying emotion, the client should be encouraged to express the anger directly and to set appropriate limits with whomever is the focus of the insult. If loneliness is the prevalent emotion, the client should be encouraged to make use of his or her support system, such as the members of a mutual-help group or friends.

Compulsive Masturbation

Persons who have been emotionally and/or physically neglected frequently turn to self-stimulation as a way of coping with the isolation they experience. The underlying emotions are often loneliness, shame, anxiety, and fear. Similar to the child who self-soothes by rocking him- or herself when alone, masturbation serves to numb the adult's awareness of unpleasant emotions.

When a client reports being a compulsive masturbator, it is vital that the psychotherapist obtain a behavioral and emotional description of what is leading the client to use this label. In some religious groups, any masturbation is viewed as sinful.

Once an individual has demonstrated that he or she can abstain from compulsive masturbation, it may be appropriate for one of the treatment goals to include learning to masturbate in a noncompulsive manner—to begin to view masturbation not as "self-abuse," but rather as "having sex with someone you love." One technique that many of my clients have found helpful is to masturbate without the use of fantasy. I recommend that fantasy be avoided because fantasy by definition is not being focused on the present moment in reality. Clients report that when they stay focused on their body and the sensations they are creating, rather than on mental images, they masturbate less frequently but experience more physical and emotional pleasure and fewer shame responses or compulsive urges.

Bestiality

Compulsive use of animals for sexual purposes seems to be the result of severe neglect, but it can also be a re-creation of an abuse experience.

In cases of the former, the child has been so isolated from other humans that his or her primary relationships have always been with animals. Many of us know the pain that people go through following the loss of a beloved pet, but few of us can imagine the grief over the loss of an animal when it has been the main source of companionship and even a sex partner. I witnessed the intense weeping of a client who had not formed any meaningful relationships with humans until becoming a member of a therapy group, when he determined that he would be unable to stop his compulsive sexual behavior with his dog and decided to "find a new home for her." His pain appeared to be no less than the pain of losing a spouse.

Individuals who as children were forced by adults to be sexual with animals may develop obsessions or compulsive behaviors focusing on animals. In these cases, the emotional/affectional relationship is usually not present. The animal is objectified, viewed only as a tool to bring relief from the compulsive urge.

Sadochism/Masochism (S/M) and Bondage/Discipline (B/D)

In sadochism/masochism (S/M) and bondage/discipline (B/D) cases, the individual is pairing emotional fear, physical pain, and sexual excitement. In one case in which I have been involved, all of the individuals had been bound and beaten as children while either being accused of sexual thoughts or acts or being called names of a sexual nature (prick, motherfucker, slut, pervert, etc.). Sometimes the beatings took place across the parent's bed, where they may have been stripped by the parent, and the breasts and genitals were often the targets of the blows. In some cases, the child's arms were tied to the bedposts so that he or she could not masturbate during the night. I want to be clear here that I am not referring to couples who find excitement in restraining one another during sex but to individuals who compulsively seek to be humiliated and beaten to the point of actual injury.

Affairs

In some cases, the client is reenacting the parental history of affairs. Although the child was never overtly sexually abused (touched), he or she did witness a parent being sexual outside of the marriage. Even if the child never actually observed the parent in the act of sexual intercourse, he or she may have been introduced to the parent's lovers, required to keep secrets regarding affairs, left in the car or other room while the parent was being sexual, or used as an excuse by the parent to leave the house ("I'm taking the kid to the zoo. We'll be back in a couple of hours," when in fact the parent was going to visit his or her lover).

Childhood romantic or sexualized relationships with a parent, sometimes termed *covert incest*, are also commonly at the root of an adult pattern of extramarital affairs. The affairs recreate the dynamics of the child-parent relationship. One cannot assume that the opposite-sex parent was the "partner" (e.g., mother and son, father and daughter); the parent can form such relationships with a child of the same sex. During the client's childhood, the parent took the child on "dates" and generally treated him or her as one would treat a lover, even if no genital sexual contact took place.

Anonymous Sex

I find that clients who take part in anonymous sexual encounters were frequently children who were molested outside of the home. I use the term *sexual encounters* rather than *sexual relationships* because in many cases, the individuals do not exchange words or even see one another's faces (e.g., the use of a "glory hole" bored in the stall wall between toilets in a public restroom through which a man inserts his penis so that the other man may perform fellatio). The word *relationship* implies relating to a person rather than merely interacting with a part of a person.

Telephone Sex

Individuals engaging in telephone sex often overheard parental sex or a parent disclosing sexual problems or fantasies in graphic detail. Again, I am not referring to a child hearing muffled sounds through the wall, but rather the situation in which the adults leave both their door and the door to the child's room completely open. In other cases, an individual spent childhood isolated from others and phone sex is an attempt to form a relationship. The use of 12-step-based mutual-help groups and group therapy is helpful for these individuals. As a therapist, one must be sensitive to the level of affection that the compulsive user of phone sex services may develop for the person on the other end of the telephone line. Several of my clients have constructed elaborate fantasies about how these pseudorelationships would somehow become real and lead to marriage.

Indecent Calls and Letters

Most of the content of indecent calls and letters with which I am familiar involves sexualized anger. The theme of the speech or writing is not lovemaking or romance but angry, even violent, sexual acts. In the majority of cases, the anger is being expressed at strangers and not at the person who has mistreated the individual in childhood. I describe this situation as "having the right fight with the wrong person." The therapeutic task is to facilitate the client appropriately focusing his or her anger toward those who actually were hurtful.

Indecent or Invasive Touch (Frotteurism)

The *DSM-III-R* (American Psychiatric Association, 1987) defines frotteurism as "recurrent intense sexual urges and sexually arousing fantasies involving touching and rubbing against a nonconsenting person. It is the touching, *not* [italics added] the coercive nature of the act, that is sexually exciting" (p. 283). However, my clients report that the excitement of "copping a feel" is the result of "getting by with something forbidden." These same persons have had histories in which a parental figure tickled them or gave them a backrub that resulted in genital, buttock, or breast contact done in a covert manner.

Compulsive Use of Pornography

A sign of an addictive pattern with the use of sexually explicit materials is the need for ever-increasing graphic detail (e.g., a man who becomes bored with *Playboy*, moves to *Penthouse*, and then to even more graphic magazines, and then to XXX videos).

When inquiring about a client's use of pornography, the therapist is encouraged to ask about the client's definition of pornography and to examine his or her own definition of pornography. For example, many people do not think of *Playboy* as pornography because it also contains nonsexually focused materials, such as interviews with political figures or articles on sporting events. One may also find people who use nontraditional visual objects for sexual stimulation, such as newspaper ads for women's undergarments or clothing catalogs. The reader is reminded that the use of sexually explicit material is not gender specific. In spite of gender stereotypes, numerous women compulsively use pornography.

Again, the goal of the compulsive behavior is important to comprehend. The man who can provide from memory the names of the *Playboy* playmates for the past 10 years is someone who is seeking a relationship with a woman but is somehow prevented from forming an actual intimate relationship with one. To such a person, the loss of his pornography collection represents the loss of the relationship and can cause great grief.

In my experience, compulsive users or collectors of pornography often had access to their parents' pornography collection during childhood. In such cases, the therapeutic task is to learn what the child learned about him- or herself and sex as a result of this exposure.

Crossdressing

Crossdressing, the wearing of clothes intended for members of the other sex, is a poorly defined term. Does the wearing of a man's shirt or boxer shorts by a woman constitute crossdressing? Would a man wearing an earring be defined as crossdressing? What if he had two earrings and they were the long, dangling style? Rather than become involved in such a value-ladened topic, I address those clients who self-identify themselves as engaging in crossdressing. I will not be addressing men from groups such as the Radical Fairies who wear dresses and other stereotypically women's clothing as political statements. All of the clinical cases with which I have been familiar involve men who wear clothing that is clearly designed for women, such as bras and pantyhose. In every case, they came from families in which masculinity was not valued or was even seen as shameful. In several of the cases, the women of the family dressed the male children as girls until they entered school or were old enough to protest. For these men, the wearing of women's clothing provided them with a sense of being acceptable and was experienced as soothing. However, they also experienced shame related to their practices. After disclosing their crossdressing in a men's therapy group, and being validated as masculine and acceptable, they reported that their interest in crossdressing continued to decline until it was almost totally eliminated.

■ Treatment Issues

After working with sexually compulsive clients for any length of time, one becomes aware of the ritualized aspect of their behavior (e.g., the man whose pornography must be arranged in a particular fashion or the woman who must spend hours preparing herself and her clothing before leaving to seek a new sexual partner). The effect of these rituals includes the induction of trance; in other words, these people are involved in self-hypnosis. Clients frequently describe common trance phenomena such as time or body distortion while discussing "cruising," or being in adult bookstores or "strip joints."

This ability to induce trance can be used within the recovery process as well. Twelve-step-based mutual-help groups (e.g., Sex Addicts Anonymous, Adult Children of Sexual Dysfunction, etc.) make use of ritual to begin and end their meetings. Individuals can create healing rituals to replace compulsive/addictive rituals. Persons who are overly bonded to a parent due to the relationship having been romantic or sexualized may perform a ritual of divorce, complete with divorce papers that are read aloud.

The therapeutic task is to determine what is the reasonable, acceptable goal of the behavior and then to find methods to obtain the goal.

Overall, the therapeutic task when treating those with sexual compulsiveness is to help clients determine what is the reasonable, acceptable goal of the behavior and then to find new, less emotionally expensive methods to obtain the goal. For example, if one is lonely, it is certainly acceptable to seek the company of others. However, if the only relationship that has been available is that with a character in a pornographic film, the loneliness will continue and even increase once the film has ended. The client would benefit from having access to a therapy group or mutual-help group so that an intimate, mutually rewarding relationship could be formed that will lead to a decrease in the client's loneliness.

Merely stopping the compulsive behavior is not enough. As they say in Alcoholics Anonymous, "There's more to it than puttin' the plug in the jug!" Once the compulsive behavior has been arrested, the therapeutic task becomes acquiring healthy sexual behaviors. Clients who are attending 12-step-based mutual-help groups ought to be encouraged to make use of the Overeaters Anonymous model of recovery,

TABLE 4.1 Some Characteristics of Healthy Sexual Behavior

1. Within one's values
2. Safe
3. Respectful of self and others
4. Honest
5. Spontaneous and playful
6. A result of intimacy and adds to intimacy
7. Lack of shame
8. The drive can be satisfied
9. Freedom of choice

SOURCE: From Hunter (1992). Reprinted with permission of the author. [Now available from Mic Hunter, 2469 University Avenue West, St. Paul, MN 55114]

which involves eating in moderation, rather than the Alcoholics Anonymous model of recovery, which involves ceasing all intake of alcohol. For those recovering from sexual abuse and compulsive sexual behavior, sex is not the problem; the misuse of sex is the issue. Therefore, I provide clients with a list of characteristics of healthy sexuality for them to use in determining whether to take part in a specific sexual act at a particular time (see Table 4.1).

PART TWO

Helping Adult Survivors
With Special Needs

Treatment of the Very Difficult Sexual Abuse Survivor

Robert S. Mayer

In the course of practicing psychotherapy for the past 25 years, I have encountered numerous patients whom I have had great difficulty treating or even maintaining in a treatment situation. In an effort to help them, I constantly tried to increase my skills. I did this by talking to scores of people, reading numerous books, and attending many conferences. During the course of this intellectual journey, I learned techniques that the proponents claimed they had used with great success. I also saw many of these strategies work brilliantly in workshop demonstration groups, but when I attempted to duplicate them in my office, I was generally unsuccessful.

While working with this category of patient, at times I have felt frustrated, incompetent, and angry. To my embarrassment, on some occasions, I have acted out my anger verbally on the patient or may have been responsible for destroying the treatment situation.

This chapter will describe the very difficult patient and present a theoretical hypothesis that I have evolved over the years that helps me understand these patients better.[1] Based on this theory, tempered by mistakes I have made over the years, it will present an approach and practical techniques that I found helpful.

■ The Patient and the Problem

The patient prototype to which I am referring is an individual who presents some combination of sexual, physical, and emotional abuse as a child. The patient's character structure tends to be complex and intense. In general, it can be obsessive, compulsive, paranoid, schizoid, borderline, histrionic, dependent, or narcissistic—or in many cases, some combination of the above.

The patients referred to in this chapter have many of the following character traits: They are controlling, grandiose, manipulating, and fragile; they have a history of difficult and unstable interpersonal relationships; they have a low tolerance for affect, and many of them act out in various ways. The acting-out behavior can take a myriad of forms, such as substance abuse, sexual addictions, suicide threats and attempts, and/or physical abuse to themselves or others.

Many also have identity disturbances. They are not sure of who they are psychologically or sexually. Almost all engage in frantic efforts to avoid real or imagined abandonment. Most expect, without sufficient basis, to be exploited or harmed by others. They question the loyalty of friends and their therapist and read threatening meanings into benign remarks or events. They also can be impulsive and can bear grudges. They are easily slighted and quick to react with anger and counterattack. They are exploitative, have a lack of empathy for others, and can be obsessive compulsive and perfectionistic.

Most are painophobic and will employ numerous strategies both conscious and unconscious to avoid pain or discomfort. This includes, among other things, painful childhood memories or the discomfort of taking responsibility for their actions. Even more astonishing, others are painophilic. While professing that they "hate" the pain, they do numerous things that to the observer appear to either keep them in pain or increase their pain. For example, some want their therapists to help them remember a traumatic experience and willingly, even while protesting, relive the trauma with what appears to be the full emotional impact time and time again without resolution. Others expose themselves, consciously or unconsciously, to situations that trigger a reliving of one of their childhood traumatic experiences. Some even give themselves physical pain by an act such as cutting and then reporting that it felt good as the razor blade cut the arm and the blood started to flow, or the release they felt when they put oven cleaner on their mucous membranes.[2]

Almost all of the patients with whom I have had difficulty have major entitlement issues, although to the outside observer, these expectations of life and the therapeutic situations are not commensurate with reality. These patients do not view it that way and will use every manipulative skill at their disposal to obtain their expectations.

To further confound the practitioner, many of these patients are very high functioning. A number of them hold advanced degrees and high-powered jobs. Many work in the helping professions, such as medicine, nursing, or psychotherapy.

The patient's character structure may be obvious during the initial therapeutic contact or during treatment. Alternately, it may flower slowly or erupt without warning. These patients have been reported before by many practitioners and are generally referred to as having a narcissistic or borderline character disorder (American Psychiatric Association, 1987; Kernberg, 1975; Masterson, 1981).[3]

As treatment progresses, I gradually become aware that (a) nothing I ever learned or was told would work does; (b) the patient's demands start to drown me in a sea of entitlement; and (c) the patient will not follow the normal rules of therapy, which, as I was taught, are that he or she has to come, pay, and talk, in that order.[4]

The patient may come to sessions sporadically but then will not talk because he or she is too frightened. Perhaps he or she cannot even get to the office because the therapist is on the 15th floor and the patient is afraid to ride the elevator alone because an abuse once occurred in an elevator. In this particular case, my supervisee found herself going downstairs to take the patient by the hand to bring her into the office.

Another patient entered my office and stood against the wall with her back to me. When she was not doing that, she hid behind the patient chair.

At other times, something I have said either inadvertently or purposefully triggered a spontaneous abreaction. Many times, this occurred with only 5 minutes of the session remaining and another patient waiting outside. All of the techniques that I learned to close the abreaction failed (Fein & Kluft, 1991; Kluft, 1984, 1991; Sacks, 1988; Steele, 1989).

When I finally firmly closed the sessions, I spent the next several months being verbally attacked by the patients for violating them just as their fathers did when their fathers raped them. One stopped payment on the check, another threatened to sue me, and others simply terminated therapy and accused me of being brutal, uncaring, unempathetic, and not understanding.

Many of these patients have attempted to manipulate me into violating various aspects of my personal and professional code of ethics. When I refused and held my ground, the therapy degenerated into an endless struggle over the issue.

Some of these patients have constantly belittled and devalued me to a point where I found myself questioning things about myself that I thought were resolved. Because of one patient, I even reentered therapy to take care of these new/old deficiencies.

Typically, a patient will present a problem and request help. When I attempt to meet the request, the patient rejects the help and often gets worse or engages in some new, bizarre form of acting-out behavior.

When using hypnosis, which I was taught and believe is a major therapeutic tool to treat dissociative patients (Allison, 1980; Bliss, 1986; Braun, 1984; Erickson, 1967; Milton H. Erickson, personal communication, November 1977; Kluft, 1984; Mayer, 1988; Putnam, 1989; Ross, 1989; Sacks, 1988, 1990; Spiegel, 1987), it has often failed miserably, even with a highly hypnotizable patient.

My hypnotic failures have exhibited a wide range. Some patients will not go into a trance. Others become somnambulant and are impossible to talk to or very difficult to bring out of the hypnotic state. Others go into a trance, yet become selectively mute or deaf in the trance state. Still others go into a trance and spontaneously relive a traumatic experience. The list goes on.

Self-mutilation or suicidal threats and actions bother me the most. I was taught that standard procedure in handling these problems is to negotiate a no-harm contract with the patient (Fein, 1990; Fein & Kluft, 1991; Kluft, 1988; Sacks, 1988). Needless to say, with these patients, they will either not negotiate the contract, or if they do, they find a way to violate it.[5]

On another occasion, I took a course in cognitive therapy and was very impressed. The instructor discussing this type of patient firmly suggested that my job was to dispel the patient's cognitive distortions (Fein, 1990). When I attempted to do so, I was met with accusations that I was using mind control on them just as their abusers did.

As can be expected from the above partial list, I have often experienced an extreme countertransference reaction to the actions of this type of patient. I have sometimes obsessed about the patient, talked endlessly to colleagues, and in general, to my professional chagrin, gave them more of my mental energy than the rest of my caseload. I have also made the mistake of doing things for the patient that I would never do for another patient, rationalizing that if I met just this one demand, trust would be built and I would be able to help the patient move from transference acting out to a working transference.

On other occasions, I found myself thinking that I should phone the patient to see if she or he is all right after a particularly emotional session in which a trauma was remembered.

At other times, I debated hospitalizing the patient, not sure whether it was best for the patient or me.

I have been tempted to accept phone calls from this type of patient at all hours of the night and once stayed in phone contact with a patient while I was on vacation.

At another time, I allowed a patient to convince me to lower my fee. This was requested in the middle of treatment while the patient was going through a particularly tough memory and had difficulty maintaining a job. Later, I learned that the patient was not in the dire financial straits that was reported to me.

I could report even more serious breaches that I have heard from experienced supervisees. One adopted her patient, and another married his patient. Both attempted to continue treatment after the legal arrangement had been consummated. My strangest experience, on more than one occasion, was finding myself conducting *marital* therapy between the patient and therapist.

■ Theory

Object relation theorists hypothesize that character disorders are a result of arrested development in a developmental stage (Mahler, Pine, & Bergman, 1975; Masterson, 1981). They also like to correlate the disorder to the developmental stage and age that the arrest took place. Yet they have difficulty explaining the presence of more than one character pathology in a single human being. They have even more difficulty explaining high functioning in combination with a severe low level character disorder (Masterson, 1981).

Other theorists have argued that people who have been abused at an early age are prone to dissociation, using dissociated parts of themselves to contain the traumatic material in order for them to survive the family system and function (Allison, 1980; Bliss, 1986; Kluft, 1984, 1988; Mayer, 1988; Putnam, 1989; Ross, 1989). A result of all of this is one of the dissociative disorders, such as Multiple Personality Disorder (MPD) or Dissociative Disorder Not Otherwise Specified (DDNOS) (American Psychiatric Association, 1987).[6]

I hypothesize that there is an interaction between trauma and developmental arrest, and this type of patient is difficult because of the severity and duration of the abuse. The trauma either causes a developmental arrest or magnifies a preexisting maturational deficiency. If the child is being abused over a long period of time and has developed to a fine degree the ability to dissociate, or split off parts of the self, then it becomes obvious that there could be any combination of *DSM-III-R* character pathology, as well as any level of functioning. The model for this would be a classic case of MPD in which different characterological traits, pathology, or developmental stages can be observed in different personalities (Bliss & Bliss, 1985; Mayer, 1988, 1991; Schreiber, 1973).

I view the patient's acting-out behavior as either a regression in the service of his or her ego or having been learned from an earlier stage of development in which strategies appropriate to that age obtained the desired results. The results are such things as getting cared for, stopping the abuse, or decreasing or eliminating the pain. I always try to remember Freud's dictum as well, which is that a patient acts out what he or she does not remember (Freud, 1913/1973).

I also believe that only a part of the patient has entered treatment to get better. Another part of the patient has entered therapy simply to get relief from pain or to redo his or her history in a positive way. This results in expectations that the therapist will take care of them or take the pain away in some easy, magical way. If any pain surfaces, they act quickly to deaden it with an antiquated strategy. Various acting-out behaviors often achieve this endpoint. Even though patients request help from the therapist, the last thing they really want is to go into the pain and feel it with the original intensity.

> The last thing patients really want is to go into the pain and feel it with the original intensity.

Paradoxically, the severe complex character structure can serve the patient in the therapeutic situation by protecting him or her from the feelings connected with the trauma. When threatened by feelings, the patient can engage in some characterological action that might stimulate a countertransference reaction in the therapist. For example, when patients feel anxious or threatened, they may demand that the therapist alter the dynamics of the therapeutic relationship. They have a belief that if the therapist does this, they will feel better. The demand is usually so extreme that it will violate the therapist's ethics and cannot be met. This can lead to endless discussions, and arguments may occur over the issue.

Obviously, while engaging in such discussions, the trauma cannot be explored or processed. If the discussion progresses to an argument, therapy might end. The patient then can blame the therapist for the therapeutic failure, and the abuse of childhood remains unresolved.

■ Treatment Strategies

As an overview, my treatment plan consists of establishing a working alliance, decreasing destructive behavior, and then working through the trauma. Of course, this is easier said than done. Because the character and acting-out behavior is in place to obliterate the cognitive and emotional memory of the abuse, the patient who was raped as a child by an adult in a trusting role, such as his or her parent, does not trust easily. Therefore, any attempt to achieve trust will most likely be met with increased transference acting out in one form or another.[7]

I have been most successful when I have based my treatment on standard psychotherapeutic technique through a theoretical framework of what I believe to be normal child development. I try to understand the developmental stages of the child and the functions that they serve, and then help the patient to pass successfully through them. Hopefully, this will build an ego that can tolerate greater degrees of affect so that the trauma can be therapeutically processed.

Understanding these stages of development helps. I can view the patient's behavior as survival strategies rather than acting out, which is pejorative. This reframing helps me to keep any countertransference in check and to be able to be understanding and empathetic toward the patient's behavior.

My general developmental understanding follows the work of Margaret Mahler and James Masterson (Mahler et al., 1975; Masterson, 1981). First, there is a symbiosis with the mother, obviously necessary for survival. At this stage of life, the normal child has a love affair with life, thinks the world is his or her oyster, and the nurturant and providing objects in his or her environment are there to serve and to make everything perfect. In this stage, the child is omnipotent, grandiose, and filled with entitlement; believes that he or she is unique; requires constant attention and admiration; and, in general, because self and object are fused, does not see the world as different from him- or herself. Failure in this stage produces a Narcissistic Personality Disorder.

At a later stage, which Margaret Mahler calls rapprochement, the child starts to move out, becomes autonomous, but needs to check in occasionally with the mother for reassurance and supplies. If the mother is unavailable, the child experiences the terror of abandonment. If the mother is too clinging, the child has the terror of engulfment. Failure in this stage produces a Schizoid or Borderline Personality Disorder.

During normal, healthy maturation and growth, through mirroring, and through empathetic responses to frustrations, these stages are worked through with the help of the parent. Eventually, the child starts to develop some sense of separation and reality, as well as an ego that can handle life's frustrations and disappointments (Mahler et al., 1975; Masterson, 1981).

I try to structure a therapeutic situation designed to recreate these stages of development. At first, I want a symbiotic holding environment, and then gentle frustration that is met with understanding and empathy. I am always aware that the patient can be in the rapprochement stage temporarily and need either temporary supplies or encouragement to individuate. For example, when the patient brings in business or professional problems, or outside victories or defeats, I listen empathetically and am quite willing to discuss them. This long period of preparatory work with cycles of gratification and frustration builds an alliance and ego for the later abreactive work (Spotnitz & Meadow, 1976).

The beginning step in treating the very difficult patient is the same for any patient. Start the therapy correctly and hope that many problems can be avoided from the beginning. The goal is to give the patient the feeling that he or she is wanted and liked, and will be treated well, and that there are boundaries and limits. The initial phone contact as well as the first session are crucial. At this juncture, the patient may attempt to manipulate the therapist for more time than is necessary to make contact and make an appointment. Or in the first session, the patient may do something else that violates the frame. If the therapist gives in, that gives the patient a message that manipulation works.

Childhood fantasies of being taken care of will be fulfilled. If the therapist holds too firmly, the patient will feel that the therapist is uncaring and nonnurturing. Obviously, these situations must be handled with great care. Manipulative demands to stretch boundaries have to be gently resisted with empathetic understanding.

I am always conscious of the trauma survivor's difficulty in tolerating affect, especially anxiety. Psychoanalytic technique was developed to stimulate anxiety, which the theorists believed stimulated memories from the unconscious. In working with the trauma survivor, I have found psychoanalytic technique to be counterproductive. Anxiety has to be reduced or the patient will act out, decompensate, or destroy treatment.

Anxiety can be reduced and managed by many techniques. If the therapist is a real object to the patient, it helps. Just as a child in rapprochement needs contact, so does this type of patient. Anxiety is further reduced if the therapist proceeds slowly and cautiously. This period, rather than being viewed as a waste of time, can be used to gain as much understanding as possible of how the patient functions, while working to form an alliance. I do this by showing interest, either verbally or through my body language and/or facial expressions. If I need to know something, I am very careful not to address the question to the ego. I have found that ego oriented questions such as "What are *you* feeling?" stimulate anxiety by making the patient feel as if he or she is being attacked. Instead, I will ask the same question in an object-oriented way. For example, I might say, "How did that make you feel?" or "Are there any feelings going through your body at this time?" In this manner, I avoid stimulating a defensive reaction from the patient by avoiding what the patient hears as an accusatory "you."

I also attempt to teach patients anxiety management techniques that they can use on their own. These include self-hypnosis, journal writing, warm baths, talking to friends, joining a support group, or many other such things that come out of conversations with patients. I am also in favor of anxiety-reducing prescription medication if necessary.

> *Going slowly often can be difficult because many patients want the therapist to immediately dig up the trauma.*

Going slowly often can be difficult because many patients come in and want the therapist to immediately dig up the trauma. In my experience, precipitously exposing the trauma has rarely been successful. Trying to abreact the trauma, even at the patient's request, can create unexpected, intolerable anxiety in the patient. This can be akin to the patient being traumatized again and at best he or she regresses into one of the past characterological strategies that worked as a child. At worst, there is a suicide attempt or some other form of self-harm and/or decompensation requiring a hospitalization, hopefully in a hospital that has a well-trained, experienced, dissociative disorders unit.

During this period, I also try to help patients strengthen their egos and decrease or eliminate any acting-out behavior. Acting-out behavior can be controlled by helping patients to become aware of the behavior and its destructiveness to them. With some patients, it is relatively easy to do this by simply confronting the behavior. For example, if a patient describes how he or she purposely cut his or her arm, I might confront the behavior by saying, "It is curious that you would take such a chance with your life." If the patient is one who would hear my comment as attacking rather than one of helpful concern, I would know that what I call confrontation is counterproductive, and I would try a different approach. Using the above example, I would say, "I suspect that you must have been in a lot of pain to do that to yourself." Knowing the patient better, I might say, "Given your childhood, I can understand how cutting yourself would make you feel better and perhaps even give you control over the pain."[8]

I have found that another way that ego is built is through cycles of understanding, as well as empathetic responses when the patient experiences frustration. In the treatment situation, this is accomplished by maintaining a firm therapeutic frame and boundary, which patients, like children, need and hate. They will try often to stretch these limits. When the patient tries to manipulate the boundaries, the best response is an empathetic interpretation. For example, if the patient has difficulty in leaving the treatment room when the session is over, I might say, "I am sorry that we have to end now, I know that you are upset," or "I know that it is hard for you to leave now, perhaps you would like to sit for a few minutes in the waiting room before you have to go outside." If the patient complains that I will not take his or her phone calls at all hours, I might say empathetically, "It would be nice if I could be available to you at all hours." Aside from acting as ego-strengthening techniques, this type of nonattacking, empathetic response demonstrates that the therapist is a solid, reliable, constant object with whom the patient can experience the hurts of childhood.

I also believe that the therapist who is working with a trauma survivor must be a real object who is emotionally available, rather than the neutral analyst that I was trained to be. For example, if the patient asks me a direct question, if possible I will answer it rather than reflect it back to the patient. If one does not do that, the patient has the regressive childhood experience of going to his or her mother for supplies and finding no one home, which stimulates anxiety and brings in a character defense.

In this context, I am as open as I can be, scrupulously honest and direct, but I will not share details of my personal life other than those of a structural nature, such as whether I am married, my age, my training, my degrees, where I am going on vacation, and so on. I will also do so only on the patient's request, always remembering which one of us is the patient.

I view a patient talking about his or her occupation or other matters not as a resistance but as part of a rapprochement phase, and I am more than happy to discuss his or her business successes, frustrations, and failures. Of course, being a real object is meant therapeutically. Given the patient's stage of development, I believe that a real, separate, object-oriented relationship with him or her is impossible. I also always assume health on the part of the patient. For example, when I go on vacation, I do not ask patients if they want a covering therapist. I assume that they can take care of themselves; however, I will fulfill the demand if asked. Any other stance infantilizes patients and encourages acting out.

As early as possible, if a patient is dissociative, I train him or her hypnotically. I teach the patient how to go into a trance, how to come out, how to do simple hypnotic techniques, and how to find a safe hypnotic place. This is done for the purpose of establishing a holding environment so that the patient can feel free to go into the pain (Kluft, 1991). Learning and experiencing controlled hypnosis helps the patient gain control over involuntary dissociation; and, as with all of us, by mastering a new task, confidence and ego are built (M. H. Erickson, personal communication, April 18, 1977). In addition, a tool is built in that can be used later by the therapist in a myriad of ways, such as controlling a crisis or retrieving memories.

> *Learning and experiencing controlled hypnosis helps the patient gain control over involuntary dissociation.*

During this period, I test patients to see which interventions will be most effective. Confrontation of defenses or behavior as illustrated above works well with patients who are more borderline than narcissistic. They seem to be able to take the confrontation and hear it as caring and integrate it into their egos, thus strengthening them (Masterson, 1981). One can see if this works quite easily. Patients will demonstrate some affect and the behavior will change. If patients are more narcissistic than borderline, they react negatively to confrontations. They hear it as an attack and quickly defend. Unfortunately, this leaves a very narrow window of therapeutic entry to the narcissistic patient. The only avenues I have found are mirroring. The mirroring is effective because most likely the patient is demanding it because he or she did not get proper mirroring from the parent.

Interpreting on the basis of patients' vulnerability helps decrease their sense of shame, as well as self-attack. The interpretation shows patients that the therapist understands them and is not criticizing them. Constant repetition of this technique starts to build in an internal defense against the internal critical and attacking voice. It also is one way to teach them a self-soothing device. This is often a long, arduous process that is prone to countertransference reactions in the therapist, especially if the therapist had a narcissistic mother who required constant mirroring. Unfortunately, there are very few short-term therapeutic rewards for the therapist while engaging in this process except those of mastering the craft.

During this period, I am also hoping to help both the patient and myself to have a very good cognitive understanding of the patient's life history. This will be very helpful when traumas surface because there will be a place to put them in perspective.

When the patient is ready and I feel I have as good an alliance as I can get with someone who has been abused, the trauma is then examined. This is a crucial countertransference stage because in general, with a painophobic survivor, he or she will regress into a frustrating, treatment-destructive, countertransference behavior. It is at this time that James Masterson's borderline triad serves me (Masterson, 1981). Elimination of the behavior causes anxiety, and anxiety causes the defense to reform. Working through the defense again causes anxiety, and so it goes.

When pitfalls occur, my strategy is to cognitively appeal to the healthy part of the patient's ego. Invoking the golden rule sometimes works well. People who have been treated unfairly as children in general do not like to treat themselves or others unfairly.[9] If I make a mistake, I never defend myself, but I apologize and explain the reasons for my actions. This technique has the additional benefit of role modeling for patients: nondefensive, honest, open behavior.

At some point in the therapy, it becomes apparent that a patient has gone through the initial stages and is ready for abreactive work. I judge this by a number of criteria: The acting-out behavior has greatly decreased; the patient is not as sensitive to the way I phrase things; and the patient seems more interested in finding out what happened to him or her as a child than in getting it fixed magically by the therapist. One major clue is that the theme of the sessions is more about the patient's childhood than complaints about the therapist or day-to-day events.

> *People who have been treated unfairly as children in general do not like to treat themselves or others unfairly.*

It should be noted that therapy is by no means smooth sailing from this point on. Most likely, the patient will revert back to a defensive behavior, with which we will have to deal again.

I have found that when I scrupulously and empathetically adhere to these rules, the therapy with these difficult patients is generally manageable. It is manageable because it starts off correctly, gives the patient the proper therapeutic message of the therapeutic task, and allows him or her to feel understood and as safe as possible. The treatment may seem long, it may seem to the therapist that nothing is being done and nothing is happening, and yet a solid base is slowly being built.

Many cases have been difficult because I got off to a bad start and had to retreat. Taking away what has been given creates a very difficult situation. The only thing I have been able to do is to explain to the patient what happened, that I made an error, and it would be therapeutically better for him or her if we did it differently. Sometimes this works; continuing along the old path has always failed.

However, there still are some patients who have great difficulty from the beginning. Hyman Spotnitz argued that any patient could be cured if the therapist was willing to join him or her long and far enough (Spotnitz & Meadow, 1976). I tend to agree with this. However, this position must be balanced between the reality of outpatient therapy and the needs of the therapist. The therapist is not required to treat everyone who comes into his or her office. Some patients' egos may be so damaged that they require more care than is physically or emotionally possible in an outpatient setting.

In summary, the key to working with the so-called difficult patient is to start the therapy correctly and to maintain control over the counter-transference. The former has to be done with great empathy and under-standing of the patient. The latter is best accomplished when the thera-pist reframes what we have been calling either acting-out behavior or character pathology to strategies used by the patient that were learned when he or she was a child to attempt to solve the problems of a nightmare of a childhood. This reframing will convert a pathological countertransference reaction from the therapist to an empathetic, un-derstanding action. Constant repetition of this by the therapist will form a therapeutic alliance and a working transference, build patient ego, and lead to a successful conclusion of therapy. In addition, the therapist must be prepared to be patient, go slowly, and not gratify the patient more than is necessary to maintain the treatment process.

■ Notes

1. Thanks should be given to the members of my Thursday afternoon study group, in which many of these techniques and theories were tried and developed, and results obtained and analyzed from the participants. Additional thanks to Judith Pearson, Ph.D., an associate at the Masterson Institute in New York City, for her help in clarifying many of the characterological concepts used in this chapter.

2. Bessel van der Kolk argues that extreme pain can cause the release of endorphinlike substances in the brain that, like a narcotic, either decrease the pain or cause a euphoric state (van der Kolk, 1988).

3. I think the use of the term *disorder* shows a lack of understanding of the problem and sets up a pejorative mindset in the practitioner. In addition, I have noticed that some therapists use these terms pejoratively, probably because of the difficulty of working with this class of patient.

4. They cannot be treated if they do not come to session, and the therapist is not happy if they do not pay. Talking is least important because they can always be made to talk (Spotnitz & Meadow, 1976).

5. Patients agree not to cut themselves until they talk to me. At some point they call (talk to me), tell me they are going to cut themselves, and then hang up. I have learned to add to the contract "see me" instead of "talk to me." But, as can be expected, if they want to violate the contract, they will.

6. Why one patient ends up with MPD and another with DDNOS is not yet clear. I believe that it has to do with the age at which the initial abuse took place.

7. Interestingly, I have observed that these patients appear to trust deeply, but I do not believe that they really trust or ever will during the therapeutic situation. The best that can happen is a leap of faith or an agreement from them that they will do the work anyway.

8. Sometimes, I might empathetically respond by telling the following story: "When I was studying with Milton Erickson, who was in terrible pain from arthritis, polio, and two strokes, I once watched him push his Adam's apple toward the back of his neck. I alarmingly said, 'Dr. Erickson, what are you doing? That must be very painful.' He replied, 'Yes, it is very painful, but the pain I cause myself is much easier to bear than the pain I cannot control' " (M. H. Erickson, personal communication, April 1976).

9. Some people obviously do not follow this rule. They identify with the aggressor and treat people as brutally as they were treated, which is probably the reason children still get abused, as well as some of the other horrors of our civilization.

Stages of Recovery and Relapse Prevention for the Chemically Dependent Adult Sexual Trauma Survivor

Caryl Trotter

Susan is a recovering alcoholic. She attends AA but keeps herself isolated and doesn't have much to do with others. Her husband tries to help her get out of herself, but she resists his attempts and considers this nagging. He often feels she is "somewhere else," even though she is employed and maintains relationships with others. Their sexual relationship is at a standstill and Susan appears increasingly depressed. She made one attempt to talk to her counselor about her depression and sexual dysfunction, but was advised that her sobriety would be severely threatened if she got into heavy feeling work so soon in her recovery. Her husband has more than once considered leaving the marriage, even though he loves Susan, and Susan has more than once considered drinking again to ease the pain and guilt she feels.

John has been in a chemical dependency outpatient program for the past 2 months after an intervention by his employer and his wife. He was having trouble concentrating at work and was coming in later and later each day, or not showing up at all. He was frequently distant with his wife and children and snapped at them for the smallest thing. His wife attempted to talk to him several times about his drinking, but John insisted he was just going through some rough times and he would soon cut down. In a routine assessment through his treatment program, he revealed to his counselor that he had been molested by his brother as a child, but had long ago resolved it. Upon this disclosure, the counselor showed animated interest, defocused on his alcoholism treatment, and insisted that John have a direct confrontation with his brother. John felt confused and fearful at this proposal and regretted bringing up the subject. He made excuses to stop his counseling and vowed that he could stay sober without anyone's help.

Both Susan and John are survivors of childhood sexual trauma and are in a double bind. In Susan's case, her counselor fails to understand that Susan is showing signs of posttraumatic stress resulting from her abusive childhood. John's counselor is overly invested in initiating intensive therapy and neglects the fact that John is likely to return to drinking if he defocuses on secondary issues. Both Susan and John are prime candidates for *reciprocal relapse,* that is, a condition in which the symptoms of one disorder can trigger symptoms of another disorder and create the potential for relapse. If Susan's posttraumatic symptoms become acute, they are likely to trigger cravings to drink. In John's case, had he proceeded with the confrontation, he probably would have been emotionally overwhelmed and would have returned to chemical use. He is already a relapse candidate because he failed to master recovery tasks that are necessary in early sobriety. Alcohol abuse by either Susan or John will impede their recovery process because it blocks their ability to feel the emotional pain necessary for motivation in therapy. Susan requires a dual focus on her posttrauma symptoms and her substance abuse. John primarily requires treatment for alcoholism while postponing any intensive abuse work until his sobriety is stronger, if then.

Professionals in the chemical dependency field historically are not well trained to identify and treat symptoms resulting from childhood trauma, particularly sexual abuse. It has traditionally been held that the counseling focus for the newly recovering person should be simply staying sober the first year and that "psychological" issues should not be addressed. This approach is also mirrored in AA meetings and other 12-step groups. On the other hand, professionals in the mental health field historically are not well trained in identifying chemical addictions and tend to view substance abuse as a symptom of underlying emotional problems. Consequently, many chemically dependent survivors are in a double bind: Some begin having symptoms early in their recovery and are not given practical treatment supports, or they are not adequately assessed for serious addiction so that treatment never progresses. Overfocusing either on rigid sobriety while ignoring post-trauma symptoms or on issues secondary to serious addiction can create for the recovering person the potential for relapse.

■ Understanding the Role of Chemicals in Sexually Traumatic Families

Many adult survivors report that their early use of alcohol and other drugs or their compulsive behaviors are related to childhood abuse experiences. The drugs and behaviors serve a survivor in numerous ways:

- They increase the survivor's own tendency to dissociate in order to reduce or avoid emotions associated with being abused
- They interfere with the memory storage of traumatic experiences
- They create some level of well-being or enable the survivor to remain "neutral"
- They release inhibitions against expression of painful emotions or rage
- They release inhibitions against sexual expression either for closeness needs or for the need to express hostility
- They create social groups that have few demands but in fact may resemble the originally abusive family system

According to the traditional medical model of addictions, there appears to be a strong intergenerational transmission involving certain biological and genetic factors. There is compelling evidence that children born into alcoholic families have a 15% chance of also becoming alcoholic (Winoker, Cadoret, Dorzab, & Baker, 1971). Other studies support a physiological vulnerability toward addiction (Goodwin, 1979; Pollock, Schneider, Gabrielli, & Goodwin, 1987; Shukitt, Goodwin, & Winoker, 1972).

We must not, however, ignore other powerful influences occurring in addictive, abusive family systems. Perhaps the most important of the psychological/familial factors are the psychological and physical abuse coupled with neglect of premorbid alcoholic children by their alcoholic parents.

Just as having chemically dependent parents creates a greater potential for addiction for adult children, being abused as a child also appears to be a setup for many survivors to become chemically dependent later in life. One study indicates that sexually abused female crisis center clients were 10 times more likely to have a drug addiction history and more than twice as likely to have an alcoholism history than were the clients in the comparison group, who had not been sexually abused (Briere & Runtz, 1989).

Whereas some addicts use chemicals to get high, the victims of early childhood abuse use them to get by.

Treating the adult survivor in a traditional 12-step program that insists on abstinence is not so simply attained. The substance abuse is more often deeply embedded within the family system as well as chronically used for the survival of posttraumatic stress. As clinicians, we must acknowledge that whereas some addicts use chemicals to get high, the victims of early childhood abuse truly use them to get by. To ignore these very real differences is to invite relapse and to deny appropriate treatment.

John Briere (Briere & Runtz, 1992) has expanded the definition of addictions to include a number of compulsive behaviors designed to reduce tension. Among these behaviors designed to distract, anesthetize, calm, or otherwise aid dissociation from abuse-related distress are substance abuse, sex "addiction," bingeing and purging, self-mutilation, and high risk-taking. Briere cites relatively predictable steps that generate tension-reducing behaviors:

1. The survivor experiences or anticipates an interpersonal stressor regarding perceived abandonment, injustice, or betrayal with a lover or authority figure.

2. The stressor creates for the survivor understandable current dysphoria, but because of the similarity to childhood abuse, it restimulates or exacerbates unresolved feelings of rage, anxiety, and emptiness resulting in an "overreaction" to the stressor.

3. The psychic pressure combined with the survivor's dread of painful feelings and lack of ability to regulate affect motivates (a) dissociation, including detachment from the consequences of self-destructive behaviors, and (b) a search for any means to reduce tension.

4. This process results in one or more tension-reducing behaviors designed to provide at least one of the following: temporary distraction; interruption of dissociative or dysphoric states; anesthesia of psychic pain; restoration of control; sensory input incompatible with distress; temporary feeling of emptiness; self-calming and soothing; relief from guilt or self-hatred; and provision for perceived need for punishment.

These tension-reducing behaviors are thought to be learned during and following traumatic childhood experiences, when immediate relief was critical to the young child's survival. Because of the overwhelming pain and the victim's subsequent reliance on these relatively primitive defenses, there is little motivation to learn more sophisticated responses to stress as the child develops. For the clinician, the treatment can be slow and frustrating, and client "resistance" can be interpreted erroneously as manipulative.

■ Assessing the Chemically Dependent Adult Sexual Trauma Survivor

Considering the reality that the majority of chemically dependent people seeking treatment are likely to have experienced some childhood trauma, and that the majority of sexual trauma survivors are likely to engage in some type of tension-reducing behavior that might include substance abuse, it is important to have at hand useful and reliable assessment instruments, whether in the chemical dependency field or the mental health field. For some clients, it may be ill-advised to begin addressing trauma issues early in the recovery process. For others, posttrauma symptoms may begin appearing early, so that postponing trauma work is not possible or clinically advisable. All survivors must be carefully assessed for substance abuse because the chemicals not only negate any positive effects of therapy but also may be creating for the client a life-threatening situation. Either way, the clinician is advised to assess the client early in treatment both for the presence of addictions and for sexual trauma.

Assessing for Chemical Dependency

Assessing for the presence of substance abuse takes practice and sensitive timing. The clinician should ask questions in a matter-of-fact way regarding what the client drinks, how much, how often, and when, where, and how chemicals have been a problem in any area of the client's life. Certain questions (e.g., "How do you feel when you drink?" "What does alcohol/drugs allow you to feel, do, or be that without it you would not be able to feel, do, or be?" "When do you most often want to use?") can supply a great deal of information. There are numerous screening tools to determine the presence of substance abuse. Clinicians are advised to check with their community drug and alcohol programs to determine which instruments are being used successfully. As clinicians assess for the presence of substance abuse, they are encouraged strongly to keep in mind that the clients in front of them may be trauma survivors, so that their chemical use may be unique to tension reduction of trauma-related issues.

Assessing for Sexual Trauma

There are numerous assessment instruments designed to address childhood sexual trauma experiences. They are cited in the professional literature (Briere, 1989; Briere & Runtz, 1992, Courtois, 1988) as well as in popular self-help books (Bass & Davis, 1988; Blume, 1990). As with assessing for chemical dependence, identifying early sexual trauma in an adult should be addressed in a matter-of-fact way during routine psychosocial assessment. It needs to be noted, however, that like alcoholism, survivors tend to deny, repress, or avoid disclosing that they were abused, or they may make no connection between their current problems and earlier maltreatment. Also, because many survivors have learned a high tolerance for intolerable behavior, as clinicians we must describe inappropriate sexual behaviors rather than merely ask the client if he or she was sexually abused. Many clinicians report that an initial assessment of sexual trauma may reveal little or no significant history, and that not until later in treatment are such experiences revealed. This delayed disclosure may be due to the lifting of repression, the clearing of the brain from the effects of chemicals, and greater trust in the therapist as the treatment proceeds.

Before beginning an assessment, there are several general assumptions that need to be understood.

1. Attempt to normalize the trauma. Explain to your client that the presence of psychological trauma is common to those having chemical dependency or emotional problems.

2. Be available to follow up on a disclosure. If you are limited in time, training, or resources, it may be better to acknowledge the current significance of the abuse and describe the services you or a referent can provide.

3. Allow the assessment to unfold over time and in whatever format appears to work best for the survivor. Because of trust issues, as well as the problem of remembering trauma, the survivor may not disclose early in treatment. Therefore, allow that assessment will be an ongoing part of treatment. Assessment formats include pencil and paper questionnaires, clinical instruments designed to assess for the presence of posttraumatic stress disorder (PTSD) and dissociation, and interview guidelines to be used by the clinician.

4. Do no harm. This statement should seem evident, but we must be highly respectful of the fact that we may be asking about some of the most shaming, terrifying experiences of this client. We must frame our questions with great care.

5. Do not go witch-hunting. This is meant figuratively as well as literally. Too many therapists are overly invested in seeking out disclosures of severe childhood sexual trauma and may, in fact, suggest to clients that their current problems are related to abuse as yet undiscovered. In this time of backlash, when therapist credibility is at an all-time low, we must be cautious not to suggest the presence of disremembered abuse or sadistic abuse unless there is adequate clinical evidence and rationale.

Once these general assessment guidelines are followed, more direct questions may be asked regarding early sexual trauma. What follows are some typical questions usually asked early in treatment regardless of the treatment setting.

1. When you were a child or teenager, did anyone ever kiss you in a way that had to be kept a secret?
2. When you were a child or teenager, did anyone ever touch your body in a way that had to be kept a secret?
3. When you were a child or teenager, did anyone ever make you touch their sexual parts and ask you to keep it a secret?
4. When you were a child or teenager, did anyone ever look at you in a sexual way, watch you dress, or invade your privacy in a sexual way?
5. For any of the above experiences, did anyone ever use physical force or threats?

Other questions that could ascertain whether sexual maltreatment occurred could include the presence of stepparents, stereotypical gender roles, "absent" parents through addiction or emotional problems, presence of drug-addicted or alcoholic parents and stepparents, social and emotional isolation within the family and between siblings, role and boundary confusion, and violations of power and authority.

Many survivors use drugs and alcohol for the management of trauma memories. Some become addicted, and others do not. Some require lengthy periods of sobriety before embarking on recovery from childhood issues, whereas some are able to begin their abuse recovery early in sobriety. To help in determining who, when, and how to approach trauma-based therapy, there are three classifications of chemically dependent survivors: active addiction/repressed trauma issues; active addiction/active trauma issues; and active trauma issues/reactive chemical use.

Active Addiction/Repressed Trauma Issues

Survivors with active addiction/repressed trauma issues have a genetic predisposition and family history for addiction and/or alcoholism. They show increasing tolerance for chemicals over time plus physical withdrawal when chemicals leave the body. With chemicals requiring 6 to 18 months to completely clear the body, establishing sobriety must be the primary issue. Posttrauma symptoms (i.e., flashbacks, intrusive traumatic memories, acute anxiety precipitated by abuse-related stimuli) are usually absent. These survivors may report sexually traumatic memories with little distress, or they may be amnesic for such experiences. Because of heavy chemical use, these survivors have been isolating themselves from the triggers that would activate memory or the dysphoria that accompany the memories. These triggers tend to begin for these survivors later in their recovery as they seek greater levels of personal involvement.

These survivors can be given forewarning that the childhood trauma experiences that they disclose may become problematic for them as they proceed in treatment. Clinicians should advise amnesic survivors that sometimes childhood memories that may be disturbing might emerge later in their recovery and may require counseling attention. It may be helpful to administer an assessment for the presence of current PTSD (Briere & Runtz, 1988), although clinical experience has shown that if these instruments are used in the first several weeks after detox, they are somewhat unreliable.

Because the major treatment task for this type of trauma survivor is the establishment of sobriety, treatment approaches include inpatient chemical dependency programs, outpatient programs, individual and group therapy, and AA and other appropriate 12-step groups. Survivors are encouraged to seek treatment for sexual trauma only when sobriety is well established or when trauma-related symptoms become acute enough to interfere with early chemical dependency recovery tasks.

Active Addiction/Active Trauma Issues

Survivors with active addiction/active trauma issues are like those in the first category in terms of their genetic predisposition for addiction, tolerance, and withdrawal symptoms. They have sought relief from trauma-related symptoms through chemicals, and when the chemicals leave their systems, the repressed emotions quickly surface, creating for these survivors a dual diagnosis of chemical dependency and post-trauma symptoms (PTSD, major depression, anxiety disorders, panic attacks). For successful recovery, both problems must be treated simultaneously because there is a high risk of relapse if the survivor is not offered healthy, sober ways of managing the posttrauma symptoms.

This dually diagnosed survivor should be given a thorough sexual trauma assessment that focuses on the unique way that chemicals have been used for tension reduction of abuse-related dysphoria. Although the establishment of sobriety is still the priority for this type of survivor, trauma-related symptoms, beliefs, and behaviors will probably need to be addressed early on in therapy so that relapse is not as great a possibility. The use of individual and group therapies for trauma resolution should be coupled with substance abuse counseling and attendance at 12-step groups. These survivors may find some of the basic tenets of 12-step philosophy contradictory to trauma-based therapy, including the notion of "character defects" and turning one's will over to a higher power.

Active Trauma Issues/Reactive Chemical Use

Survivors with active trauma issues/reactive chemical use react to trauma-related issues by seeking self-medication through drugs and alcohol, but do not become progressively addicted over time. By treating the trauma-related issues directly, the need for chemical reliance usually decreases. Because of the negative effects of chemical use on therapy, abstinence is strongly recommended.

Because these survivors drink or self-medicate and are not addicted, the best assessment and treatment approaches are trauma focused. The survivors should be warned that they are at risk for addiction and that they need to abstain during the course of treatment because chemical use slows down necessary memory acquisition and interferes with affect regulation. Treatment approaches include individual and group therapies that are trauma focused and addiction sensitive.

■ A Developmental Model of Recovery

Numerous authors have suggested that a developmental approach to recovery from childhood traumas is the most effective (Brown, 1988; Herman, 1992a; Putnam, 1989; Sgroi, 1989; van der Har, Brown, & van der Kolk, 1989). Most focus on the establishment of a strong therapeutic alliance and symptom reduction followed by the exploration and metabolization of memories and positive personality change. With the chemically dependent sexual trauma survivor, a developmental model becomes particularly important in reducing relapse potential. The model for recovery from addictions described by Terence T. Gorski (1989) details recovery tasks that must be accomplished in increasingly difficult sequence. The developmental model that follows is designed to be used along with Gorski's model, which is aimed at the establishment and maintenance of sobriety, symptom reduction, and relapse prevention through warning sign management. The model contains five stages: Transition, Stabilization, Early Recovery, Middle Recovery, and Ongoing Recovery. Each stage builds on the former and allows the recovering survivor to move forward and backward in the model according to need.

Transition: Preparing for Recovery

This is a pretreatment stage during which the trauma survivor is experiencing symptoms of overwhelming stress and is attempting to cope with that stress using outdated defenses such as substance abuse, isolation, and other tension-reducing behaviors. The following are typical occurrences during this stage.

Increased posttrauma symptoms. These range from flashback and intrusive images to problems with sleep, panic attacks, and sexual dysfunction. These symptoms, perhaps once only rare nuisances, become serious enough to disrupt everyday life and threaten important relationships. What was once a drinking problem or the use of drugs to temporarily reduce physical pain has become a serious addiction. Survivors may become focused on seeking, taking, and recovering from chemical binges. They may be involved with substance-abusing social groups that greatly resemble their abusive family systems, and these groups may revictimize the survivors.

Family crisis. Growing up in a sexually abusive family requires the children to become hypervigilant and distrustful of others. As a result, adult survivors commonly have difficulty becoming involved in healthy relationships and, in fact, are often involved in relationships that are neglectful, exploitative, or abusive. During this pretreatment phase, the survivors may be experiencing sexual battles with their partners, threats of abandonment by the partners, or serious codependency to the extent that the survivors are acutely depressed. Some survivors are also highly tolerant of aggression in their relationships and may be victims of domestic violence.

Memory triggers. Many adult survivors never forget their early trauma experiences. Many others repress or dissociate the memories altogether. The process of maturation, emotional and perhaps physical safety from the perpetrator(s), and the involvement of trusting adult relationships can trigger memories of trauma. Although the return of memories appears to be directly related to the safety felt by the survivors, such memories can wreak havoc on the survivors' relationships. Flashbacks can, and usually do, occur during intimate sexual contact. Husbands, heretofore benign and loving fathers, are viewed with suspicion by female survivors. Wives of male survivors do not understand how their spouses could be so affected as grown men.

Developmental blocks. Human beings progress through predictable and necessary developmental stages. This pretreatment difficulty describes when survivors are unable to set healthy boundaries for themselves and with others, to act as separate individuals, and to find healthy ways of nurturing themselves while establishing support systems.

Failing coping mechanisms/negative drug and alcohol consequences. Defenses such as denial, dissociation, and minimization serve the abused child well at the time, but they outlive their usefulness once the child matures and enters more complicated interpersonal relationships. Likewise, the original anesthetizing qualities or emotional permissiveness of chemicals are now replaced with consequences such as damaged relationships and interference with work productivity.

Addicted survivors usually enter treatment for their substance abuse due to these chemical consequences and, once in treatment, realize that there are many other contributing reasons to their loss of control over chemical use. Typical trauma-related triggers that motivate the entrance into treatment include intimacy and sexual dysfunction, pregnancy or children reminding a female survivor of her young victimization, and the death or confrontation of the perpetrator(s). The transition phase ends when survivors learn by the consequences that they cannot safely use addictive chemicals and that their usual ways of coping with stress no longer work: They attend a 12-step meeting, enter a drug and alcohol treatment center, or seek individual therapy.

Stabilization

This stage of recovery is perhaps the most important of the model. It is during this phase that sobriety-based recovery is begun and trauma-focused symptom reduction is established. Addicted survivors must recognize the alcohol and other drug consequences in their lives and profess their loss of control over the substance. They must determine the function of chemicals as a tension-reducing behavior and strive toward more effective ways of managing the stress of everyday life as well as trauma-related triggers and memories. For many clinicians, brevity of time and treatment objectives will require that the survivors terminate treatment once their reliance on tension-reducing behaviors has decreased and sobriety has been attained. Survivors in longer term care will return to this stage over and over because these behaviors tend to be immediately effective for reducing tension, and few alternatives appear to the survivors to work as well. Some of the tasks of the stabilization stage are as follows.

Establishing a diagnosis that is based on a description of behaviors more accurately defines the survivor's experience.

Breaking through denial: Assessment and diagnosis. Each survivor must be given a thorough assessment for chemical addiction, the presence of sexual trauma, and the degree of interference with early recovery tasks. Establishing a diagnosis that is based on a description of behaviors rather than classifications of pathology more accurately defines the survivor's experience. This includes a thorough explanation of typical PTSD and other psychiatric diagnoses that are normalized as understandable reactions to early sexual trauma.

Recognizing tension-reducing behaviors. Such behaviors as substance use, self-mutilation, compulsive sexual activity, and bingeing or chronic overeating are ways that victims distract and soothe themselves in the face of the overwhelming confusion and terror of sexual trauma. Usually there is an interpersonal trigger that creates for the survivor contemporary distress coupled with a restimulation of unresolved, trauma-related emotions. An inability to bear such psychic pressure combined with an inability to manage strong emotion leads a survivor to dissociate, detach from the potential negative consequences of self-destructiveness, and seek any available means to alter the tension. These behaviors, although immediately effective, create for the survivor eventual guilt and self-loathing, and an increasing sense of loss of control when trauma-related issues arise. Consequently, the survivor is likely to have reinforced the belief that anything related to the original sexual trauma is not to be addressed.

The task in this aspect of stabilization is to intervene wherever one can by (a) noticing which situations trigger a self-destructive response; (b) learning affect-regulation skills through desensitization, deep breathing, visualizations, and normalization of intense emotion; (c) learning cognitive reframing by becoming aware of abuse-distorted beliefs and substituting more accurate and contemporary alternative beliefs; and (d) learning self-supportive behaviors by challenging negative self-talk, and learning techniques designed to ground the survivor and distract him or her from intrusive thoughts or images.

Managing shock and stress by creating safety. Uncovering the reality of being sexually abused is accompanied often by immense shock and loss. Children usually make sense of their abuse by keeping their abusers "good" while somehow blaming themselves for the abuse, defining it as just punishment for crimes they must have committed. Focusing on the trauma causes survivors to reevaluate everything they thought about themselves, their abusers, and the world. This can create enormous stress both emotionally and cognitively, so that sometimes survivors appear psychotic. Safety can be created in the treatment setting through the beliefs and attitudes of the clinician and staff.

Survivors can be taught ways to manage their self-destructive behaviors and emotions. Medication may be carefully prescribed to help contain sobriety-threatening emotions, as well as other techniques including breathing and relaxation. Stress must be reduced to a minimum and the survivors' lifestyles must be prioritized. Many survivors must be taught nondestructive self-care, including healthy ways of eating and sleeping, and establishing environmental safety with others.

Assume a survivor identity. Part of the effectiveness of 12-step groups is the immediately shared culture of the thoughts, beliefs, experiences, and language connected to chemical abuse or other compulsions that have identified with a 12-step approach. Identifying oneself as a survivor discourages denial of sexual trauma, supports the understanding of trauma-related behaviors and defenses, and provides for the client a "road map" for future treatment through others who have preceded them.

Establishing a therapeutic alliance. This task incorporates the philosophy of treatment, the therapeutic structure, and the establishment of therapeutic goals. The philosophy of treatment should be a phenomenological approach, that is, understanding the survivor's symptoms as pragmatic reactions to trauma-related stress rather than pathological disorders. In defining the therapeutic structure, safety is ensured (i.e., therapy will not reenact the original betrayal of abuse); the boundaries and expectations of therapy are outlined; and the role of the therapist as a supportive witness to the survivor's experience versus an expert in psychiatric pathology defines the parameters of the therapeutic relationship as more egalitarian with a mutual commitment to the survivor's success.

Successful completion of the stabilization phase of sexual trauma recovery happens when the survivor has the capacity to self-soothe, tolerate painful emotion, and rely on some degree of social support. Other short-term goals that are relevant to this stage of recovery include creating internal and external safety, improving the survivor's functioning in the world, teaching the survivor how to contain and suppress painful memories and emotions, teaching the survivor self-soothing, providing psychoeducation regarding the long-term effects of childhood trauma, teaching medication management, and teaching stress reduction and management.

The goals for the stabilization phase of chemical dependency recovery include (a) thinking clearly, recognizing and identifying feelings, exercising judgment, and controlling behavior; (b) stabilizing the motivating crisis that brought the survivor into treatment; and (c) managing any acute physical and psychosocial problems that could jeopardize early sobriety, including the management of postacute withdrawal.

Postacute withdrawal, a group of symptoms that occurs as a result of abstinence from addictive chemicals, can mimic PTSD, depression, and dissociation. The symptoms include an inability to think clearly, memory problems, emotional overreactions or numbness, sleep disturbances, stress sensitivity, and physical coordination problems. Clinicians are encouraged to take their time in making an accurate diagnosis of PTSD or another diagnosis besides substance abuse in the first several weeks of sobriety, and allow for the survivor's system to clear the chemical damage. Survivors need to be educated as to what is postacute withdrawal and that the treatment includes management of stress, healthy diet, aerobic exercise, and relaxation, all on a regular basis.

■ The Twelve Steps of Alcoholics Anonymous

1. We admitted that we were powerless over alcohol—that our lives had become unmanageable.
2. Came to believe that a Power greater than ourselves could restore us to sanity.
3. Made a decision to turn our will and our lives over to the care of God *as we understood Him.*
4. Made a searching and fearless moral inventory of ourselves.
5. Admitted to God, to ourselves, and to another human being the exact nature of our wrongs.
6. Were entirely ready to have God remove all these defects of character.
7. Humbly asked Him to remove our shortcomings.
8. Made a list of all persons we had harmed and became willing to make amends to them all.
9. Made direct amends to such people wherever possible, except when to do so would injure them or others.
10. Continued to take personal inventory and when we were wrong promptly admitted it.
11. Sought through prayer and meditation to improve our conscious contact with God, *as we understood Him,* praying only for knowledge of His will for us and the power to carry that out.

12. Having had a spiritual awakening as the result of these steps, we tried to carry this message to other alcoholics and to practice these principles in all our affairs.[1]

In a 12-step program, Steps 1 through 3 support the moving through the stages of transition and stabilization. Step 1 of the Twelve Steps of Alcoholics Anonymous reads:

We admitted that we were powerless over alcohol—that our lives had become unmanageable. (Alcoholics Anonymous, 1976, p. 59)

This step encourages the addicted survivor to make an intellectual and emotional connection between problems experienced and the misuse of chemicals.

Step 2 reads:

Came to believe that a Power greater than ourselves could restore us to sanity. (Alcoholics Anonymous, 1976, p. 59)

This step supports the survivor in understanding that (at least some of) their "insanity" is chemically induced, that there are attitudes and beliefs that prevent them from seeking help, and that they can recover only with outside help.

Step 3 reads:

Made a decision to turn our will and our lives over to the care of God *as we understood Him.* (Alcoholics Anonymous, 1976, p. 59)

This step supports the survivor's entrance into the principles and the culture of the 12 steps, which provide a language, identity, and guideline for living for attaining sobriety.

Alcoholics Anonymous has a high success rate for its followers and is still considered by many the best source for securing long-term sobriety. Recovering addicted survivors are encouraged to follow 12-step principles as best they can, realizing that the original steps were created without consideration for chemical use as a survival method for horribly abused children who had few other options for psychic escape. When certain ideas or principles threaten the survivor—or worse, contradict trauma-focused therapy—the treatment plan must be reassessed.

Early Recovery

This phase of treatment is focused on recalling the trauma, looking inward to develop trust and awareness in one's self, and beginning to develop trust in others. Many clinicians ask about the timing and sequence of inquiring about the past. In general, trauma-focused clinicians tend to weigh the extent of intrusive symptoms, including the degree of postacute withdrawal, the level of dissociation or chemically induced confusion and numbing, and the degree of overwhelming affect (anxiety, depression, rage, etc.) against the survivor's available resources (e.g., mental functioning, ability to self-soothe, and ability to ask for external support). If the survivor is in crisis, has acute chemical- or trauma-induced symptoms, is deeply dissociated, or is socially isolated or in an unsupportive home environment, it is wise to continue to focus on stabilization and provision of support. The clinician focuses on the day-to-day maintenance of sobriety and the basic recovery steps necessary for such maintenance, normalizes the survivor's current experience, validates previous recovery successes, and works toward increasing the survivor's feelings of safety and self-control. Once it is determined that the survivor can safely focus on more potentially affective-laden material, the following steps are suggested.

Understanding that the abuse is at the core of his or her problems by reconstructing trauma experiences. One goal of such reconstruction is to integrate the various aspects of consciousness (the image memory, the associated feelings, the kinesthetic sensations, and the meaning applied to the experience) that were understandably partitioned off for the psychic survival of the child (see Steele & Colrain, 1990). Another goal is to uncover enough memory so that current problems in living begin to make sense and the survivor learns that he or she can tolerate intense levels of feeling when the memories are processed. This desensitization and reframing are healing in the therapeutic setting as well as creating in the survivor immunity for memories that will emerge well after treatment has terminated.

There are essentially two types of memories: those that are accessible and those that are fragmented or dissociated. Memories that are available to survivors can indicate what happened, how they feel about what happened, and how they perceive those particular experiences to be influencing them now. Processing memories is useless unless there is adequate cathartic release and examination of cognitive distortions.

Encouraging the uncovering of fragmented or dissociated memories usually requires some type of "triggering" stimulus such as age regression; bridging current affect to earlier, similar emotional states; hypnosis; and expressive therapies. One must proceed with caution in using these techniques, remembering that the psychic curtain that hides these memories has protected the survivor well and may wreak havoc if pulled down too quickly. Certainly, the ethical clinician is sensitive to any of his or her own agendas and needs regarding the uncovering of traumatic events. Generally, it is best to proceed conservatively with little use of intrusive techniques unless the survivor's current level of dysfunction is directly connected to defense against a particular traumatic memory.

The pacing required in processing memory is important, as is the sequence of the work. It is advisable to use the first part of the session to focus on present issues of sobriety and trauma-based symptoms, moving on to past issues and memory reconstruction, and ending the session with a return to the present with plans for self-care and maintenance of abstinence.

Assigning meaning to the trauma. It has been stated that one person's trauma is another person's bad day. It is important to understand that we are treating survivors' perceptions of their experiences. Therefore, we must carefully ascertain a survivor's unique meaning placed on the trauma, the relationship he or she had with the perpetrator, issues surrounding trust and betrayal, and the survivor's level of culpability, as well as issues regarding humanity, cause and effect, and good and evil.

Redefining defenses as coping strategies. There are few, if any, trauma-based symptoms that cannot be reframed to be understood as ways to keep the abused child psychically safe. The term *character defects* and lives of "insanity" contradict this idea and must be interpreted carefully to the survivors. They must come to understand that their defenses are normal reactions to abnormal situations, retaining the notion that they do have greater control over their lives now and that greater choices exist.

The major goals of early recovery from addictive chemicals include accepting the disease of addiction and learning how to function without alcohol or other drugs. Just as it is important to understand current trauma-based symptoms by processing memories, the addicted survivor must be educated about addictive disease and the resulting life problems. A structured recovery program allows both the physical healing to occur and survivors to learn to value sober living.

Steps 4 and 5 of the 12-step program could be useful at this stage of recovery. Step 4 reads:

> Made a searching and fearless moral inventory of ourselves. (Alcoholics Anonymous, 1976, p. 59)

This step encourages substance abusers to complete a personal inventory of both strengths and weaknesses. To do this means to confront the ways that keep them defended against the need to complete such an inventory (denial, grandiosity, etc.), to choose an experienced person to assist in the process, to create a list of questions about areas of concern in their lives, and to complete the inventory by writing a list of strengths and weaknesses. There are numerous guides available to assist them in this process, including the Big Book of AA (Alcoholics Anonymous, 1976). Survivors are cautioned about the use of the term *character defects*, which is defined as those destructive thoughts, feelings, and behaviors that drive psychic pain and invite relapse. Although some of these "defects" may have arisen because of the addiction (they would not have formed had the survivor not become an addict), other personality characteristics may, in fact, be posttraumatic stress reactions.

Experienced, trauma-focused clinicians are seriously questioning traditional psychiatric diagnoses that were largely created without consideration of the long-term sequelae of child abuse. Many of the criteria that define borderline personality disorder, for example, have been associated with symptoms of posttraumatic reactions (Herman, 1992a). It may be more fruitful during this inventory to ask questions that focus on how the survivors still may be attached to their abusive families, how their defensive behaviors may be appropriate responses to chronic child abuse, and how they can move beyond a victim identity and learned helplessness. In essence, the survivors are reframing their thoughts, feelings, and beliefs about themselves, others, and the world from their new perspective as sober survivors.

Step 5 is simply the instruction to confide in another person what has been learned from Step 4. It reads:

> Admitted to God, to ourselves, and to another human being the exact nature of our wrongs. (Alcoholics Anonymous, 1976, p. 59)

Although it sounds simple, such a feat is usually accomplished with a great deal of emotional exposure. Secrets that carry great shame, guilt, and fear must be revealed for successful recovery. Many people who have witnessed Step 5 have told me that this is when they hear disclosures of childhood sexual trauma. It is hoped that survivors are able to choose people who are not only experienced in traditional Step 5 disclosures regarding the harm coming from addictive chemical use but also sensitive to the harmful effects of sexual trauma. A successful Step 5 results in caring, warmth, and respect for the survivor's struggles. The survivor is able to feel unconditional respect, which helps him or her to come out of the emotional isolation necessary to survival.

Middle Recovery

This stage of recovery from sexual trauma focuses on mourning the multiple losses that the survivor has incurred directly due to the perpetrator's actions as well as the responses of those around the survivor during and after the abuse. The survivor begins to look at his or her family with more objective, adult eyes, redefining the sexual abuse as the responsibility of the offender and of those who failed to protect the victim(s). The following steps are helpful to completing this stage:

Recognizing the abusive family system. During this phase, the survivors examine various aspects of the dynamics, beliefs, and destructive behaviors of their family system, especially if the sexual trauma was incestuous. They come to understand the various ways their normal needs for trust and attachment were twisted and exploited to meet adults' needs. They come to understand how "normal" children grow and develop, gaining an increasing empathy for themselves and their defenses aimed at survival. They mourn the loss of their "real" mothers or fathers, and more, they mourn the loss of their attachment to their imagined parents, whom they now realize did not love them in the way they had fantasized. They mourn the loss of bodily integrity, their healthy sexuality, their comfort and pride in their genders, and their delight in their own sexual arousal to their chosen partners.

Some survivors resist mourning because of its immense pain and confusion of feelings. Some find it much easier to stay angry and resentful at the perpetrators or nonprotecting adults. Some resist mourning because they are still very attached to the offenders. To admit loss might invite feelings of outrage that would threaten what sem-blance of love they feel they might have. Resistance to mourning might look something like this:

"I'll hurt you the way you hurt me." (seeking revenge)

"I forgive you." (needing to remain loyal to the abuser, pardoning the abuser's crimes, and minimizing or rationalizing the damage perpe-trated) (For an alternative view on forgiveness, see Hunter, 1990, pp. 112-114.)

"I'll sue you." (survivor remains a victim to the offender's whims)

Assigning responsibility to the perpetrator(s) and unprotective family members. Briere and Runtz (1992) and others speak to the "abuse dichot-omy." This belief system created by the child is similar to:

I'm being hurt because I am bad. Because parents are always right and do things for my own good, they must be punishing me because I have been bad. It is my fault that I'm being hurt/punished, and I am as bad as I am being punished. Because I'm hurt often and deeply, I must be very bad.

This dichotomy speaks to the intense need that children have to make sense of the insanity of the abuse by making themselves bad and requiring punishment, and therefore keeping their parents good. The alternative is terrifying. As the adult survivors examine this defensive way of thinking and come to understand the exploitation involved, they are able to reframe their belief in their "malevolence."

Challenging learned helplessness. Abused children have few choices in accommodating to abuse other than complying and adjusting whatever they can to keep themselves as physically and psychically safe as possible. This leads them to believe they are helpless in making proac-tive choices. In this stage, such powerlessness is confronted, creating for the survivors renewed interest in their present lives and beginning the process of looking outward.

During the middle recovery period from chemical addiction, the primary goal is to move beyond the early, intense, structured recovery program that helped the survivor attain abstinence, to a more balanced lifestyle that is sobriety centered. The focus is no longer simply getting through the day sober, but more on the normal activities of work, family, and social time with friends and family, as well as having time for self-nurturance, relaxation, healthy eating, and exercise.

Early recovery from both addictions and sexual trauma focused on attaining sobriety and stabilizing trauma-based symptoms. It is supported by an intense recovery program such as the principles of the 12 steps and psychotherapy for trauma-based issues and symptoms. During this time, the sexual trauma is intentionally remembered and understood. Adopting a dual identity of alcoholic/addict and trauma survivor supports the client through this period of recovery. The 12-step principles give the addicted survivor a ready-made culture that guides his or her path.

Middle recovery, unlike early recovery, may be less intense. The focus is less on internal experience and more on the family dynamics that supported sexual exploitation, as well as on balanced, sober living. Steps 6 and 7 can support the process of examining which coping mechanisms from the past (character defects) are continuing to give problems in everyday life and consequently are interfering with relationships and goals.

A friend once told me that in order to really understand the concept of "survivor," a person must first come to understand that he or she was a victim. Some survivors become attached to their defenses and even feel entitled to them. For instance, one client believed that her friends should be available to her at all times because no one had been there for her as a child. I explained to her that no one could change how she was treated in the past, but that we could not realistically expect others to make up for the losses.

In Step 6, addicted survivors are asked to examine aspects of their personality that no longer work for them. This step reads:

> Were entirely ready to have God remove all these defects of character. (Alcoholics Anonymous, 1976, p. 59)

The phrase sometimes used regarding this step is "getting sick and tired of being sick and tired." Survivors must look at their behaviors with themselves and others and determine which of the behaviors no longer works. Those behaviors that were once adaptive and accommodating to the sexual trauma must be examined for their contemporary usefulness. Many survivors are terrified about giving up behaviors that simulate safety, but they must do so in order to continue their normal growth and development.

Step 7 is a natural outgrowth of Step 6. It reads:

Humbly asked Him to remove our shortcomings. (Alcoholics Anonymous, 1976, p. 59)

In this step, recovering persons ask God to remove those characteristics
that block one from practicing humility and self-awareness. In Step 6,
addicted survivors acknowledge their self-defeating behaviors and
indicate a willingness to change. In Step 7, survivors realize that they
cannot change lifelong destructive behaviors in isolation, and they ask
for help. They come to understand that they cannot live full and
meaningful lives without humility—the true validation of who they are,
including their strengths and weaknesses.

Late Recovery

This phase of recovery is sometimes desired by survivors early in
their treatment process. It is the time when they confront the crimes of
their sexual trauma, detach from the abusive family system, and work
on personality change, which includes each developing a true sense of
a self. This is a time of reconnecting with themselves and the ordinari-
ness of everyday life. There are two tasks in this phase of treatment:
confrontation and developing a self.

Confrontation and Separation

I feel it is important for all sexual trauma survivors to confront their
abusers and nonprotective adults in a *symbolic* way. Several clients of
mine have attempted to directly confront their abusers from childhood
and have been met with very vocal denials, admonishments, and,
unfortunately, delayed sexual and physical assaults. Judith Herman
(1992a) directs clinicians to never underestimate the current danger of
abusers, even though it may have been many years since they abused
the clients. Some abusers will reenact their original threats against the
adult children, including threats of loss, suicide, and even homicide.
Alternately, a symbolic confrontation might include an angry letter
written to the abuser that is witnessed by the addicted survivor's
support group. The survivor might wish to select a few group members
to perform a psychodrama in which he or she confronts various family
members and then "disposes" of them. Such confrontations claim for

the survivor nonresponsibility for the sexual abuse and help him or her to separate from the traumatic experience, the exploitative values, and the abuser's shame. The goal of confrontations is to detach from any symbols of hope that the abuser will ever come to love the survivor in the way he or she has fantasized.

Some survivors must make difficult decisions regarding physical separations from their abusers, especially if the abusive families are less dysfunctional now, and if the survivors want their own children to have a relationship with their grandparents. Other decisions must be made about who else in the family must know of the abuse so that other potential victims are protected.

Developing a Self

Survivors face the tasks of surpassing their original identities of victim and survivor and of developing a new self. They must separate out those aspects of their personalities that are still "reactive" or have been created to defend against aspects of the sexual trauma. They must look for new ways to believe, feel, and act according to their own choices. One of the typical areas of hard work during this phase is the reowning of their sexuality. Up until now, they may have been ruled by sexual flashbacks, having certain sexual practices off limits, or feeling ashamed and limited sexually. During this task, they learn to take back control over their arousal patterns, learn how to separate out which sexual practices are pleasurable for them, and learn to leave any sexual shame behind.

The treatment goals for addiction recovery are very similar to those of a trauma focus, including the personality changes necessary for positive self-esteem, healthy intimacy, and the ability to live a productive, happy life. Some addicts must understand the dynamics of their childhood dysfunctional families to determine which beliefs may now affect their sobriety. Support groups such as Adult Children of Alcoholics have proved very helpful in understanding the rules and behaviors in alcoholic families and how they are passed on to adult children.

Steps 8 and 9 follow the tasks of late recovery very nicely. They include identifying those people who have been harmed due to addiction and the effects of the abuse, and making amends to them. Making amends is not a quick, easy apology. Rather, this process is an honest attempt by addicted survivors to acknowledge that they have hurt others and that they are sorry and are willing to do what is necessary to make things right again.

Step 8 is really very simple, with little interpretation required. It reads:

Made a list of all persons we had harmed and became willing to make amends to them all. (Alcoholics Anonymous, 1976, p. 59)

The addicted survivors make a list of all the people that were harmed by their addiction and identify what needs to be done to make things right. Then they make a list of the people who have hurt them, and they forgive those people. Step 8 is completed when survivors identify by the consequences if making amends would further harm themselves or others.

Step 9 is the process of making amends set up in Step 8. It reads:

Made direct amends to such people wherever possible, except when to do so would injure them or others. (Alcoholics Anonymous, 1976, p. 59)

First, survivors determine that they have established a strong sobriety program, for this emotional process can set up a relapse if they are not careful. Then they make a concrete plan of when and how to approach the persons on the amends list. Making amends are then approached by survivors admitting the reality of their addiction, by recognizing the harm it has caused, and by making commitments to repair the damages.

Survivors might also include in this amends process those persons who have been harmed from the effects of the survivors' sexual trauma. This might include issues around trust, outbursts of anger, and emotional abandonment within an important relationship. It should be explained that such reactions are related originally to the sexual abuse, and the survivors now realize that they are capable of making more objective, adult choices over their reactions toward others.

From an addictions point of view, the act of forgiveness is critical to staying sober.

Many survivors have a very difficult time with the 12-step principle of the need for forgiveness. This principle states that when one has been harmed, there are two choices: to forgive or to resent. Resentment, sometimes referred to as recycled anger, causes stress, which causes new pain and problems in life. This vicious cycle can lead to intolerable pain leading to relapse. Therefore, from an addictions point of view, the act of forgiveness is critical to staying sober. However, from the viewpoint of sexual trauma survivors, the possibility of forgiving their abusers creates for them despair, rage, and sometimes loss of faith in the 12-step program in general.

It is my experience that many survivors do not wish to forgive their abusers unless the abusers first ask for such forgiveness. The likelihood of this happening is rare, so I suggest the option of detachment. This way, survivors do not have to say "I forgive you," but rather, "I separate from you and your harm, your shame, your humiliation. I trust that my Higher Power will reckon with you in an appropriate manner. I let you go." Addictions counselors suggest that recovering people write an unmailed letter to those they wish to forgive, listing what the other person did that was harmful, how they felt about it then and how they feel about it now, and that they forgive them. I would suggest that similar letters be written to abusers, but that survivors write clearly that they hold the abusers absolutely responsible for their actions. The letters might conclude with a "turning it over" and the revelation that the survivors are strong enough now to move beyond revenge.

Some survivors have a very difficult time moving beyond revenge. Rather than suggesting that they repress revenge fantasies, it may be advisable to bring the fantasies to a head by asking survivors to say out loud, in great detail, just what they would like to do or have done to the abusers. Allowing these fantasies to be verbalized and normalized often causes the intensity of revenge to decrease rapidly.

A last point regarding late recovery is that early in their treatment, many survivors want to directly confront their abusers, indicating that they have no expectations as to the outcome. I have yet to determine this to be true. Usually survivors want the abusers to make their own amends, offer apologies, and ask the survivors how they can make it up to them. Some survivors want their abusers to hurt as much as they have been hurt. Others want to force their abusers into treatment so that new relationships might be formed. It is critical that before the survivors make plans for any direct confrontation, or making amends, for that matter, that their physical and psychic safety be determined. It is necessary to put off confrontations until the survivors are stable in their sobriety and have developed enough ego strength and ability to self-soothe so that the outcome of any confrontation does not seriously threaten them.

■ Ongoing Recovery

By the time the chemically dependent survivors reach this level in their recovery, they may have been in treatment for 2 to 5 years. This phase of recovery does not end, but rather continues throughout the remainder of the survivors' lives. Once isolated, stigmatized, and utterly despairing, adult survivors now begin the reconnection with others. Many survivors who have been in my groups for several years admit to me at this time that they would rather begin finding friends who are NOT survivors. They feel very guilty about this at first until they understand that they have outgrown the constraints of an identity connected to the past. The aspects of ongoing recovery involve learning to establish boundaries, create healthy relationships, and pass on to others what they have learned in recovery in an effort to protect the next generation. These recovery tasks include the following:

Learning to establish boundaries. Sexually traumatized children have every boundary violated. This stage encourages the survivors to learn the necessity of setting limits with others for physical, emotional, and sexual safety. They learn that boundaries can be flexible and can be more or less resilient according to whom they are with and the social situation. Many survivors experiment with setting sexual boundaries with loved ones, and relationship upheavals are normal and expected. It is not easy for the partners of survivors, who may be used to unrestricted sexual expression, to be told that their behavior must change for the strength of the relationship. Survivors also learn to discriminate trustworthy people from those who are untrustworthy, rather than distrusting everyone or allowing everyone into their personal space.

Learning how to have healthy relationships. This process is merely determining whether current relationships are supportive of the survivors' ongoing recovery. If they are not, those relationships must be terminated. If they are, then the survivors work on expanding existing relationships or creating new ones that do not reenact earlier abusive intimacies and that are reciprocally healthy. There are many books and guides specifically for recovering people on the establishment of such healthy relationships (see Hunter, 1992).

Passing it on—protecting the next generation. Many survivors vow to stop the sexual abuse legacy with their generation. This declaration is good and necessary, but we must ask how they plan to do so. One choice that some survivors make is to tell their children about their own traumatic experiences. This is a method that addresses the children's safety rather than a vengeful disclosure. Making amends to the children about trauma-related problems may be important. Survivors may wish to alert other family members about abusers who still have access to children. Other survivors may wish to take political action to join in the prevention effort to stop child abuse. This may take the form of helping other victims, providing community education, and making political and legal efforts toward protecting children. All of these efforts raise public awareness.

Ongoing recovery from chemical dependency involves maintaining an effective recovery program, watching for relapse warning signs, solving the problems of everyday life, and productive living. These tasks are supported by the remaining Steps 10, 11, and 12.

Step 10 reads:

Continued to take personal inventory and when we were wrong promptly admitted it. (Alcoholics Anonymous, 1976, p. 59)

It is recommended that inventories be taken in the morning and at night. Morning inventories ask what the survivors need to do today to maintain their recovery program and act responsibly. Evening inventories ask the survivors to determine what they have done well today, what they have done poorly, and how they can remedy whatever they have done poorly. Any warning signs regarding addiction or trauma-related behaviors need to be assessed and intervention used if necessary. Such inventories should be a practiced part of the survivors' lives, so that when problems arise they may be quickly handled before they are denied or dissociated away. Many survivors find that writing in a journal from the very beginning of their recovery journey is a vital part of their healing. These journals mark the way of progress and show up any patterns or situations that could create a relapse progression.

Step 11 is the step of spirituality. It reads:

Sought through prayer and meditation to improve our conscious contact with God *as we understood Him*, praying only for knowledge of His will for us and the power to carry that out. (Alcoholics Anonymous, 1976, p. 59)

In the first 3 steps, addicted survivors come to believe in a Higher Power just to get sober. Many find that the Higher Power they come to know during Step 11 is quite a different source of courage, strength, and hope.

Many sexual trauma survivors have had to "worship" their abusers, so these survivors come reluctantly to the understanding of another, benevolent God. Step 11 asks survivors to make a decision to believe in a Higher Power and to call it God. Next, survivors are asked to make a decision that it is possible to develop a deep personal relationship with the God of their understanding and to practice daily prayer that the relationship can grow and strengthen. Survivors are then encouraged to acknowledge to themselves and others ways in which they have changed as a result of their spiritual experiences. Many recovering survivors balk at the idea of "surrendering" to their Higher Power and trusting that they will receive spiritual support in hard times. This process is erroneously interpreted as a submission that reenacts feelings of victimization. Survivors need ample support in understanding that their Higher Power can be a symbol of their own active choosing, from a religious God to aspects of nature.

A basic slogan within AA is, "In order to keep it, you have to give it away." This reflects the task of Step 12, which reads:

> Having had a spiritual awakening as the result of these steps, we tried to carry this message to other alcoholics and to practice these principles in all our affairs. (Alcoholics Anonymous, 1976, p. 60)

Recovering survivors recognize that through their practice of the previous 11 steps they have had a spiritual awakening and now carry the message of strength and hope to other addicted survivors. They are in a position to tell their own stories of what it was like to be addicted and to suffer the life-threatening effects of sexual trauma. They are able to speak to their need to pursue sober lives through abstinence and the personal and relationship changes needed to maintain sobriety. They are also able to model how they have made active choices to live meaningful, productive, sober lives. This process of sharing in recovery is provided with no expectation of compensation or personal reward, but with humility. Survivors continue to participate in 12-step meetings, sharing their experience, strength, and hope. They live their lives on the basis of the 12-step principles because the steps are compatible with their unique trauma reactions and recovery needs. Survivors realize that they must continually strive in their spiritual growth, recognizing that they will never achieve perfection.

■ The Relapse Process

Recovery from chemical dependency and sexual trauma is not a process of straight-line growth. Most people recover in stages, during which they come to understand the nature of their addiction and the dynamics of their sexual trauma, spend time applying and integrating new knowledge in their daily lives, and then coast for awhile before the need arises for more growth. It is common for recovering people to backslide from time to time, usually when they are trying out new skills or are under unusual amounts of stress. This stop-start process is normal and is to be expected.

Some survivors, however, do not make it through the recovery process, becoming stuck in the face of change and eventually falling back on old behaviors that temporarily provide psychic relief but create even worse problems in the long run. Some of the more common "stuck places" for survivors include (a) denying and minimizing the impact and effects of the sexual trauma; (b) continuing to insist that the sexual abuse was their fault; (c) continuing to use tension-reducing behaviors that are self-destructive; (d) being more invested in others than in themselves; (e) isolating themselves and withdrawing from the very people who could be helpful; and (f) going through life crises, which include serious depression, suicide attempts, life-threatening chemical use, or self-destructiveness.

If these stuck places are not interrupted so that recovery may begin anew, a full-blown relapse is not far away. The term *relapse* is commonly used to refer to those chemically dependent people who begin to use alcohol and other drugs after a period of sobriety. Although certainly addicted survivors do relapse in this way, they also relapse to former conditions of the trauma-related reactions of classic PTSD, tension-reducing behaviors, and victimizing situations. The general course toward relapse is from denial of the consequences of chemical addiction and/or sexual trauma, coupled with an exacerbation of one or more high-risk factors that the survivors bring to their recovery. Then it takes only a minor trigger to set into motion the relapse process.

A relapse is a progression of events that is interrelated and causally connected and that, when set into motion, culminates in the eventual abuse of chemicals and/or posttrauma symptoms. Survivors' vulnerability toward relapse depends on what high-risk factors they bring with them into treatment and their immunity against triggers in the environment. Mismanagement of these trigger events can lead to internal dysfunction (difficulty in thinking, affect modulation, memory containment, stress management, and self-blame), external dysfunction (avoidance, crises, immobilization, hypervigilance, withdrawal, helplessness), loss of control (boundaries, judgment, self-destructiveness, revictimization, emotional and physical collapse), and deterioration (suicide attempts, chemical abuse, psychosis). The key to preventing relapse is for survivors to identify their high-risk factors, successfully manage trauma-related triggers, and learn potential warning signs of impending trouble. Typical high-risk factors and trigger events are discussed below as well as a typical progression from internal impairment to serious relapse behaviors.

> *The key to preventing relapse is for survivors to identify high-risk factors, manage trauma-related triggers, and learn warning signs of trouble.*

High-Risk Factors

Many recovering survivors come to treatment with strikes against them. These risk factors do not cause survivors to relapse; the factors just make relapse more likely to happen. The following are some of the more common risk factors:

1. *History of severe abuse.* This includes those survivors whose sexual trauma was significant in duration and frequency, included multiple perpetrators, included physically forced penetration or intercourse, and occurred at a very early age. It also includes survivors whose perpetrators were significantly older than they.

2. *Severe posttraumatic symptoms.* The flashbacks (including visual, auditory, olfactory, and kinesthetic), nightmares, survivor guilt, and so on are so severe as to cause major disruption in survivors' everyday lives.

3. *History of ritualized sadistic abuse.* This type of abuse nearly always includes physical abuse; bizarre features include quasi-religious rituals involving living sacrifices as well as mind control of the victims. Drugs and alcohol are readily used to anesthetize victims and create dissociation.

4. *Chronic reliance on tension-reducing behaviors.* Such dependence disallows learning of new, more sophisticated ways of managing stress. The persistent pairing of self-destructive behaviors with repetitive thoughts serves only to further embed the accompanying negative beliefs.

5. *Isolation or living a victim lifestyle and self-neglect.* The recovery skills that are learned by survivors are quickly negated if they continue to live attached to abusers. Likewise, if survivors neglect their basic needs for

eating, sleeping, and medical care, the mind and body are left unsupported in the energy required for recovering.

6. *Recanting.* This occurs when survivors take back previously disclosed sexual trauma. This is a very common tactic for abused children, who attempt to remain loyal to their abusers. Adult survivors also will occasionally take back their claims of abuse, which necessarily involve revealing the truth and creating for them overwhelming emotional dissonance.

Trigger Events

The relationship between the number of high-risk factors and the intensity of a particular trigger determines whether survivors will begin to relapse. Survivors with fewer high-risk factors will require a greater stressor to trigger internal problems. For survivors with many high-risk characteristics, it will take only a minor trigger to set off difficulties in their thinking and affect modulation. Trigger events specific to recovering survivors typically involve interpersonal stressors that evoke perceived betrayal, threat, abandonment, fear, or severe conflict with someone they love or with an authority figure. These trigger events typically fall into the following categories:

1. *Sexual encounters.* For the survivor, these experiences can reenact feelings of victimization and classic PTSD symptoms of flashbacks of the abuse.
2. *Medical procedures.* These necessary experiences (pelvic exams, dental procedures, tests requiring physical constraints) can also evoke PTSD symptoms and feelings of helpless dependency.
3. *Confrontations with the abuser.* Survivors may regress to an emotional time in their lives where they feel frozen in fear and shame.
4. *Death of the abuser.* This physical separation may facilitate the lifting of repression leading to recall of the abuse.
5. *Memories.* Survivors' children may trigger age-regressed memory or reveal to the survivors their own vulnerability as a child.
6. *Disclosures of sexual trauma.* Survivors may be triggered by negative reactions that they receive on disclosing their sexual trauma or they may be startled by disclosures from their children and other relatives.
7. *Revictimizations.* Many victims of rape and domestic violence have repressed memory triggered during and after assaults on them as adults.
8. *Media intrusion.* Many survivors enter treatment after having viewed a talk show or movie that so closely resembles their own abuse that they exhibit posttrauma symptoms.

Internal Dysfunction

Experiencing any one of the above triggers can cause severe stress. The tasks involved in managing a trigger include identifying it, understanding the unique meaning and impact, updating the meaning from a here-and-now perspective, and making plans for managing it more effectively in the future. Ignoring or dissociating from a trigger or, worse, relying on tension-reducing behaviors can quickly create for the survivor symptoms of internal dysfunction. Descriptions of the symptoms of internal dysfunction include:

1. *Difficulty in thinking clearly.* This involves symptoms of dissociation (feeling detached, numbed, or out-of-body), "trance logic" (the dissociated thinking that from a child's perspective explained the abuse), obsessive thinking, and loss of rational reasoning.
2. *Difficulty with affect modulation.* Natural feelings of anger and anxiety become rage and panic attacks.
3. *Difficulty in containing memories.* Survivors lose touch with the reality that they are safe as images and sensations intrude on their lives.
4. *Difficulty in eating and sleeping.* Survivors' posttrauma symptoms may make sleeping without nightmares difficult, and eating becomes a source of solace or overcontrol.
5. *Difficulty in stress management.* Many survivors tend to tolerate enormously high levels of stress and slow down only when major disaster strikes, such as severe illness or emotional collapse.
6. *Difficulty in placement of responsibility.* This is a slippage into denial regarding the abusers' responsibility for the trauma as well as the survivors' responsibility for recovery choices.

External Dysfunction

If the internal problems are not resolved, survivors are likely to begin showing external signs that their lives are breaking down. This is a progression of feelings and behaviors caused from chronic buildup of stress and denial of previous warning signs of internal dysfunction. Some of the typical signs of these external problems include:

1. *Avoidance and symptomatic behaviors.* These behaviors, designed to avoid thinking or feeling about sexual trauma, include a variety of tension-reducing activities such as acting out (sexual promiscuity, risk-taking, binge eating), acting in (depression, isolation), and resistance to recovery activities.

2. *Crises.* Many survivors have been labeled with borderline personality disorder due to their propensity for a crisis-centered life. Interestingly, nearly all of the criteria that make up the diagnosis for the disorder have been connected independently to posttrauma reactions. Such crises may be attempts at distraction for survivors who welcome the familiarity of adrenaline and chaos.

3. *Immobilization.* Internal and external chaos create for survivors the inability to take any further action. A clinical depression often follows.

4. *Hypervigilance and anxiety.* The immobilization of depression sometimes evokes in survivors the need to be hypervigilant and anxious toward others even though others may wish only to help.

5. *Social withdrawal.* Survivors isolate themselves from 12-step meetings, friends and family, and treatment providers, and sometimes are unable to continue at work.

6. *Confusion and overreaction.* Survivors' thinking is impaired; they become confused and overreact to benign situations and people.

7. *Learned helplessness.* This perception comes out of survivors' inability to effect any change over their sexually abusive experience coupled with their position of insubordination.

Loss of Control

If the symptoms of external dysfunction are left untreated, behavioral loss of control will follow. During this period, survivors are unable to control their behavior or care for themselves adequately. Typical responses include:

1. *Loss of boundaries.* This might take the form of survivors permitting offensive contacts by other adults or making inappropriate demands on children.

2. *Poor judgment.* Survivors make poor choices regarding safety, relationships, and self-care.

3. *Inability to seek help.* Survivors deny the need for further help and refuse any offers.

4. *Option reduction.* Survivors begin to feel that there may be no way out other than insanity, suicide, or chemical use.

5. *Emotional and/or physical collapse.* This may take the form of panic attacks, psychosis, severe depression, or the development of a serious disease or disorder.

6. *Revictimizations and reenactments.* Because of the combination of loss of boundaries, poor judgment, and the need for avoidance, it is not uncom-

mon for survivors to be revictimized through rape, domestic violence, or sexual servitude.

Deterioration

It is at this time that survivors will turn to drastic measures to survive. Typically, they will make a serious suicide or homicide attempt, begin abusing drugs or alcohol, and/or develop psychiatric problems, all requiring hospitalization.

■ Relapse Prevention Through Warning Sign Management

Chemically dependent survivors have a strong tendency toward chemical and posttrauma relapse. Appropriate action by survivors and their support systems can interrupt, if not prevent, relapse before the consequences become tragic. The following steps directly parallel relapse prevention planning for chemically dependent nonsurvivors:

1. *Stabilization—regaining control.* These are the very steps the survivors took in the beginning of treatment, including emotional containment, self-care and self-control, and cognitive reframing. It may be important to temporarily increase the number of 12-step meetings and counseling sessions and to reduce stress to a minimum.

2. *Assessment—figuring out what happened.* Usually, this requires looking for the trigger that set into motion the relapse progression and unraveling the dysfunctional thoughts, feelings, and behaviors that went along with it. Assessing the current level of self-care and accommodating for any high-risk factors is important.

3. *Education.* It is essential that survivors learn about the process of recovery and how relapse occurs, whether chemical relapse or the return of posttrauma symptoms and behaviors. They need to understand how postacute withdrawal and classic PTSD affect recovery.

4. *Warning sign identification.* This is the basis of relapse prevention planning. These are the "red flags" that warn of impending problems often triggered by high-risk situations. Chemically dependent survivors are encouraged to undertake the following process:
   • Review the list of warning signs by reading the progression listed above (internal dysfunction through deterioration)
   • Put an asterisk beside no more than three signs that apply

- Rewrite the warning sign in their own words
- Tell a story about an experience in which the warning sign manifested, and a story about a future event that is likely to create the same warning sign
- Identify the thoughts, feelings, and compelling actions that occur with the warning sign

5. *Warning sign management.* Once warning signs are identified, an action plan must be created. Survivors identify, predict, and plan for triggers by attempting to avoid them or integrating them into daily life. High-risk factors are acknowledged and accommodated. A concrete daily schedule is helpful to structure behavior that allows for triggers and high-risk situations.

6. *Daily review of recovery.* Relapse prevention means planning on a daily basis activities that will help manage difficult situations, memories, and feelings; this reflects Step 10. Activities might include counseling sessions, meetings, support groups, journal writing, letters of encouragement to themselves, and affirmations.

7. *Involvement of significant others.* Chemically dependent survivors cannot recover alone. They require a support system that is informed of the survivors' warning signs with specific instructions on intervention.

8. *Follow-up and reinforcement.* As recovering survivors embark on more intimate relationships, they will continue to uncover new triggers and responses related to the past and will require ongoing vigilance over warning signs. Some survivors plan checkpoints, such as every 3 months, to review their warning signs and make changes as necessary.

■ Planning for the Future: The Need for Reciprocal Treatment Planning

This chapter has indicated the need for treating the long-lasting effects of sexual trauma concurrently with treating chemical dependency. The majority of chemically dependent people have suffered some type of psychological trauma, and for many this includes sexual abuse. Some have serious posttrauma symptoms at the beginning of their addictions recovery, and some do not. The challenge before clinicians of both disciplines of chemical dependency and mental health is to assess recovering survivors individually and provide adequate treatment for both difficulties as needed. This humane balance not only is necessary clinically to attain and maintain sobriety but also to acknowledge and respect the adult survivor's tragic history. The two diverse professional fields can no longer afford to protect territories, but rather must bring to one another the best in treatment philosophies and strategies. This requires open minds, humility, and respect, and sometimes a sense of humor. As survivors are offered the best of both worlds, they are ensured a type of serenity described in The Promises of the 12 Steps:

> If we are painstaking about this phase of our development, we will be amazed before we are half-way through. We are going to know a new freedom and a new happiness. We will not regret the past nor wish to shut the door on it. We will comprehend the word serenity and we will know peace. No matter how far down the scale we have gone, we will see how our experience can benefit others. That feeling of uselessness and self-pity will disappear. We will lose interest in selfish things and gain interest in our fellows. Self-seeking will slip away. Our whole attitude and outlook on life will change. Fear of people and of economic insecurity will leave us. We will intuitively know how to handle situations that used to baffle us. We will suddenly realize that God is doing for us what we could not do for ourselves. (Alcoholics Anonymous, 1976, p. 83, reprinted with permission)

As I completed this manuscript, our field was being challenged strongly by "false memory syndrome" thinking. The debate over delayed memory has become one of many issues, I'm sure, that will attempt to admonish those who are courageous enough to speak their horrific truths. There has never been a more critical time for those of us who care for survivors to band together in support of their truths. It is not a time to polarize.

I envision a growing awareness of the need for an expansive approach to the treatment of childhood trauma and its enormous consequences. My vision includes closing the gap between disciplines so that our suffering survivors may benefit from all treatment philosophies and modalities available to them. My vision includes increasing tolerance and expanded clinical interpretations for the wide range of behavioral symptoms that early abuse brings about. This vision includes understanding the nature of dissociation and its role in the use of chemicals, the nature of traumatic memory and its tendency to be revealed later in life, and the personality adaptations necessary for the victim to survive. With these understandings, perhaps we will refer to recovery as a stepwise journey inviting the support and wisdom of many. Perhaps we will refer to relapse as something we need to anticipate rather than staunchly attempt to prevent.

In spite of the challenging times in front of us all, I believe that this work not only is valuable but has enormous social and political ramifications for our children and our planet. When I feel overwhelmed with the enormity of it all, I take solace in a story I was told about a tourist who came across a fisherman walking a beach that was strewn with thousands of beached starfish. As the fisherman was slowly easing one of the animals back into the water, the tourist asked how that could possibly make any difference considering the thousands of other starfish that would die under the hot sun. The fisherman answered, "It will make a huge difference to the one I just put back in the water."

■ Note

1. The 12 Steps are reprinted here with permission of Alcoholics Anonymous World Services, Inc. Permission to reprint the Steps and the Promises does not mean that AA has reviewed or approved the content of this publication, nor that AA agrees with the views expressed herein. AA is a program of recovery from alcoholism *only*—use of the 12 Steps and the Promises in connection with programs and activities that are patterned after AA, but that address other problems, does not imply otherwise.

7

Strengthening the Heartline

Working With Adult Survivors of Childhood Sexual Abuse and Their Partners

Betty Button

Allen Dietz

Professionals who work with adult survivors of childhood sexual abuse generally recognize the consequential role that supportive partners can play in healing. Because much of the active recovery from abuse must be accomplished in the survivors' daily milieus between therapy sessions, their personal relationships can form an integral part of the framework of healing. When professionals encourage and reinforce constructive relationships and offer support to caring partners, survivors' progress and well-being can be enhanced tremendously. This chapter emerges from our more than 6 years' experience in the following areas: personally navigating the healing process as survivor and partner; presenting continuing education seminars on survivor relationship issues, where we learn much from the professionals who participate; and conducting workshops for survivors and their allies—our fellow travelers and our most valued teachers.

If a relationship is to endure the stresses of a survivor's recovery, decisions along the healing path must be made jointly by the partners. It is unrealistic to expect a partner or a relationship to remain static while the survivor surges through the dynamic process of recovery. In the words of an applicable maxim, "One can never step twice into the same river." The couple must share a commitment to change.

■ Impact on Partners

For a partner who stays closely involved as a survivor heals, the positive long-term impact can be very powerful. Intimately sharing in such personal growth can result in a realignment of priorities and life goals. Partners have unique chances to assess what is truly important to them in a relationship, to confront their own issues, to develop new life skills, and to deepen interpersonal commitments. As they work together through the healing process, survivors and their partners can seize opportunities to discover untapped strengths in themselves and in each other.

Among the general population, little is known about the dynamics and effects of sexual abuse, and even less about the healing process. It is not surprising, then, that a partner would be terribly confused when a survivor reveals a history of abuse and seeks therapy to heal from the trauma. Partners may question whether the abuse actually happened, wanting desperately to believe it did not. They may be tempted to ask, "How could you not remember something so significant?" or "Maybe you just saw it in a movie and it seems real now." After all, survivors often doubt the abuse themselves. There is only limited information to alleviate partners' uncertainty about the healing process and their role in it.

It is common for a partner to feel betrayed by a survivor's lack of "full disclosure." At the beginning of the relationship, the survivor may not have conscious memories of the abuse or awareness of its lasting effects on his or her life. As the survivor changes in unpredictable ways during the healing process, the partner may feel further betrayed. Prior to learning about the abuse and its aftereffects, the partner may have established a positive and close relationship with the survivor's family. He or she may then feel duped as illusions are shattered. One partner compared this to finding himself on a runaway roller coaster when he did not even know he had bought a ticket to the amusement park.

Many survivors are prompted to enter a healing process when strong, painful emotions begin to surface. These "leaking feelings" are overreactions that are out of proportion to the situation and may be directed toward the people closest to the survivors, such as intimate partners, children, other family members, and friends. For example, a survivor accidentally breaks an inexpensive dish and begins to sob uncontrollably. Her partner tries to use humor to console her, reminding her they'd never really liked that dish anyway. The survivor becomes angry and accuses the partner of not taking her feelings seriously. The anger intensifies as the survivor concludes that the partner no longer cares about her and must want to end the relationship.

It can be interpreted that survivors feel safe and comfortable enough around their allies to allow strong feelings to emerge. Such behavior, however, can obviously damage relationships if it continues. Survivors must learn to channel their emotions constructively. It is indeed a challenge to identify survivors' reactions that are disproportionate to the situation at hand without discounting those that are legitimate within the current context.

As survivors get in touch with the original trauma and the depth of its impact, they generally feel worse before beginning to feel better. Partners who are not familiar with the healing process may doubt whether it is actually working. They may question the capability of the therapist and other professionals involved, and may attempt to interfere with the survivors' personal decisions regarding healing.

> *As survivors get in touch with the original trauma and its impact, they generally feel worse before beginning to feel better.*

A partner's feelings of isolation and loneliness may heighten as the survivor withdraws emotionally and/or physically at various stages of recovery. If the survivor chooses to curtail his or her social interactions, the partner is automatically affected. It is easy for a partner to assume that none of his or her own acquaintances is dealing with similar challenges because healing from sexual abuse is a rare topic in "polite conversation." When a partner tries to develop allies, it may be extremely difficult to find support. Family members, friends, and coworkers may distance themselves due to discomfort with abuse issues, an unwillingness to learn or understand, or perhaps their own unresolved personal issues.

Partners must come to grips with major upheavals involving the present, the future, and even their perceptions of the past. It can seem that nothing is as it was before. Inevitably, original expectations and plans for the relationship will be at least temporarily modified. Resources, which may have been limited in the first place, are now being almost totally redirected into healing. It is only natural that partners are faced with grieving a number of related losses.

Whereas survivors struggle to pinpoint and release blocked anger, partners frequently may have much easier access to their own. Partners are likely to be struck by the unfairness of the current situation in terms of having to expend their energy and resources to repair the damage inflicted by others long ago. There may be resentment toward anyone even remotely connected to the abuse or the healing process, and toward people whose lives are seemingly free of such major obstacles.

A partner's anger would naturally be directed toward the perpetrator(s) and toward family members and others who did not protect the survivor as a child. However, for a variety of reasons, the survivor may also be on the receiving end. The partner may at some level believe that the survivor could have prevented the abuse and thus avoided the pain and drain involved in healing. Survivors who have been functioning for years without any apparent effects may be criticized by their partners for no longer being willing or able to compartmentalize the trauma. Partners may pressure survivors to speed up the healing process, especially as symptoms begin to abate. To complicate matters further, partners may feel guilty about any anger that they have toward the survivors regarding the abuse or the therapeutic process.

Guilt may also arise over the partner's inability to rescue the survivor from the childhood abuse or to help the survivor avoid the pain that necessarily accompanies effective healing. The partner may even begin to feel directly responsible for the survivor's healing, tying his or her self-image to the survivor's fluctuating emotional state. As the process intensifies, partners sometimes feel they should be able to ignore or postpone their own needs, and that survivors should not be asked for any assistance or support. These "super-partners" may then experience guilt for failing to meet their own unreasonable expectations.

Some unhealthy dynamics can emerge that later prove problematic. A partner may remain in a relationship with a survivor out of a sense of duty or pity or out of fear that the survivor could not withstand his or her departure. Behaviorally and semantically within the relationship, the survivor may be characterized as "sick," and the partner "well." The partner may state or imply that the survivor is "crazy," weak, flawed, or incapable of functioning on his or her own. Assuming a "martyr" stance, the partner may take over an inordinate amount of what had been the survivor's tasks and responsibilities in the household or in the relationship. Little thought is given to prioritizing the tasks or questioning whether some of them might be done less often, less perfectly, or eliminated altogether. When a partner's sole identity is as a caretaker, the survivor must remain "sick" in order to feel confident that the relationship will continue. The obvious corresponding message is that if the survivor recovers, the partner might leave.

As the stress and pressure of the healing process mount, many partners themselves experience reactions similar to those of the survivor. These symptoms can include overwhelming physical, emotional, and spiritual fatigue, as well as posttraumatic stress disorder (PTSD) symptoms such as sleep disturbances, nightmares, and hypervigilance. Even shame is not unusual among partners of survivors. A partner may develop "secondary shame" about the survivor's abuse history, or a partner may question the implications of having chosen to become involved with a survivor, even if the abuse was not remembered or disclosed when the relationship began.

Partners have closely observed survivors' unhealthy coping styles, some of which seem to work at least temporarily. Among these are compartmentalizing, denial, self-blame, substance abuse, a fatalistic attitude, and emotional withdrawal or numbness. It is not surprising that partners may adopt similar behaviors as the stress of the survivors' healing process becomes more intense.

Sadness and depression are often experienced by partners. The sadness precipitated by learning that a loved one was victimized as a child can be compounded by living with a survivor's ongoing depression. The partner may become frustrated over the slow pace of the healing process and his or her own powerlessness to improve the survivor's outlook. Maintaining a positive approach to life or any optimism about the future is an increasing challenge.

Accompanying childhood sexual abuse survivors through the healing process causes partners to reevaluate some of their own basic assumptions. For example, many partners have grown up around traditionally negative attitudes regarding psychotherapy. Suddenly they are being asked to acknowledge the value and appropriateness of seeking professional help. Partners learn firsthand that the effects of childhood trauma do not diminish on their own.

Living with a survivor who is healing can trigger feelings or memories within the partner. A partner may discover previously blocked memories of having been abused or neglected or become aware of dysfunction in his or her family of origin. At this point in one survivor's therapy, it may seem impossible to envision his or her partner also embarking on a healing process. It must strictly be a matter of individual choice, but healing side-by-side can be and has been done by many couples. Relationships involving two survivors have the advantage of some basic mutual understanding, but the stresses can be extremely complex. It is very important that the couple has dependable and competent support systems outside the primary relationship. Of course, some partners choose not to begin therapy immediately on detecting unresolved issues, and others may resist or remain in denial indefinitely. Serious conflict may arise if one person in the relationship is working toward personal healing and growth and the other is actively choosing not to do so.

Once a survivor discovers that sexual abuse is the source of persistent difficulties in his or her life, there can be a sense of relief at finally discovering something concrete on which to focus an active healing process. The survivor's partner may find himself or herself at the opposite end of the emotional spectrum. Partners often report feeling they have lost all power over their own lives. It appears to them that stability and predictability have disappeared and that events outside their control are now driving the relationship. Once the "dam has broken," partners may feel overwhelmed, helpless, and left out. Without warning, new memories or buried emotions may surface, totally consuming survivors' energy and attention. Their partners may be tempted to say, "Just go ahead with the process and let me know when you're finished."

As a couple's attention and resources shift toward the survivor's healing, the balance within the relationship can be upset and their lifestyle seriously disrupted. As the therapeutic process consumes more and more of the survivor's energy, the partner may feel resentful or jealous. The partner may begrudge the increasing amount of time the survivor is spending in solitude or on self-care. The survivor's sharing personal details with a therapist and others involved in the healing process may be threatening or unsettling to the partner.

Sexual intimacy is usually affected in some significant way as therapy progresses, because the survivor's sexuality is among the last areas to heal. From the partner's perspective, this is extremely painful and unfair. Terrifying or devastating memories may intrude at the most unexpected and undesirable moments in the intimate lives of survivors and their partners. It is quite distressing for a partner suddenly to be perceived as a perpetrator within a survivor's flashback. In essence, both the survivor and the partner may both feel victimized by these intrusions into their most intimate moments.

As a survivor moves deeper into the process of recovery, it is common for the partner to examine his or her commitment to the relationship. There is no way to predict what changes the process ultimately will bring about in the survivor, in the partner, and in their interactions with each other. Partners may question their own ability or willingness to sustain the pressures inherent in the process. At the outset, a partner's fear of the unknown is probably justified. As partners learn about abuse issues and the healing process, and as couples together begin to overcome some of the obstacles involved, this fear can lessen tremendously.

■ Assessing the Status of Relationships

The patterns created in a survivor's past are often played out through involvement in unsafe, unhealthy, or otherwise unsatisfying relationships. It follows, then, that the primary relationship in which a survivor finds himself or herself at the outset of the healing process may be faulty. The compartmentalization required to remain in an unhealthy relationship while attempting recovery can run counter to the survivor's integration.

As couples begin a healing process, it may be important to analyze the "payoff" for healing as opposed to maintaining the status quo. At some level, one or both partners may not want the process to succeed. For example, the roles of "caretaker" and "sick person" may be ingrained in the relationship. A partner may be serving as a "buffer," making all decisions relating to issues outside the relationship in order to reduce the survivor's stress. As the survivor becomes more assertive and attempts to reclaim some of the decision making, tension within the couple may result. The partner may feel threatened, perceiving that one of his or her primary roles in the relationship is being usurped. When working with couples, it is important to discuss the roles in the relationship and the language used to define those roles. How will those roles change during the course of the healing process and what impact will those changes have on the relationship? Anticipating role changes and dealing with them proactively can prevent the intentional or un-witting sabotage of the process.

The partner may have a vested interest in maintaining the survivor's people-pleasing or "superhuman" behaviors. This can be acted out in a variety of ways, including insisting on a return to "the way things used to be," setting deadlines for healing or making unilateral decisions to stop paying for therapy, pressure to hurry the process, demanding sex, or orders to "snap out of it." This type of reaction may indicate a profound lack of awareness of the complexity of the healing process and can have an irreparable impact on the relationship. When therapists notice signs of such pressure, they should point them out and examine their destruc-tive potential. Early in the course of therapy, therapists should educate partners and survivors about the nature and goals of the healing process and discuss realistic time frames and therapeutic milestones.

Early on, when working with a survivor and his or her partner, it is crucial to assess the relationship's inherent strengths and each individ-ual's commitment to it. What is the "glue" that bonds the partnership? Why was the relationship initiated and why are the partners remaining together now? Do the reasons given indicate a solid foundation?

As partners jointly embark on a healing journey, emotional safety within the relationship is essential. At the outset, uncertainty about the process and its results may be overwhelming. The couple's trust in commitments made within the relationship can provide at least a de-pendable base. The signs of a trusting relationship will be unique to each couple. Throughout the healing process, couples should discuss and continue to refine their definition of trust. Specific illustrations of trusting and trustworthy behavior should be offered by each partner and common ground negotiated. For example, a survivor may not want his or her partner to talk with anyone outside the relationship about the survivor's abuse history or therapy. The partner, however, may feel the legitimate need to discuss the impact of the healing process on his or her life and on the relationship. The couple should seek a mutually acceptable solution that allows the partner much-needed personal sup-port without jeopardizing the survivor's emotional safety. Areas for negotiation could include the level of detail to be disclosed and appro-priate settings (e.g., a support group) or people involved (e.g., a thera-pist or close friend). Discussing each other's needs and working out a reasonable compromise will help to build trust in each other.

The couple's ability to communicate clearly and directly with each other should be assessed. Is the communication style open, honest, and straightforward, or are messages embellished? Do partners expect "mind-reading"? Does one get angry when the other is unable to anticipate what's expected without a direct request? The hidden agendas that were so fundamental to the communication styles of many survivors' families of origin are often carried over into their adult relationships. We frequently hear comments such as, "If my partner loved me, he or she would know what I want or need without my having to say it." The assumption is, of course, "If the request must be spoken, it means my partner doesn't love me." Mindreading and unspoken motives can significantly undermine a couple's ability to communicate and should be addressed early in the survivor's recovery.

Couples are challenged to learn and apply new skills as they move through the healing process. Do they solve problems constructively? Can they adapt quickly to new situations? How have they handled past crises in their individual lives and in their relationships?

Support systems for each partner and for the relationship must be developed and actively used. At the beginning of the process, the therapist should assist the couple in identifying and analyzing systems that are currently available to them and in planning to construct others that could be beneficial. What external support (e.g., therapists, friends, church, support groups) will be accessible to the couple throughout the healing process? What current systems in their lives (e.g., family of origin, friends who do not understand, overly stressful working environment) might work against healing? Are there some available sources of support (e.g., friends, support groups, family, church, therapists) on which the couple is not presently relying? What others (e.g., support groups, supportive friends) could be developed?

> *Survivors are asked to accord themselves top priority in the allocation of time, money, and other resources.*

Many survivors report having to "go on faith" in making the decision to heal. The basics of the process seem foreign. Ironically, survivors are asked to accord themselves top priority in the allocation of time, money, and other resources, usually without the accompanying self-esteem to justify it. Supportive partners can provide some much-needed reassurance and motivation.

Healing from sexual abuse is an evolving process, necessitating the continual assessment and ongoing monitoring of the relationship by the therapist and by each partner. In our work with survivors and their partners, we use the following list as basic indicators of a healthy relationship:

- Individuals in the relationship are honest in their interactions with their partners and with other people
- The couple has a direct and straightforward communication style, containing no hidden messages or assumptions
- The amount of time spent together and spent working on the relationship is sufficient from each partner's perspective
- The partners' senses of humor are compatible; they are able to laugh together
- The degree of physical closeness in the relationship is acceptable to both partners
- Each person maintains his or her individual identity within the relationship, resulting in true interdependence
- Partners demonstrate respect and common courtesy toward each other, even when they disagree
- There is a willingness to seek outside help or support when needed, together and individually
- There is a solid commitment from both partners to making the relationship work
- The couple exercises good problem-solving skills or is willing to develop or improve them

In contrast, we offer the following list of "danger signs," which could indicate potential relationship problems:

- One or both partners sacrifice individual identity to the relationship; independent decisions or activities are lacking
- Physical, emotional, and/or verbal abuse is present
- Overt or implied threats are common in the couple's communication
- There is destructive involvement of other people; for example, outsiders meddle in the personal business of the couple, attempt to convince partners to take sides against each other, or attempt to cause jealousy between them
- Communication is absent or minimal; feelings go unexpressed
- Manipulation is used by one or both partners
- There is a lack of trust between the partners
- There is evidence of growing resentment within the relationship that is not openly acknowledged or addressed

- The relationship is not a major priority for one or both partners
- A child is "triangulated" into the parents' relationship (i.e., asked to play a role more appropriately suited to an adult partner, such as providing significant emotional support)
- Adopting a "win or lose" approach to problem solving, partners do not seek compromises or mutually acceptable solutions
- Partners are unwilling or unable to find humor or playfulness together
- The degree of physical closeness within the relationship is not acceptable to one or both partners

What follows in Table 7.1 is a relationship assessment questionnaire used in our weekend workshops for couples. This exercise is designed to help define the underpinnings of relationships. Differences or concerns that emerge as couples share their responses to this questionnaire should be discussed and explored; areas of conflict that remain unresolved should be taken into therapy. For a relationship that is not built on a firm foundation, the prospects of surviving an intensive healing process are less than promising.

Having a long-range vision can help couples weather the upheavals that accompany the healing process. Together they must "toss an anchor into the future" to help pull them through the rough times ahead. This anchor is composed of the core that attracted them to each other, their collective experience, their love for each other, and the dreams they share for the years ahead.

An equitable balance of power within the relationship is essential. Open discussion and negotiation of individual and shared responsibilities can enhance the process of recovery. Therapists can appropriately suggest or even facilitate this exchange. We have conceptualized the following list from our personal experience:

1. The survivor is not responsible for the abuse and its aftereffects. Once the connections between dysfunctional coping styles and the sexual abuse history become apparent, however, the survivor should take responsibility for attempting to make healthy choices for the present and future. Survivors and partners must understand that intellectual awareness does not bring about automatic change.
2. The survivor is responsible for charting and implementing his or her own healing process, with support and guidance from professionals and other allies.

TABLE 7.1 Questionnaire on Intimate Relationships

Instructions:

Spend some time individually answering each of the following questions about your current relationship, to the best of your ability. Be sure to give at least one example to illustrate or support each of your answers. When you are finished, discuss your answers with your partner. The goal of this exercise is to help you find the cornerstones of your relationship—those aspects on which you can build for the future—and to identify areas of concern that may merit additional work.

1. How did I decide to get involved in this relationship in the beginning? What core features attracted me to my partner?
2. Would I be likely to become involved in this relationship if I could make the choice again? What are my reasons for this answer?
3. Regardless of my answer to the preceding question, am I willing to work to maintain this relationship now? Do I believe my partner is willing? Would either or both of us be unwilling to seek outside help or counsel if our relationship were in serious trouble?
4. Do I have, and am I encouraged by my partner to have, my own identity?
5. Do I feel loved and liked by my partner? Do I feel respected by my partner? Do I ever feel used or manipulated by him or her?
6. Do I love, like, and respect my partner?
7. Do I feel that my partner makes unreasonable demands of me?
8. Can I be honest and direct with my partner? Can I express a feeling or opinion without fearing I'm jeopardizing the entire relationship?
9. Is the amount of time my partner and I spend together adequate, if not ideal?
10. Do my partner and I share humor and play? Do I ever feel that my partner is laughing *at* me instead of *with* me? Am I comfortable when we play together?
11. Does my partner remind me of anyone in my family or of previous partners? If so, whom? Is this connection positive, negative, or both?
12. Do I feel jealous of other people, things, or activities in my partner's life?
13. Do I trust my partner? Do I feel my partner trusts me?

3. The survivor is responsible for communicating as directly and honestly as possible with his or her partner. A survivor may, of course, choose not to discuss certain issues with his or her partner, but should not expect automatic support or understanding regarding information that has not been disclosed.
4. The partner is responsible for assessing his or her own commitment to the relationship for the duration of the healing process and beyond.
5. The partner is not responsible for "healing" the survivor, nor is it appropriate for the partner to pronounce that the survivor is "cured."

6. The partner is responsible for communicating as directly and honestly as possible with the survivor.

7. Both partners are responsible for working toward mutually acceptable solutions as problems arise, particularly regarding day-to-day issues. It is not feasible to put a relationship totally "on hold" while the survivor heals.

■ Involving Significant Others in the Healing Process

Partners of survivors can influence the healing process in a variety of ways, from energetic support to active sabotage. Professionals working with survivors can offer immense help by eliciting partners' active involvement and by providing guidance regarding their participation. A partner's ability to be supportive begins with an understanding of the effects of childhood sexual abuse and the basics of the healing process. Therapists can assist by suggesting educational material to partners who want to learn. Excellent basic information on abuse and the healing process can be found in such books as *Outgrowing the Pain* (Gil, 1984), *Abused Boys* (Hunter, 1990), *Victims No Longer* (Lew, 1988), *The Courage to Heal* (Bass & Davis, 1988), and *The Courage to Heal Workbook* (Davis, 1990). Among the useful new books that have been written specifically for supportive and involved allies are *Outgrowing the Pain Together* (Gil, 1992) and *Allies in Healing* (Davis, 1991). An increasing number of video- and audiotapes are being developed on sexual abuse and healing issues.

> *Partners of survivors can influence the healing process in a variety of ways, from energetic support to active sabotage.*

In Table 7.2, we offer a list of "do's and don'ts" for partners and allies of survivors that can be customized to address a couple's specific circumstances.

Partners can take active steps to combat the isolation they may feel. Resources such as the books and tapes previously mentioned can provide validation. Relevant newsletters convey factual information and offer partners an opportunity to communicate with their peers and with other readers through creative writing and artwork. Several periodicals that partners have found helpful are noted in the bibliography

TABLE 7.2 Do's and Don'ts for Partners and Allies

Do's	Don'ts
Do learn about abuse effects and the healing process.	Don't overwhelm the survivor with your own anger.
Do use and encourage the survivor to use empowering language.	Don't pronounce a "cure" or try to hurry the healing process.
Do support the survivor in making his or her own choices.	Don't set timetables or give ultimatums to the survivor.
Do validate the survivor's feelings.	Don't take outbursts personally.
Do encourage therapy and other active steps toward healing.	Don't be a "martyr."
	Don't isolate yourself.
Do respect personal limits and interpersonal boundaries.	Don't force cheerfulness on the survivor.
Do communicate openly about sexuality.	Don't insist that the survivor forgive.
Do help find time and resources for the healing process.	Don't try to do the healing for the survivor.
Do learn to play.	
Do find time to be with the survivor.	
Do find time to be apart from the survivor.	
Do serve as a healthy role model.	
Do listen to the survivor.	
Do blame the offender(s) rather than the survivor.	
Do plan for crises.	
Do be honest about your own feelings	
Do acknowledge progress toward healing.	
Do reinforce strengths of the survivor and the relationship.	
Do believe in the survivor and in the healing process.	

at the end of this chapter. We encourage therapists to review material carefully prior to recommending it to clients to help ensure that the material is safe, timely, and appropriate.

Formal support groups can offer much-needed validation of the range of feelings and reactions commonly experienced by partners. Fortunately, support groups for partners are becoming increasingly prevalent. In our experience, rape crisis centers have been consistently responsive in offering groups for adult survivors of childhood sexual abuse and their partners.

Therapists can help to lay a solid foundation for healing by discussing frankly with survivors and partners the time frame, commitment, and financial, emotional, and spiritual resources that are typically required. At key points in the process, the therapist may want to consider bringing the partner into the survivor's sessions. For example, as the therapy enters particularly difficult periods, it may be useful to devote a few sessions to providing information to the couple about the potential impact on the relationship. These interactions also can be used to assist with skill building and goal setting and to reinforce the couple's commitment to their relationship. Key points may include times when the survivor is feeling suicidal; when significant medication issues arise; when the survivor is in periods of severe dissociation; when and if inpatient treatment is indicated; when and if relationship issues are interfering with the healing process; and when changes occur in the survivor's view of sexuality. Shifts in sexuality may be noticeable, for example, when traumatic flashbacks are intensifying or when therapy is focusing heavily on early childhood memories.

Objective sources of professional support may be needed for the partner and for the couple. This may take the form of an individual therapist for the partner and still another to address the relationship issues. Because the loyalty and focus of the survivor's therapist rightfully will be directed toward the survivor, he or she should not also serve as the partner's individual therapist unless there is absolutely no alternative. Consultation from time to time, with the survivor's permission, can be constructive, however.

Connecting with other survivor/partner couples, either formally in workshops or support groups, or informally in social settings, can be worthwhile. Sharing experiences and perceptions with couples who are in various phases of healing can help survivors and partners view their healing as reaching a series of milestones, rather than as a singular event.

It is crucial for survivors and their partners to be able to share information with each other about the healing process as it is happening. They should be encouraged to create ongoing outlets through which each can express feelings and frustrations safely and nondestructively. Because educational or experiential activities on communication skills, effective problem solving, and goal setting can be useful adjuncts to therapy, professionals may want to consider referrals in these areas.

Laura Davis presents a number of useful communication skills and problem-solving exercises for couples in *Allies in Healing* (Davis, 1991).

Intensive sex therapy may not be indicated until the survivor has completed a substantial portion of the healing process. It is important that the survivor's therapeutic focus during this time is on recovering from the childhood abuse. In the meantime, a sex therapist can assist couples in devising a workable, short-term approach to sexuality. A sex therapist consulted for this purpose should be familiar with the effects of childhood sexual abuse and the process of recovering from it. Once childhood issues cease to overshadow the survivor's life, when flashbacks and dissociative episodes have diminished significantly or have subsided, and when the therapeutic focus turns predominantly toward the adult ego state, current sexuality issues may be appropriately addressed.

A number of promising new resources are available for survivors and partners who are working toward healing their sexual relationships. One of the first works devoted to survivors' sexuality is *Incest and Sexuality: A Guide to Understanding and Healing* (Maltz & Holman, 1987). Maltz has followed it with *The Sexual Healing Journey: A Guide for Survivors of Sexual Abuse* (Maltz, 1991). Laura Davis's *The Courage to Heal Workbook* (Davis, 1990), which covers a broad range of survivor-related topics, includes several sexual healing exercises for couples. Mic Hunter has recently written *Joyous Sexuality: Healing From the Effects of Family Sexual Dysfunction* (Hunter, 1992).

In most aspects of survivor/partner relationships, we advocate constructive compromise as a means of resolving conflict. There may not be any middle ground, however, if all sex feels abusive to the survivor. In sexual relationships, we believe that the survivor must have the right to specify sexual activity that is acceptable to him or her and to be allowed to stop if uncomfortable

> *When negotiating sexual intimacy, survivors and their partners are challenged to communicate with openness, commitment, and maturity.*

feelings emerge. These boundaries should be arranged with the partner before sexual activity begins. As a survivor learns to set sexual limits that feel comfortable, he or she must be able to trust that these limits will be honored by the partner.

When negotiating sexual intimacy, survivors and their partners are challenged to communicate with a degree of openness, commitment, and maturity that is rare in most relationships. From personal experience, we highly recommend cultivating a shared sense of humor. From reading comics in the funny pages, to sharing humorous experiences from the workday, to watching comedy shows or movies together, sharing nonthreatening activities that make both partners laugh can increase intimacy and trust. Couples who successfully negotiate the often volatile issue of sexuality during the healing process go a long way toward establishing lasting trust.

Partners often feel a very human longing for the survivor and the relationship to return to how things were before the effects of the abuse intruded. This is generally not a realistic goal for a healing process designed to break the survivor's unhealthy coping styles, which likely include dysfunctional relationship patterns. It is therefore advisable for survivors and their partners to refine continually their mutual goals as the healing process evolves. Several examples of constructive support-building exercises for couples are found in Yvonne Dolan's *Resolving Sexual Abuse* (Dolan, 1991).

In the preliminary stages of the healing process, couples should identify recurring problems in their relationships. If these patterns cannot be permanently resolved at that time, survivors and their partners should at least attempt to adopt temporary agreements. We recommend that they not undertake long-term relationship therapy during the most intense portions of a survivor's individual recovery because the healing process itself brings on such massive changes. It is imperative that the survivor make his or her healing the overriding priority. Many survivors have learned that it is quite easy to be lured away from the hard work of healing from abuse, particularly by the needs of others.

Professionals can help survivors build solid support systems by encouraging their partners to be there for the duration of the healing process. A partner is likely to ask, "What's in it for me?" The following considerations can help foster the needed motivation:

- The abuse symptoms usually do not ameliorate without intervention; in fact, they will probably worsen and negatively affect the relationship
- Working together on the healing process has great potential for strengthening relationships, enhancing mutual understanding, and deepening commitments
- Each partner will be challenged to learn or refine skills that can be applied to future crises

- Both partners will have opportunities for meaningful personal growth
- The healing process affords an examination and reassessment of one's priorities and values
- Survivors and their partners are challenged to discover and nurture their inner strength and spiritual resources
- The couple will have an opportunity to construct a "family of choice," comprising friends and allies who are truly supportive
- The healing process offers a creative challenge that can result in an unequaled sense of achievement
- Through healing, a couple can acquire extraordinary empathy for others who are grieving or in crisis
- If they so choose, the couple may ultimately use their healing experience to help others, to raise awareness of abuse-related issues, to strive to improve the systems involved, or to work toward prevention

When a relationship is permeated by dysfunctional patterns, ending it may be the healthiest option. For some couples, acknowledging the mere viability of leaving allows them to feel less "trapped"; paradoxically, they may then choose to shift their energy toward improving the relationship. A decision to end the partnership should not be viewed as failure. In fact, the healing process may actually be enhanced. Separation may free both partners to do individual healing that was not possible together.

Through the recovery process, survivors can achieve liberation from the intrusive control that sexual abuse has exerted over virtually every aspect of their lives, including their decisions regarding intimate partnerships. Caring professionals and other supportive allies can help survivors learn to make conscious choices, within and outside the context of relationships, that above all are conducive to their healing.

■ Bibliography

The following are survivor-related periodicals with frequent articles about partner and relationship issues:

The Healing Woman, The Monthly Newsletter for Women Survivors of Childhood Sexual Abuse, P.O. Box 3038, Moss Beach, CA 94038 ($25/year).

Many Voices: Words of Hope for People With MPD or a Dissociative Disorder, P.O. Box 2639, Cincinnati, OH 45201-2639 ($30/year).

Treating Abuse Today: An International Newsjournal of Abuse Survivorship and Therapy, 2722 Eastlake Avenue East, Seattle, WA 98102 ($36/year).

The Need for a Multidimensional Approach to the Treatment of Male Sexual Abuse Survivors

Larry A. Morris

■ Research on the Abuse of Males

Although research on male victims of childhood sexual abuse has not been as extensive as the research on female victims, the efforts date back to some of the earliest studies of child abuse. The information gleaned from these studies is compelling. For example, in 1929, Hamilton found a prevalency rate of 20% for females and 22% for males (Hamilton, 1929). In 1937, Bender and Blau suggested that male risk of sexual victimization was equal to that for females (Bender & Blau, 1937). In 1956, Landis reported a rate of 35% for females and 30% for males (Landis, 1956). Without presenting specific numbers or rates, DeFrancis (1969) concluded, "Boy victims are numerous" (p. 1).

Survey research results reported in the 1970s and 1980s regarding male child sexual victimization were mixed. Finkelhor (1979) found that 5% to 9% of college males surveyed reported childhood sexual victimization, whereas his survey of Boston parents revealed that 6% of the men had been sexually victimized as children. A random sample of Texas driver's license holders by Kercher and McShane (1984) revealed a sexual abuse rate of 3% for males and 12% for females. Clinical studies suggest male sexual abuse rates ranging from 11% to 17% (DeJong, Emmett, & Hervada, 1982; Ellerstein & Canavan, 1980; Farber, Showers, Johnson, Joseph, & Oshins, 1984; Pierce & Pierce, 1985; Showers, Farber, Joseph, Oshins, & Johnson, 1983). This range is consistent with the 15% rate reported by the American Humane Association (1978). Looking at the international scene, Baker's (1985) study of the prevalence of child sexual abuse in Great Britain found that 8% of the males surveyed there had been victimized. More recently, Lisak (1993) studied 595 male college students living in the Boston area. Twenty-nine percent of his sample reported childhood sexual abuse, some of whom (16.6%) also reported being physically abused.

Based on studies of male sexual perpetrators, Prentky (1984) suggested that male children are sexually victimized at a rate higher than reported in the clinical literature. For example, Groth (1979) found that 28% of convicted male sex offenders selected male child victims exclusively, whereas another 21% selected their victims on the basis of convenience only. Groth, Hobson, and Gary (1982) reported that male children are targets in about 30% of sexual offenses committed by adult males. Also of interest is the finding by Freeman-Longo (1986) that 40% of a sample of male rapists reported being sexually abused as a child by females. (See also Condy, Templer, Brown, & Veaco, 1987; Petrovich & Templer, 1984; Ramsey-Klawsnik, 1990.)

A cautionary note: The childhood sexual abuse literature today is questioned even by some of its principal contributors. This is especially the case regarding assessing the prevalence of child sexual abuse. But even with all the research quandaries, the data still point to a prevalence rate from 3% to 31% of male children, compared to 6% to 62% of female children. Nielsen (1983) has noted that male victims comprise 25% to 35% of the caseloads of clinicians working in the childhood sexual abuse area. Thus clinicians no longer require yesterday's challenge to admit to the presence of child sexual abuse (Sgroi, 1975). Today, virtually no experienced clinician can deny that the consequences of these aberrant interactions are manifested clinically in the lives of many male children and adult survivors of childhood sexual abuse.

Negative Effects of Abuse

In their landmark review of the sexual abuse literature, Browne and Finkelhor (1986) documented that many sexually abused children suffer negative effects that may endure. They posited that the impact may occur within a 2-year period from the abusive experience (initial effects) or endure into adulthood (long-term effects). Initial effects appear to be anxiety, depression, anger, and inappropriate sexual behavior. Long-term effects may include depression, self-destructive behavior, anxiety, distrust, isolation, sexual maladjustment, substance abuse, and poor self-esteem. Studies reviewed by Browne and Finkelhor either excluded males or included a relatively small number of males. Urquiza and Capra (1990) used Browne and Finkelhor's model to review the literature on the impact of sexual abuse on males. For males, the initial effects appear to be behavioral disturbances and aggression, emotional reactions and self-perceptions, physical consequences and somatic complaints, and sexuality problems. Long-term effects included depression and somatic disturbances, effects on self-esteem and self-concept, interpersonal relationship problems, impact on sexuality, and addictive behaviors.

Bolton, Morris, and MacEachron (1989) suggest six categories of effects: emotional distress, behavior problems, sexual problems, cyclical victimization, sexual orientation conflicts, and prostitution.

Emotional Distress

Research studies conducted with and clinical observations of male victims indicate a broad range of emotional distress as a result of childhood sexual abuse. Common in this category were reports of depression, suicidal ideation, guilt, low self-esteem, anger, and fear. Also found were sleep disturbances, dissociation, obsessive compulsiveness, addictions, and psychoticism. Interpersonal sensitivity and relationship problems were also frequent findings. (See Adams-Tucker, 1982; Briere & Runtz, 1988; Bruckner & Johnson, 1987; Carmen, Rieker, & Mills, 1984; Conte & Schuerman, 1987a, 1987b; DeFrancis, 1969; Dimock, 1988; Dixon, Arnold, & Calestro, 1978; Freeman-Longo, 1986; Fromuth & Burkhart, 1989; Froning & Mayman, 1990; Gomes-Schwartz, Horowitz, & Sauzier, 1985; Hunter, 1990, 1993; Hunter, Kilstrom, & Loda, 1985; Kelly & Gonzalez, 1990; Krug, 1989; Lew, 1988; Myers, 1989;

Olson, 1990; Rogers & Terry, 1984; Sebold, 1987; Spencer & Dunklee, 1986; Steele & Alexander, 1981; Stein, Golding, Siegel, Burnam, & Sorenson, 1988; Urquiza, 1993; Urquiza & Crowley, 1986; Woods & Dean, 1984; Zaphiris, 1986.)

Behavior Problems

Several researchers have found a tendency for male victims to demonstrate aggressive, antisocial, and undercontrolled externalizing behaviors. A tendency toward sexualizing the behavior was also common. The abuse of substances was a frequent finding with adolescent and adult male survivors. (See Friedrich, 1990; Friedrich, Beilke, & Urquiza, 1987, 1988; Friedrich, Urquiza, & Beilke, 1986; Froning & Mayman, 1990; Kohan, Pothier, & Norbeck, 1987; Ramsey-Klawsnik, 1990; Rogers & Terry, 1984; Zaphiris, 1986.)

Sexual Problems

Sexual problems exhibited by young male victims suggest an exaggerated interest in sexual activities such as masturbation, voyeurism, and intimate clothing. Adult male survivors often report a wide range of sexual dysfunctions, including lack of desire and ejaculatory and erectile problems. They also tend to report general dissatisfaction with adult sexual experiences. (See Bruckner & Johnson, 1987; Carlson, Dimock, Driggs, & Westly, 1987; Dimock, 1988; Finkelhor, 1979; Friedrich et al., 1987, 1988; Froning & Mayman, 1990; Hunter, 1987; Johnson & Shrier, 1987; Kohan et al., 1987; Sarrel & Masters, 1982; Sebold, 1987; Urquiza, 1993; Woods & Dean, 1984.)

Cyclical Victimization

Many researchers posit a link between childhood sexual abuse and future perpetration of sexual offenses. Some suggest that male victims become victimizers as a way of mastering the trauma of their own sexual abuse. In this manner, they attempt to regain the power lost to them through the abusive experiences. Others suggest modeling of aggressive responses as the important factor. Still others point to a raw expression of anger produced by the abuse as the primary foundation for future perpetration. Clinicians typically find a combination of these factors when treating male victims/perpetrators. Although studies show that a large majority of sexual offenders are also victims of childhood sexual abuse, it is important to note that the reverse is not the case. That is, studies do not show that the majority of male survivors go on to become perpetrators. (See Becker, 1988; Becker, Kaplan, Cunningham-Rathner, & Kavoussi, 1986; Briere & Smiljanich, 1993; Cantwell, 1988; Condy et al., 1987; Fehrenbach, Smith, Monastersky, & Deisher, 1986; Freeman-Longo, 1986; Friedrich & Luecke, 1988; Groth, 1979; Johnson, 1988; Longo, 1982; Petrovich & Templer, 1984; Ramsey-Klawsnik, 1990; Rogers & Terry, 1984; Summit, 1983; Zaphiris, 1986.)

> *Although a majority of sexual offenders are also victims of childhood sexual abuse, the reverse is not the case.*

Sexual Orientation Conflicts

One of the most frequently occurring problems with males who have been sexually abused by other males is confusion about sexuality and sexual orientation (Bruckner & Johnson, 1987; Dimock, 1988; Hunter, 1990; Lew, 1988; Myers, 1989; Olson, 1990). This confusion often produces homophobic responses of all types. Although some clinical studies suggest a link between the sexual victimization of male children and subsequent homosexual and/or bisexual behavior, most cases do not resolve themselves in that manner (Bell & Weinberg, 1981; Brunold, 1964; Finch, 1967; Finkelhor, 1984; Johnson & Shrier, 1985; Woods & Dean, 1984). Gonsiorek (1993) suggests that some young males become especially vulnerable to victimization by older males due to a preexisting tendency toward a homosexual orientation. If molested by a male, these victims may go on to choose a homosexual lifestyle; however, this path may have been followed without the victimization experiences.

Prostitution

Prostitution usually is viewed by the general public as an adult female activity. Males participate by purchasing the services offered by females. Certainly, children do not sell themselves to others for sexual purposes. However, not only do Janus, Scanlon, and Price (1984) propose that some children become prostitutes, but they also suggest that prostitution among boys may occur at about the same rate as among girls. They also found that nearly 40% of a sample of young male prostitutes reported a history of child sexual abuse prior to their involvement in prostitution. Additional family problems such as substance abuse, physical abuse, neglect, and parental discord also accompanied the sexual abuse. Case studies presented by Burgess, Hartman, McCousland, and Powers (1984) suggest that many sexually abused male children may turn to exploiting others or else continue their own victimization through prostitution (see also Coombs, 1973; Ginsburg, 1967).

■ Assessment

As can be seen by any review of the empirical and clinical literature, many sexually abused males experience some form of negative effects. The noted medical team of Kempe and Kempe (1984) even suggest that males do worse in this regard than females. However, each male may have a different response to the sexually abusive event depending on a number of factors (Conte & Schuerman, 1987a, 1987b). Some males exhibit few negative consequences of sexual abuse even when the activities appear serious, such as repeated forced penetration. Others may exhibit severe emotional problems following a seemingly less serious sexual event, such as a one-time fondling experience. Some clinicians become so perplexed by these types of cases that they convince themselves that their patients are not "in touch" with either the sexual abuse or the negative consequences. After all, how can someone endure forceable rape at 10 years of age and not show serious problems? And how can just one occurrence of fondling at 9 years of age lead to subsequent perpetration of sexual offenses?

Although there is agreement that such cases occur, little agreement exists regarding why they occur. Part of the problem seems to rest in the pervasive philosophy that negative consequences must follow sexual abuse, and the more serious the abuse, the more damage we should expect. For example, Eisenberg, Owens, and Dewey (1987) found that health professionals believed that intercourse would result in greater and longer lasting harm to the victim than fondling. This attitude is too limiting for clinicians and may lead to serious misconceptions about the impact of childhood sexual abuse. Individual differences may be the norm rather than the exception and, at the very least, the male victim's idiosyncratic responses to the abusive situation must be considered as important as the abuse itself. Male victims also may display emotional and behavioral problems that existed prior to the abuse or occurred following the abuse, but may be the result of factors unrelated to the sexual abuse. In these cases, the clinician is faced with the complicated task of determining which role the various contributing events played in producing the array of presenting dysfunctions.

Male victims may display emotional and behavioral problems that may be the result of factors unrelated to the sexual abuse.

For these reasons, clinicians should also assess the impact of child sexual abuse in terms of the relative contribution to the individual's various disturbances. This approach provides for a more objective and precise evaluation of the subjective effects of the abuse experiences. Proposed here is a model that is relatively simple, not too unfamiliar to most experienced clinicians, and consists of four components: nominal impact, secondary impact, contributing impact, and primary impact.

Nominal impact. This category may be the most controversial because it proposes that some children may be sexually abused and show few negative effects. The importance of this category, however, should not be overlooked. Some sexually abused children and some adults who were molested as children are often placed inappropriately in therapy programs with a focus on personal victimization issues when, in fact, the person took the abuse in stride and has no sexual victimization issues to resolve. In these cases, therapy most likely will be nonproductive.

This category may be the most difficult to ascertain with males because of their tendency to deny or mask victimization. Even so, a clinician should be aware that some males are telling the truth when they report that personal victimization was not present or was minimal and now resolved. The following case illustrates these points well.

> After 2 years of being sexually abused by his stepfather, John reported the abuse to a trusted adult male. No one had suspected that John was being sexually abused because he seemed like a pleasant 14-year-old who earned excellent grades and was very popular with peers. At the time of disclosure, John indicated that he hated his stepfather for what he did to him, but now that it was over, John wanted to "forget about it and be just a regular kid again."

John was placed in a therapy group for molested adolescents. After a few sessions, he began to complain that he was tired of talking about the abuse. He expressed that he didn't need to resolve the victimization issues because they were mostly resolved at the time he decided to disclose. He denied any inappropriate angry feelings or emotional problems. John's grades remained high and he continued to do well in interpersonal relationships. He did not appear anxious or depressed. He also denied any budding sexual problems. John's mother, teachers, and other trusted adults reported observing no indications that John was suffering from an emotional, sexual, or behavioral disturbance.

Concerned that problems would surface later, John's therapist and mother insisted he remain in therapy for at least 1 year. Under protest John complied, but he did little except attend the session. At the conclusion of the 1-year period, therapy was terminated as promised. Annual follow-up contacts continued to find a well-adjusted young man whose only major complaint was having been required to attend therapy sessions well beyond what he considered necessary.

Secondary impact. Within this category are cases of documented instances of childhood sexual abuse, but the abuse appears to be secondary to other events and/or factors in the person's life. For example, an individual may exhibit emotional and behavioral problems consistent with those found in other cases of sexual abuse, but the sexual abuse events may have been only one part of an array of factors producing the dysfunctions. In some cases, the dysfunction may have been present prior to the sexual abuse. Consider the following cases.

Throughout childhood, Al was emotionally and physically abused by an alcoholic father and other family members. His mother often abused Al even more severely than did his father. His siblings were also abused, and strife among the children was common. At about 10 years of age, Al was molested by an uncle several times. Although Al told his parents about the abuse, they did not believe him and no action was taken to provide therapy for him.

During Al's first years in school, he was either detained or placed in classes for the mentally retarded. He reported being treated as retarded by his family and educators throughout his childhood. Teasing about his slow intellectual abilities also occurred from peers and family members.

Although Al did not engage in the usual dating activities as an adolescent, he reported sexual experiences with a couple of age-appropriate females during late adolescence and early adulthood. As a young adult, Al was arrested for molesting a young female family member. Although

Al admitted to inappropriate sexual activities with this girl, he denied engaging in sexual behavor with any other children. No reports of inappropriate sexual behavior with other children surfaced.

Psychological evaluations revealed that Al functioned mostly at a borderline or below intellectual level. A learning disorder rather than mental retardation was suggested. Al appeared to be seriously lacking in social skills and seemed to understand only the rudimentary aspects of social interactions. He was also experiencing a significant amount of emotional distress characterized by low self-esteem, social anxiety, low self-confidence, depression, fear, guilt, and confusion.

Although Al was molested as a child, his subsequent emotional, sexual, and behavioral problems appear related more to his history of physical and emotional abuse by family members and his undiagnosed learning disability than to the sexual abuse. However, the sexual abuse appears to have exacerbated his emotional problems and confused him even further regarding appropriate interpersonal and sexual responses.

Art remembers his childhood fondly and he reported no unusual family experiences. Parents were described in mostly favorable terms. As a preteen, Art enjoyed sexual contact with boys his own age. He reported never being interested in females of any age. When Art was about 10 years old, older and more aggressive males would occasionally "ask" Art to masturbate and fellate them. He complied, but never considered these experiences as abusive or traumatic. Rather, Art saw himself as a willing partner in childhood sexual exploration activities even though the boys were older by at least 5 years. However, his sexual interest in males remained at the prepubescent level. As an adult, Art established a "loving" relationship with several prepubescent boys and eventually seduced each child into a sexual relationship.

Although Art was technically molested as a child, he did not perceive the experiences as sexual abuse. He reported being attracted to prepubescent boys from an early age, and his preference for sexual partners did not change as he grew older. A number of factors, including biological, may be the foundation for Art's sexual attraction to prepubescent males, but childhood sexual victimization does not seem to be a major contributor.

Contributing impact. Many cases of sexual abuse contain other factors that may play a significant role in the emotional and behavioral problems exhibited by an individual. Although it is tempting to focus either on the sexual abuse issues or on the other issues, it is more important for the clinician to view both as contributing to the individual's dysfunctions. The case described below seems fairly typical of those containing contributions to emotional and/or behavioral problems from sexual abuse as well as other factors.

> Throughout his childhood and adolescence, Bill's family moved frequently, allowing him few opportunities to establish peer relationships. The moves were prompted by family conflicts and frequent episodes of domestic violence. Bill's father always seemed angry, and often physically abused Bill and his mother. Both parents were alcoholics.
>
> Bill's sexual history also revealed chaotic and abusive childhood experiences. When Bill was about 9 years old, a young adult manipulated Bill into "servicing" him sexually. A couple of years later, Bill was molested by an older adolescent. When Bill was about 12 years old, his father caught him masturbating. His father seized the opportunity to teach his young son about "normal" sex by hiring a female prostitute for him. Bill responded with fear and was unable to have sex with the prostitute. Bill's father was not amused and emotionally abused Bill for not being able to perform like a man. As a teenager, Bill was also physically and sexually abused by peers.
>
> During adolescence, Bill was hospitalized for anxiety and depression. Suicide attempts were documented. Psychological and psychiatric evaluations over several years revealed deteriorating intellectual functioning, a serious learning disability, sexual confusion with performance dysfunctions, anxiety, and clinical depression.

Bill's social history reads like a horror story. He was physically, emotionally, and sexually abused by a variety of individuals. Most adult models were alcoholic and abusive in some way. Even sexual contact with peers was abusive. Thus many factors contributed to Bill's subsequent emotional instability, not just his childhood sexual abuse.

Primary impact. The major feature of this category is the finding that childhood sexual abuse is the primary cause of the individual's emotional and behavioral problems. Although other factors may exist, they appear to contribute in only minor ways to the individual's dysfunctions. Consider Dan's history.

Dan presented a history of promiscuous homosexual behavior since about 14 years of age. Although he always regretted his activities, Dan found it nearly impossible to resist the urges to frequent parks, restrooms, and other places used for quick sexual contacts. He would often engage in three to six homosexual contacts nearly every day. Dan seldom achieved orgasm through these contacts and often felt like "a sex machine for others." Although his primary sexual orientation was homosexual, he dated females and eventually married. He reported that he enjoyed the intimacy of his marital relationship and even found pleasure in the sexual activity with his wife. However, his urges to visit "glory holes" and continue his homosexual contacts with strangers remained strong and largely uncontrollable.

Dan was the only child born to his biological parents, who divorced when Dan was about 7 years old. His mother received custody and Dan saw little of his father after the divorce. He did not remember much about his father, but described his mother in favorable terms. He could not recall any form of abuse by either parent. Dan was a good student, although he was not always motivated to do his best. His peer relationships were good and, in fact, he was popular and active in extracurricular activities.

When Dan was 11 years old, a male boarder came into his room and began to make sexual advances. When Dan refused his requests, "The man simply took my clothes off and fucked me. He was large and muscular and I was no match for him. It was terrible. It hurt and he tore me up." Dan reported being terrified at the time and too afraid to tell anybody. The man subsequently established a "personal" relationship with Dan and "while it still hurt a lot, I let him do what he wanted." Dan reported having mixed feelings when the man moved about 8 months later: "I was relieved that I didn't have to experience the pain and blood anymore, but I missed his friendship."

For the next few years, Dan felt ashamed of the sexual abuse but wondered what it would be like to have a relationship like that again. At about 13 years of age, Dan was in a public restroom and was propositioned by an adult male. He allowed the man to perform fellatio but found the experience emotionally unsatisfying. Shortly after this episode, Dan began having compulsive homosexual experiences, none of which seemed emotionally or sexually satisfying.

In Dan's case, the sexual abuse by the male boarder appears to be the primary factor in Dan's subsequent compulsive and self-destructive sexual activities.

Thus, for the male victim of sexual abuse, the impact could range from nominal to severely damaging, depending on a number of environmental and individual variables. The task for the clinician is twofold: Accurately assess the nature of the abuse and its relative importance to the presenting problems, and develop an effective treatment program accordingly.

■ Multidimensional Treatment Challenges

Because it is not unusual for male victims of childhood sexual abuse to enter therapy with a myriad of problems, some of which may not be related to sexual victimization, most male survivors pose a therapeutic challenge. Even so, few techniques have been developed for the male victim specifically. Most treatment strategies for childhood sexual abuse victims are rooted strongly in the therapeutic efforts with female survivors over the past couple of decades. Although many of these concepts accommodate easily to the needs of the male survivor, Sepler (1990) cautions against using approaches with males that emphasize the helpless victim role. Groth (1983) also notes that therapy with male survivors should help in resolving issues created by the trauma but should not perpetuate a victim attitude. Males tend to eschew the victim role and may respond in unproductive ways when faced with ideas of helplessness, weakness, and lack of control. On the other hand, a number of techniques have been shown to be

> *Males tend to eschew the victim role and may respond in unproductive ways when faced with ideas of helplessness, weakness, and lack of control.*

successful in treating many of the emotional, cognitive, behavioral, and sexual problems displayed by many males regardless of etiology. Some procedures also have been adapted successfully from the treatment of other traumas irrespective of the victim's gender.

Because it is unlikely that any single therapeutic approach will capture the range of problems presented by male survivors, the clinician should consider selecting as many techniques as necessary to effect a successful recovery. Berliner and Wheeler (1987) advise that male sexual abuse victims present a multidimensional clinical challenge that may require a multidimensional therapeutic approach. Bolton et al. (1989) and Morris (1990) also propose a "multiremedial" approach to evaluating and treating male victims of sexual abuse. Historical underpinnings for multidimensional therapeutic approaches can be found in a "multimodal" model proposed by Lazarus (1971, 1976) and a "systematic eclectic psychotherapy" concept described by Beutler (1983), although neither model addresses the male survivor specifically.

As noted, male survivors of childhood sexual abuse often suffer emotional and psychological distress. Many experience difficulties with establishing positive self-concepts and interpersonal relationships. Anger, anxiety, and depression are common symptoms. A wide range of disturbances in sexuality is also reported by many male survivors, and addictions of all types are all too familiar. Many of these disorders are manifested through maladaptive cognitive and behavioral responses.

A multidimensional therapeutic approach would suggest considering cognitive behavior therapy to help identify, challenge, and restructure maladaptive cognitive distortions associated with the "damaged goods" syndrome (e.g., Beck & Emery, 1985; Ellis, 1962; Meichenbaum, 1977); to select relaxation procedures to reduce tension and anxiety (e.g., Benson, 1976; Brown, 1977; Jacobson, 1938; Luthe & Schultz, 1970; Paul, 1969a; Stroebel, 1978); to select social and heterosocial skills training (e.g., Abel et al., 1984; Bellack & Hersen, 1978; Bellack & Morrison, 1982; Curran & Monti, 1982), desensitization (e.g., Paul, 1969b; Wolpe, 1958; Wolpe & Lazarus, 1966), and/or assertiveness training (e.g., Hersen, Eisler, & Miller, 1973; Hersen, Eisler, Miller, Johnson, & Pinkston, 1973; Hersen, Kazdin, Bellack, & Turner, 1979; Kazdin, 1974, 1976) to ameliorate social skills deficits; and to consider anger management procedures (e.g., Meichenbaum, 1974; Novaco, 1975) for reducing maladaptive hostile and angry responses. Depression management techniques (e.g., Beck, Rush, Shaw, & Emery, 1979; Beck & Young, 1985; Lewinsohn, Biglan, & Zeiss, 1976; Lewinsohn & Hoberman, 1982; Lewinsohn, Youngren, & Grosscup, 1979) are also available and can be used in conjunction with other procedures when appropriate.

Several techniques have been developed to alleviate sexual dysfunctions such as erectile disorders, ejaculatory problems, and sexual desire disorders (e.g., Kaplan, 1974, 1975; Leiblum & Rosen, 1989; Masters & Johnson, 1970, 1976; Masters, Johnson, & Kolodny, 1988; Zilbergeld, 1992). Deviant sexual responses often respond well to a variety of techniques reported in the literature on treating perpetrators of sexual offenses. (For reviews, see Horton, Johnson, Roundy, & Williams, 1990; Knopp, 1984; Laws, 1989; Maletzky, 1991; O'Connell, Leberg, & Donaldson, 1990; Salter, 1988.)

Therapists such as Dimock, Hunter, and Struve (1993), Linden (1990), and Timms (1992) suggest that the use of touch and/or body movement may be helpful for a number of problems, including memory retrieval, increasing trust, improving sexual functioning and intimacy, decreasing self-destructive behavior, dissociation, and maladaptive defenses. Otani (1993) describes therapeutic approaches based primarily on a clinical model of trauma. Techniques such as psychoeducation, imagery, age regression, ego-states therapy, responsibility reassignment, and psychophysiological control are suggested. More traditional techniques based on insight, transference, countertransference, abreaction, and related concepts also can be integrated into any multidimensional treatment plan. In addition, self-help guides (e.g., Bear & Dimock, 1988) and personal accounts of sexual abuse (e.g., Estrada, 1994; Thomas, 1989) can be effective adjuncts to any therapeutic approach.

Paths to Recovery

Although individual differences should dictate treatment plans and the selection of multidimensional techniques, addressing personal victimization issues specifically is paramount to achieving success. Some therapists (e.g., Bear & Dimock, 1988; Lew, 1988) have identified various stages in this process. Hunter (1990) suggests five stages of recovery based on grief responses: denial, bargaining, anger, sadness, and acceptance/forgiveness. Some therapists view stages as steps on a path to recovery. Summarized below is a path to recovery presented by Bolton et al. (1989). Although the steps are presented in a logical sequence, few males will follow the path exactly, but all steps have been shown to be important to the recovery process for most males.

Breaking the Silence

Many male victims of sexual abuse do not disclose this information to anyone or else they wait until adulthood to tell someone, usually a therapist. Perry (1993) surveyed 256 male survivors currently in therapy. He found that 4% disclosed as a child, 4% disclosed as an adolescent, but most (91%) waited until adulthood before disclosing. Sixty-nine percent disclosed first to a mental health professional. Perry also found that 52% of his sample disclosed for the first time while in therapy with their present therapist. Of those, 55% did so at intake and 20%

disclosed within five sessions. It should be noted that 25% disclosed at various stages in therapy, including waiting until after 26 sessions.

Other studies also suggest that males are more reluctant than females to disclose sexual victimization experiences (Finkelhor, 1984, 1986; Fritz, Stoll, & Wagner, 1981; Johnson & Shrier, 1985; Knopp, 1984; Landis, 1956; Myers, 1989; Nasjleti, 1980; Nielsen, 1983; Porter, 1986; Rogers & Terry, 1984; Swift, 1979). Reasons for this are many, but most researchers and clinicians point to the male socialization experiences as being the major contributor to this phenomenon (Dimock, 1988; Finkelhor, 1984, 1986; Hunter, 1993; Lew, 1988; Morris, 1993; Nasjleti, 1980; Struve, 1990; Vander Mey, 1988). Males are socialized to be dominant, competitive, active, and powerful. Manhood is achieved by overpowering opponents and overcoming obstacles. An important part of this social ritual is to display to other males evidence of manhood. This often takes the form of collecting beautiful women, expensive toys, and other desirable trophies. Males also display by swapping stories of dangerous escapades, physical prowess, and sexual conquests. Defeats and signs of weakness receive much less play.

During traumatic events, males are expected to "take it like a man" (Summit, 1993). This means no whining, no crying, no complaining. Most males are all too familiar with the concept of "stuffing your feelings and going on," regardless of the pain. Males seldom rush to others with tales of woe and reports of victimization, especially sexual victimization. To tell someone about sexual victimization runs the risk of showing that the male was not strong enough to protect himself or he was weak and "cried" about his injuries.

If sexually abused, males either attempt to minimize the negative impact or else use various strategies to deny that the event was abusive at all. Males sexually abused by other males become especially reluctant to disclose the experience due to the additional stigma of homosexuality. Males sexually abused by females may not view the event as abusive because they are socialized to believe that males should always be willing to participate in sexual activities with females. They tend to redefine the experience as a sexual conquest or as evidence of their budding sexual prowess. Both of these denial strategies reflect a cultural bias against identifying sexual contact between adult females and male children as harmful (see Allen, 1990; Groth, 1979; Justice & Justice, 1979; Kasl, 1990; Mathews, Matthews, & Speltz, 1990; Ramsey-Klawsnik, 1990; Sepler, 1990; Trivelpiece, 1990). When the female perpetrator is the male's mother, a significant taboo is broken. Shame in these case can be so strong that it precludes discussing the event with anyone.

Secrecy allows sexual abuses to continue. Maintaining the secret into adulthood also perpetuates the damage created by the abuse. This issue is particularly troublesome for males, who are expected to remain strong and stoic in the face of adversity. Therefore, many males remain silent about their sexual abuse. The road to recovery, however, begins with breaking the silence. The male victim must first reveal his victimization before a focused treatment for the sexual abuse can begin. Although a therapist is a good place to begin, disclosing to other trusted individuals also can be a good start.

Accepting the Experience as Abusive

Many males who disclose often continue to protect themselves through various forms of denial. They may perpetuate the notion that the experience may have happened but it had little negative impact on them. These denial strategies help protect males from dealing with strong feelings and viewing themselves as weak and as victims. The imaginary link between weakness and victimization must be broken in order to successfully negotiate this step.

Separating the Abuse From the Abused

Males are expected to be strong and to protect themselves. To many males, victimization means that they were not manly enough to prevent the abuse and that they are responsible for it somehow. Many male victims fail to think of themselves as just children caught up in the adult-child power differential. Therefore, they incorrectly assume the responsibility for their abuse rather than assign the responsibility to its proper owner, the abuser.

Unpleasant Memories

Although total recall of all abusive experiences is unnecessary for achieving an effective recovery from childhood sexual abuse, remembering painful childhood memories allows the male survivor the opportunity to resolve issues rather than avoid them. Many males build powerful barriers between themselves and memories of traumatic events. Once these

d, a flood of emotionally laden material often comes
t for the therapist to inform the male survivor, in
ainful memories may emerge as he works toward

Feelings

An important part of achieving manhood is to effect control over most feelings, especially feelings associated with weakness, fearfulness, submissiveness, and dependency. Males are taught that they must conquer their "unmanly" feelings lest the feelings conquer the man. Child sexual abuse often produces unacceptable feelings. Many male victims work so hard at controlling or denying their feelings that they grow up nearly devoid of appropriate emotional expressions. Others seem unable to establish control, and they embark on a neverending quest to reduce the pain through other means such as aggressive acting out and substance abuse. Either way, most males require rather intensive therapeutic work to eventually learn to connect their strong feelings to the childhood abusive experiences, accept their feelings as valid, and develop more effective expressions of all emotions.

Mourning Lost Childhood

Like most victims of childhood sexual abuse, males have had the opportunity for normal childhood experiences snatched from them. Although all forms of child abuse pervert normal childhood developmental experiences, sexual abuse seems to be one of the most damaging. Few children are prepared for normal childhood exploratory experiences, much less adult sexual experiences. Once a child is sexualized through victimization, the opportunity to learn about sexual matters in a childhood manner is forever lost; other childhood experiences are often lost as well. For some male survivors, it is as though childhood never existed. The opportunity to learn basic trust, security, self-esteem, personal bounda-

> *Although all forms of child abuse pervert normal childhood developmental experiences, sexual abuse seems to be one of the most damaging.*

ries, healthy social interactions, love, intimacy, control, self-confidence, and children's playfulness are often gone as well.

Many male survivors attempt to recapture what was lost, but it cannot be found. The sad reality is that childhood experiences cannot be regained in adulthood, and must be mourned. However, hope is not dead. Through the mourning process, the male survivor can recover. He can also begin to learn effective adulthood strategies to establish a reasonably secure, happy, and satisfying adult lifestyle.

Self-Image

Most survivors of childhood sexual abuse feel damaged in some way. These feelings often are translated into specific ideas about the survivors' self-worth. Some male survivors believe that they have no worth at all. Others may see themselves as having worth, but their overall self-concept is negative. Childhood sexual abuse produces a faulty perception that a worthwhile person is transformed into a damaged and worthless person. This erroneous belief also perpetuates the negative effects of the abuse by keeping the person weak, seemingly powerless, and unable to assess his worth accurately. The distorted perceptions often are played out through self-destructive behaviors or, in some cases, a compulsive drive for perfection.

To reverse this process, the male survivor can be guided into a better understanding of the etiology of the negative self-image. It is important that the male survivor learn that although sexual abuse may produce negative effects, the person's worth remains intact. Then he can begin decreasing the frequency of negative evaluative statements of himself and replacing harmful thoughts with more positive ones. What follows next is altering the behavioral indexes of his negative self-image.

Relationships

Childhood sexual abuse experiences expose the child to a dysfunctional model of interpersonal relationships. The example given ignores the basis for establishing appropriate interactions such as trust, caring, and respect. Personal boundaries are shattered and trust is used to manipulate. Respect and caring are absent. Male victims often develop interpersonal strategies to help them cope with the victimization. Although the survival strategies may work during childhood, they often fail in adulthood and become a source of frustration and additional problems for the male survivor.

Because most child victim survival strategies are based on misinformation about interpersonal relationships, the adult survivor must be guided toward an accurate view of appropriate and satisfying relationships. Current relationships based on old survival ideas may need to be terminated or altered to better fit the survivor's newly emerging, healthy approach to interpersonal relationships.

Confusion About Sexuality

A premature introduction to adult sexual behavior misdirects the usual development of sexual information, feelings, and behavior. This often creates confusion about sexual matters beyond that normally experienced by children. Some male victims may confuse sexual responses with anger and power. Sexual responses and other feelings may become so intertwined that the male survivor is unable to differentiate them. Some males are simultaneously drawn to and repelled by sexual contact. Male children who were sexually abused by other males often develop considerable anxiety and confusion about their gender role and sexual orientation. Homophobic responses such as fears of all men, fears of gay men, or fears of becoming homosexual are common.

Regardless of the nature of the confusion about sexual matters, the therapist should explore sexuality issues openly and honestly with the male survivor. Dysfunctional areas then can be identified and corrected with appropriate multidimensional techniques.

Victim to Victimizer

Although many perpetrators of child sexual abuse were also sexually abused as children, most male survivors are not perpetrators. However, some male survivors express concern that they may perpetrate a sexual offense because they sometimes have thoughts and/or feelings associated with inappropriate sexual behavior, even though they have never acted out. Others worry that their childhood victimization places them in a high-risk category for future perpetration. The task of the clinician is to explore these issues in therapy and to perform a risk assessment. The survivor often needs only reassurance that he is at low risk to engage in abusive behavior. Others may need a more intensive therapeutic approach designed to address directly a higher risk for perpetration.

Confronting the Abuser

Confrontation of one's abuser may be therapeutic for some male survivors, but it is not a crucial step in establishing a successful recovery. In fact, poorly conceived and executed confrontations may result in additional abuse and trauma for the survivor. Confrontations should never be used just to express anger or to prove that the survivor is a "real man" after all. Confrontations are usually more effective after the survivor has completed successfully several other steps on the path to recovery. Once the survivor has shown progress in establishing emotional strength and control, a plan for confrontation can be explored. In this way, the survivor will require little, if anything, from his abuser in order to effect a successful confrontation. The confrontation becomes an opportunity to show emotional strength, power, and control rather than just an expression of angry feelings. Many types of confrontations can be used, but the direct type carries the highest risk for a negative outcome. Symbolic confrontations are usually less risky.

■ Conclusions and Future Directions

Within the past 5 years or so, major strides have been made in the identification and understanding of male childhood sexual abuse victims. Although no clinical outcome studies have demonstrated clearly the efficacy of specific treatments on the effects of sexual abuse on males, studies suggest that a multidimensional therapeutic approach may be useful. Drawing from a wide range of treatment techniques instead of a single therapeutic approach is likely to be more successful in addressing the multiple and complex problems often presented by male survivors. This chapter suggests using a multidimensional therapeutic approach to assist male survivors as they attempt to negotiate their paths to recovery.

The task facing both researchers and clinicians is to increase the understanding of the negative sequelae associated with the sexual abuse of males. Additional studies are needed to elaborate on extant descriptive data and to generate sound therapeutic techniques. Now is the time for the refinement and maturation of research pertaining to male victims of childhood sexual abuse. The silence is broken.

References

Abel, G. G., Becker, J. V., Cunningham-Rathner, J., Rouleau, J., Kaplan, M., & Reich, J. (1984). *The treatment of child molesters: A manual.* Unpublished manuscript. (Available from G. G. Abel, Emory University, Atlanta, GA)

Abel, G., Becker, J., & Skinner, L. (1990). *Treatment of the violent person—Crime & delinquency issues* [Monograph]. Bethesda, MD: National Institute of Mental Health.

Adams-Tucker, C. (1982). Proximate effects of sexual abuse in children. *American Journal of Psychiatry, 139,* 1252-1256.

Alcoholics Anonymous. (1976). *Alcoholics Anonymous* (3rd ed.). New York: A.A. World Services.

Allen, C. M. (1990). Women as perpetrators of child sexual abuse: Recognition barriers. In A. L. Horton, B. L. Johnson, L. M. Roundy, & D. Williams (Eds.), *The incest perpetrator: A family member no one wants to treat* (pp. 108-125). Newbury Park, CA: Sage.

Allison, R. (1980). *Minds in many pieces.* New York: Rawson, Wade.

Alpert, J. L., & Paulson, A. (1990). Graduate-level education and training in child sexual abuse. *Professional Psychology: Research and Practice, 21*(5), 366-371.

American Humane Association. (1978). *National analysis of official child abuse and neglect reporting.* Denver: Author.

American Psychiatric Association. (1987). *Diagnostic Statistical Manual of Mental Disorders* (3rd ed.). Washington, DC: Author.

Baker, A. W. (1985). Child sexual abuse: A study of prevalence in Great Britain. *Child Abuse & Neglect, 9,* 457-467.

Bass, E., & Davis, L. (1988). *The courage to heal: A guide for women survivors of child sexual abuse.* New York: Perennial Library.

Bear, E., & Dimock, P. (1988). *Adults molested as children: A survivor's manual for women and men.* Orwell, VT: Safer Society Press.

Beck, A. T., & Emery, G. (1985). *Anxiety disorders and phobias: A cognitive perspective.* New York: Basic Books.

Beck, A. T., Rush, A. J., Shaw, B. F., & Emery, G. (1979). *Cognitive therapy for depression.* New York: Basic Books.

Beck, A. T., & Young, J. E. (1985). Depression. In D. H. Barlow (Ed.), *Clinical handbook of psychological disorders* (pp. 206-244). New York: Guilford.

Becker, J. V. (1988). The effects of child sexual abuse on adolescent sexual offenders. In G. E. Wyatt & G. J. Powell (Eds.), *Lasting effects of child sexual abuse* (pp. 193-207). Newbury Park, CA: Sage.

Becker, J. V. (1989). Impact of sexual abuse on sexual functioning. In S. R. Leiblum & R. C. Rosen (Eds.), *Principles and practice of sex therapy: Update for the 1990s* (pp. 298-318). New York: Guilford.

Becker, J. V., Beitchman, J. H., Zucker, K. J., Hood, J. E., DaCosta, G. A., Akman, D., & Cassavia, E. (1992). A review of the long-term effects of child sexual abuse. *Child Abuse & Neglect, 16,* 101-118.

Becker, J. V., Kaplan, M. S., Cunningham-Rathner, J., & Kavoussi, R. (1986). Characteristics of adolescent incest perpetrators: Preliminary findings. *Journal of Family Violence, 1,* 85-97.

Becker, J. V., & Skinner, L. J. (1984). Behavioral treatment of sexual dysfunctions in sexual assault survivors. In I. R. Stuart & J. C. Greer (Eds.), *Victims of sexual aggression: Treatment of children, women, and men* (pp. 211-233). New York: Van Nostrand Reinhold.

Becker, J. V., Skinner, L. J., Abel, G., & Cichon, J. (1986). Level of postassault sexual functioning in rape and incest victims. *Archives of Sexual Behavior, 15*(1), 37-49.

Bell, A., & Weinberg, M. (1981). *Sexual preference: Its development among men and women.* Bloomington: Indiana University Press.

Bellack, A. S., & Hersen, M. (1978). Chronic psychiatric patients: Social skills training. In M. Hersen & A. S. Bellack (Eds.), *Behavior therapy in the psychiatric setting* (pp. 291-316). Baltimore: Williams & Williams.

Bellack, A. S., & Morrison, R. L. (1982). Interpersonal dysfunction. In A. S. Bellack, M. Hersen, & A. E. Kazdin (Eds.), *International handbook of behavior modification and therapy* (pp. 717-747). New York: Plenum.

Bender, L., & Blau, A. (1937). The reaction of children to sexual relations with adults. *American Journal of Orthopsychiatry, 7,* 500-518.

Benson, H. (1976). *The relaxation response.* New York: William Morrow.

Berliner, L., & Wheeler, J. R. (1987). Treating the effects of sexual abuse on children. *Journal of Interpersonal Violence, 2*(4), 415-434.

Beutler, L. E. (1983). *Eclectic psychotherapy: A systematic approach.* New York: Pergamon.

Bliss, E. L. (1986). *Multiple personality, allied disorders, and hypnosis.* New York: Oxford University Press.

Bliss, J., & Bliss, E. (1985). *Prism: Andrea's world.* Briarcliff Manor, NY: Scarborough.

Blume, E. S. (1990). *Secret survivors: Uncovering incest and its aftereffects in women.* New York: John Wiley.

Bolton, F., Morris, L. A., & MacEachron, A. (1989). *Males at risk: The other side of child sexual abuse.* Newbury Park, CA: Sage.

Bowlby, J. (1969). *Attachment and loss: Volume III.* New York: Basic Books.

Braun, B. G. (1984). Uses of hypnosis with multiple personality. *Psychiatric Annals, 14,* 34-40.

Braun, B. (1986). Issues in the psychotherapy of multiple personality disorder. In B. Braun (Ed.), *Treatment of multiple personality disorder* (pp. 1-29). Washington, DC: American Psychiatric Press.

Braun, B. G. (1988). The BASK model of dissociation. *Dissociation, 1*(1), 4-23.

Briere, J. (1989). *Therapy for adults molested as children: Beyond survival.* New York: Springer.

Briere, J., & Runtz, M. (1988). Post sexual abuse trauma. In G. E. Wyatt & G. J. Powell (Eds.), *Lasting effects of child sexual abuse* (pp. 85-99). Newbury Park, CA: Sage.

Briere, J., & Runtz, M. (1989). The Trauma Symptoms Checklist (TSC-33): Early data on a new scale. *Journal of Interpersonal Violence, 4,* 151-163.

Briere, J., & Runtz, M. (1990). Differential adult symptomatology associated with three types of child abuse histories. *Child Abuse & Neglect, 14,* 357-364.

Briere, J., & Runtz, M. (1992). *Child abuse trauma: Theory and treatment of the lasting effects.* Newbury Park, CA: Sage.

Briere, J., & Smiljanich, K. (1993, August). *Childhood sexual abuse and subsequent sexual aggression against adult women.* Paper presented at the 101st Annual Convention of the American Psychological Association, Toronto, Ontario, Canada.

Brown, B. B. (1977). *Stress and the art of biofeedback.* New York: Harper & Row.

Brown, S. (1988). *Treating adult children of alcoholics: A developmental perspective.* New York: John Wiley.

Browne, A., & Finkelhor, D. (1986). Impact of child sexual abuse: A review of the research. *Psychological Bulletin, 99*(1), 66-77.

Bruckner, D. F., & Johnson, P. E. (1987). Treatment for adult male victims of childhood sexual abuse. *Social Casework: The Journal of Contemporary Social Work, 68,* 81-87.

Brunold, H. (1964). Observations after sexual traumata suffered in childhood. *Excerpta Criminologica, 4,* 5-8.

Burgess, A. W., Hartman, C. R., McCousland, M. P., & Powers, P. (1984). Impact of child pornography and sex rings on child victims and their families. In A. W. Burgess (Ed.), *Child pornography and sex rings* (pp. 111-126). Lexington, MA: Lexington Books.

Burgess, A. W., & Holmstrom, L. L. (1979). Rape: Sexual disruption and recovery. *American Journal of Orthopsychiatry, 49*(4), 648-657.

Cantwell, H. B. (1988). Child sexual abuse: Very young perpetrators. *Child Abuse & Neglect, 12,* 579-582.

Carlson, S., Dimock, P. T., Driggs, J., & Westly, T. (1987, May). *Relationship of childhood sexual abuse and adult sexual compulsiveness in males.* Workshop presented at the First National Conference on Sexual Compulsivity/Addiction, Minneapolis, MN.

Carmen, E., Rieker, P. P., & Mills, T. (1984). Victims of violence and psychiatric illness. *American Journal of Psychiatry, 141,* 378-383.

Carnes, P. (1982). *Out of the shadows.* Minneapolis, MN: CompCare.

Carnes, P. (1989). *Contrary to love.* Minneapolis, MN: CompCare.

Christie, M. J., & Chester, G. B. (1990). Physical dependence on physiologically released endogenous opiates. *Life Science, 30,* 1173.

Condy, S. R., Templer, D. I., Brown, R., & Veaco, L. (1987). Parameters of sexual contact of boys with women. *Archives of Sexual Behavior, 16,* 379-394.

Conte, J. R., & Schuerman, J. R. (1987a). Factors associated with an increased impact of child sexual abuse. *Child Abuse & Neglect, 11,* 201-211.

Conte, J. R., & Schuerman, J. R. (1987b). The effects of sexual abuse on children: A multidimensional view. *Journal of Interpersonal Violence, 2*(4), 380-390.

Coombs, N. R. (1973). Male prostitution: A psychosocial view of behavior. *American Journal of Orthopsychiatry, 44,* 782-789.

Courtois, C. A. (1988). *Healing the incest wound: Adult survivors in therapy.* New York: W. W. Norton.

Courtois, C. A., & Watts, D. (1982). Counseling adult women who experienced incest in childhood or adolescence. *Personnel and Guidance Journal, 60,* 275-279.

Cunningham, J., Pearce, T., & Pearce, P. (1988). Childhood sexual abuse and medical complaints in adult women. *Journal of Interpersonal Violence, 3*(2), 131-144.

Curran, J. P., & Monti, P. M. (1982). *Social skills training: A practical handbook for assessment and treatment.* New York: Guilford.

Davis, L. (1990). *The courage to heal workbook: For women and men survivors of child sexual abuse.* New York: HarperCollins.

Davis, L. (1991). *Allies in healing: When the person you love was sexually abused as a child.* New York: HarperCollins.

DeFrancis, V. (1969). *Protecting the child victim of sex crimes committed by adults.* Denver: American Humane Association.

DeJong, A. R., Emmett, G. A., & Hervada, A. A. (1982). Epidemiologic factors in sexual abuse of boys. *American Journal of Diseases of Children, 136*(11), 990-993.

Dimock, P. (1988). Adult males sexually abused as children: Characteristics and implications for treatment. *Journal of Interpersonal Violence, 3*(2), 203-221.

Dimock, P., Hunter, M., & Struve, J. (1993, September). *The use of touch in psychotherapy with sexual abuse survivors.* Workshop presented at the Fifth Annual National Conference on Male Survivors, Bethesda, MD.

Dixon, K. N., Arnold, L. E., & Calestro, K. (1978). Father-son incest: Underreported psychiatric problem? *American Journal of Psychiatry, 135,* 835-838.

Dolan, Y. M. (1991). *Resolving sexual abuse: Solution-focused therapy and Ericksonian hypnosis for adult survivors.* New York: W. W. Norton.

Eisenberg, N., Owens, R. G., & Dewey, M. E. (1987). Attitudes of health professionals to child sexual abuse and incest. *Child Abuse & Neglect, 11,* 109-116.

Ellerstein, N., & Canavan, W. (1980). Sexual abuse of boys. *American Journal of Diseases of Children, 134,* 255-257.

Ellis, A. (1962). *Reason and emotion in psychotherapy.* New York: Lyle Stuart.

Erickson, E. K. (1950). *Childhood and society.* New York: W. W. Norton.

Erickson, M. H. (1967). Permanent relief of an obsessional phobia by means of communication with an unsuspected dual personality. In J. Haley (Ed.), *Advanced techniques of hypnosis and therapy: Selected papers of Milton H. Erickson, M.D.* (pp. 340-463). New York: Grune & Stratton.

Estrada, H. (1994). *Recovery for male victims of child sexual abuse* (2nd ed.). Santa Fe, NM: Red Rabbit Press.

Farber, E. D., Showers, J. C., Johnson, C. G., Joseph, J. A., & Oshins, L. (1984). The sexual abuse of children: A comparison of male and female victims. *Journal of Clinical Child Psychology, 13,* 294-297.

Fehrenbach, P. A., Smith, W., Monastersky, C., & Deisher, R. W. (1986). Adolescent sexual offenders: Offender and offense characteristics. *American Journal of Orthopsychiatry, 56,* 225-233.

Fein, C. G. (Speaker). (1990, June). *Boundaries, limits, contracts and mistakes.* Workshop conducted at the Second Annual Eastern Regional Conference on Multiple Personality and Dissociation, Alexandria, VA (Cassette Recording No. 30 a-b). Alexandria, VA: Audio Transcripts.

Fein, C. G., & Kluft, R. (Speakers). (1991, June). *Hypnotic techniques in the treatment of multiple personality disorder.* Workshop conducted at the Third Annual Eastern

Regional Conference on Multiple Personality and Dissociation. Alexandria, VA (Cassette Recording No. 33 a-d). Alexandria, VA: Audio Transcripts.

Finch, S. M. (1967). Sexual activity of children with other children and adults (commentaries). *Clinical Pediatrics, 3*, 1-2.

Finkelhor, D. (1979). *Sexually victimized children.* New York: Free Press.

Finkelhor, D. (1980). Sex among siblings: A survey of prevalence, variety, and effects. *Archives of Sexual Behavior, 9*(3), 171-194.

Finkelhor, D. (1984). *Child sexual abuse: New theory and research.* New York: Free Press.

Finkelhor, D. (1986). *A sourcebook on child sexual abuse.* Newbury Park, CA: Sage.

Finkelhor, D., & Browne, A. (1985). The traumatic impact of sexual abuse: A conceptualization. *American Journal of Orthopsychiatry, 55*(4), 530-541.

Freeman-Longo, R. F. (1986). The impact of sexual victimization on males. *Child Abuse & Neglect, 10*, 411-414.

Freud, S. (1973). Remembering, repeating and working through: Further recommendations on the technique of psycho-analysis. In J. Strachey (Ed. and Trans.), *The standard edition of the complete psychological works of Sigmund Freud* (Vol. 12, pp. 150-154). London: Hogarth. (Original work published 1913)

Friedrich, W. N. (1990). *Psychotherapy of sexually abused children and their families.* New York: W. W. Norton.

Friedrich, W. N., Beilke, R. L., & Urquiza, A. J. (1987). Children from sexually abusive families: A behavioral comparison. *Journal of Interpersonal Violence, 2*, 391-402.

Friedrich, W. N., Beilke, R. L., & Urquiza, A. J. (1988). Behavior problems in young sexually abused boys: A comparison study. *Journal of Interpersonal Violence, 3*, 21-28.

Friedrich, W. N., & Luecke, W. J. (1988). Young school-age sexually aggressive children. *Professional Psychology: Research and Practice, 19*, 155-164.

Friedrich, W. N., Urquiza, A. J., & Beilke, R. L. (1986). Behavior problems in sexually abused young children. *Journal of Pediatric Psychology, 11*, 47-57.

Fritz, G. S., Stoll, K., & Wagner, N. A. (1981). A comparison of males and females who were sexually molested as children. *Journal of Sex and Marital Therapy, 7*, 54-59.

Fromuth, M. E. (1986). The relationship of childhood sexual abuse with later psychological and sexual adjustment in a sample of college women. *Child Abuse & Neglect, 10*, 5-15.

Fromuth, M. E., & Burkhart, B. R. (1989). Long-term psychological correlates of childhood sexual abuse in two samples of college men: Definitional and methodological issues. *Violence and Victims, 2*, 241-253.

Froning, J. L., & Mayman, S. B. (1990, November). *Identification and treatment of child and adolescent male victims of sexual abuse.* Workshop presented at the Third National Conference on the Male Survivor, Tucson, AZ.

Gay, P. (1993). *Ego states therapy and eating disorder.* Unpublished manuscript.

Gil, E. (1984). *Outgrowing the pain: A book for and about adults abused as children.* San Francisco: Launch Press.

Gil, E. (1988). *Treatment of adult survivors of childhood abuse.* Walnut Creek, CA: Launch Press.

Gil, E. (1992). *Outgrowing the pain together: A book for spouses and partners of adults abused as children.* New York: Dell.

Gilbert, B., & Cunningham, C. (1986). Women's post-rape sexual functioning. *Journal of Counseling and Development, 65*(2), 71-73.

Ginsburg, K. N. (1967). The "meat rack": A study of the male homosexual prostitute. *American Journal of Orthopsychiatry, 21,* 170-185.

Glanz, K., & Himber, J. (1992). Sex therapy with dissociative disorders: A protocol. *Journal of Sex and Marital Therapy, 18*(2), 147-153.

Gomes-Schwartz, B., Horowitz, J., & Sauzier, M. (1985). Severity of emotional distress among sexually abused preschool, school-age and adolescent children. *Hospital & Community Psychiatry, 30*(5), 503-508.

Gonsiorek, J. (1993, August). Relationship of sexual abuse of males and sexual orientation confusion. In L. A. Morris (Chair), *Wounded warriors: Male survivors of childhood sexual abuse.* Symposium conducted at the 101st Annual Convention of the American Psychological Association, Toronto, Ontario, Canada.

Goodwin, D. W. (1979). Alcoholism and heredity: A review and hypothesis. *Archives of General Psychiatry, 36,* 57-61.

Gorski, T. T. (1989). *Understand the twelve steps.* Englewood Cliffs, NJ: Prentice Hall.

Groth, A. N. (1979). *Men who rape: The psychology of the offender.* New York: Plenum.

Groth, A. N. (1983). Treatment of sexual offenders in a correctional institution. In J. Greer & I. Stuart (Eds.), *The sexual aggressor: Current perspectives on treatment* (pp. 160-176). New York: Van Nostrand Reinhold.

Groth, A. N., Hobson, W. F., & Gary, T. (1982). The child molester: Clinical observations. In J. Conte & D. Shore (Eds.), *Social work and child sexual abuse* (pp. 129-144) New York: Haworth.

Hamilton, G. V. (1929). *A research in marriage.* New York: Albert & Charles Boni.

Hammond, D. C. (1978). *Hypnotic suggestions and metaphors.* New York: W. W. Norton.

Herman, J. (1992a). *Trauma and recovery: The aftermath of violence from domestic abuse to political terror.* New York: Basic Books.

Herman, J. (1992b). Complex PTSD: A syndrome in survivors of prolonged and repeated trauma. *Journal of Traumatic Stress, 5*(2), 23-45.

Hersen, M., Eisler, R. M., & Miller, P. M. (1973). Development of assertive responses: Clinical measurement and research considerations. *Behavior Research and Therapy, 11,* 505-521.

Hersen, M., Eisler, R. M., Miller, P. M., Johnson, M. K., & Pinkston, S. G. (1973). Effect of practice, instructions and modeling on components of assertive behavior. *Behavior Research and Therapy, 11,* 442-451.

Hersen, M., Kazdin, A. E., Bellack, A. S., & Turner, S. M. (1979). Effects of live modeling, covert modeling, and rehearsal on assertiveness in psychiatric patients. *Behavior Research and Therapy, 17,* 369-377.

Hohmann, K. (1989). Sexual compulsivity, not addiction. *The Phoenix, 9*(4), 1.

Horowitz, M. J. (1986). Stress response syndromes: A review of post traumatic and adjustment disorders. *Hospital & Community Psychiatry,* pp. 37, 241-249.

Horton, A. L., Johnson, B. L., Roundy, L. M., & Williams, D. (Eds.) (1990). *The incest perpetrator: A family member no one wants to treat.* Newbury Park, CA: Sage.

Hunter, M. (1985). *The membership demographic of the self-help group Sex Addicts Anonymous.* Unpublished master's thesis, University of Wisconsin, Superior.

Hunter, M. (1987, May). Membership demographics of the self-help group Sex Addicts Anonymous. Workshop presented at the First National Conference on Sexual Compulsivity/Addiction, Minneapolis, MN.

Hunter, M. (1990). *Abused boys: The neglected victims of sexual abuse.* Lexington, MA: Lexington Books.

Hunter, M. (1992). *Joyous sexuality: Healing from the effects of family sexual dysfunction.* Minneapolis, MN: CompCare. [Available from the author, 612/649-1408]

Hunter, M. (1993, August). Males who have experienced childhood sexual abuse: Recovery issues. In L. A. Morris (Chair), *Wounded warriors: Male survivors of childhood sexual abuse.* Symposium conducted at the 101st Annual Convention of the American Psychological Association, Toronto, Ontario, Canada.

Hunter, R. S., Kilstrom, N., & Loda, F. (1985). Sexually abused children: Identifying masked presentations in a medical setting. *Child Abuse & Neglect, 9,* 17-25.

Jacobson, E. (1938). *Progressive relaxation.* Chicago: University of Chicago Press.

Janus, M.-D., Scanlon, B., & Price, V. (1984). Youth prostitution. In A. W. Burgess (Ed.), *Child pornography and sex rings* (pp. 127-146). Lexington, MA: Lexington Books.

Jehu, D. (1990). *Beyond sexual abuse: Therapy with women who were childhood victims.* New York: John Wiley.

Johnson, R. L., & Shrier, D. K. (1985). Sexual victimization of boys: Experience at an adolescent medicine clinic. *Journal of Adolescent Health Care, 6,* 372-376.

Johnson, R. L., & Shrier, D. K. (1987). Past sexual victimization by females in an adolescent medicine clinic population. *American Journal of Psychiatry, 144*(5), 650-652.

Johnson, T. C. (1988). Child perpetrators—Children who molest other children: Preliminary findings. *Child Abuse & Neglect, 12,* 219-229.

Justice, B., & Justice, R. (1979). *The broken taboo: Sex in the family.* New York: Human Sciences Press.

Kaplan, H. S. (1974). *The new sex therapy.* New York: Brunner/Mazel.

Kaplan, H. S. (1975). *The illustrated manual of sex therapy.* New York: Quadrangle.

Kasl, C. D. (1990). Female perpetrators of sexual abuse: A feminist view. In M. Hunter (Ed.), *The sexually abused male: Volume 1. Prevalence, impact, and treatment* (pp. 259-274). Lexington, MA: Lexington Books.

Kazdin, A. E. (1974). Effects of covert modeling and model reinforcement on assertive behavior. *Journal of Abnormal Psychology, 83,* 240-252.

Kazdin, A. E. (1976). Effects of covert modeling, multiple models, and model reinforcement on assertive behavior. *Behavior Therapy, 7,* 211-222.

Kelberer, M. (1989). Compulsive sex part of addiction cycle. *The Phoenix, 9*(4), 1.

Kelly, R. J., & Gonzalez, L. S. (1990, November). *Psychological symptoms reported by sexually abused men.* Workshop presented at the Third National Conference on the Male Survivor, Tucson, AZ.

Kempe, C., Silverman, F., Steele, B., Droegenuelle, W., & Silver, H. (1962). The battered child syndrome. *Journal of the American Medical Association, 181,* 105-112.

Kempe, R. S., & Kempe, C. H. (1984). *The common secret: Sexual abuse of children and adolescents.* New York: W. H. Freeman.

Kercher, G., & McShane, M. (1984). The prevalence of child sexual abuse victimization in an adult sample of Texas residents. *Child Abuse & Neglect, 8,* 485-502.

Kernberg, O. F. (1975). *Borderline conditions and pathological narcissism.* New York: Jason Aronson.

Kluft, R. P. (1984). Varieties of hypnotic interventions in the treatment of multiple personality. *American Journal of Clinical Hypnosis, 24,* 230-240.

Kluft, R. P. (Speaker). (1988, October). *Treatment of multiple personality disorder.* Workshop conducted at Fifth International Conference on Multiple Personality/Dissociative States, Chicago.

Kluft, R. P. (Speaker). (1991, June). *The management of abreactions.* Workshop conducted at the Third Annual Eastern Regional Conference on Multiple Personality and Dissociation, Alexandria, VA (Cassette Recording No. 25-652-91b). Alexandria, VA: Audio Transcripts.

Knopp, F. H. (1984). *Retraining adult sex offenders: Methods and models.* Orwell, VT: Safer Society Press.

Kohan, M. J., Pothier, P., & Norbeck, J. S. (1987). Hospitalized children with history of sexual abuse: Incidence and care issues. *American Journal of Orthopsychiatry, 57,* 258-264.

Krug, R. S. (1989). Adult male reports of childhood sexual abuse by mothers: Case descriptions, motivations and long-term consequences. *Child Abuse & Neglect, 13,* 111-119.

Landis, J. (1956). Experiences of 500 children with adult sexual deviants. *Psychiatric Quarterly Supplement, 30,* 91-109.

Laws, D. R. (Ed.). (1989). *Relapse prevention with sex offenders.* New York: Guilford.

Lazarus, A. A. (1971). *Behavior therapy and beyond.* New York: McGraw-Hill.

Lazarus, A. A. (1976). *Multi-modal behavior therapy.* New York: Springer.

Leiblum, S. R., & Rosen, R. C. (Eds.). (1989). *Principles and practice of sex therapy: Update for the 1990s.* New York: Guilford.

Lew, M. (1988). *Victims no longer: Men recovering from incest and other sexual child abuse.* New York: Nevraumont.

Lewinsohn, P. M., Biglan, A., & Zeiss, A. M. (1976). Behavioral treatment of depression. In P. O. Davidson (Ed.), *The behavioral management of anxiety, depression and pain.* New York: Brunner/Mazel.

Lewinsohn, P. M., & Hoberman, H. M. (1982). Depression. In A. S. Bellack, M. Hersen, & A. E. Kazdin (Eds.), *International handbook of behavior modification and therapy* (pp. 397-431). New York: Plenum.

Lewinsohn, P. M., Youngren, M. A., & Grosscup, S. L. (1979). Reinforcement and depression. In R. A. Depue (Ed.), *The psychobiology of the depressive disorders: Implications for the effects of stress* (pp. 291-316). New York: Academic Press.

Linden, P. (1990, November). *Embodying power and love: A workshop on applying body/move ment awareness training with incest survivors.* Workshop presented at the Third Annual National Conference on Male Survivors, Tucson, AZ.

Lisak, D. (1993, September). *Research on male victims of childhood abuse: What do we know and what do we need to know?* Paper presented at the Fifth Annual National Conference on Male Survivors, Bethesda, MD.

Longo, R. E. (1982). Sexual learning experiences among adolescent sexual offenders. *International Journal of Offender Therapy and Comparative Criminology, 26,* 235-241.

Lowenstein, R. (1991). An office mental status examination for complex chronic dissociative symptoms and multiple personality disorder. *Psychiatric Clinics of North America, 14*(3), 567-605.

Luthe, W., & Schultz, J. H. (1970). *Autogenic therapy: Applications in psychotherapy.* New York: Grune & Stratton.

Mackey, T. F., Hacker, S. S., Weissfeld, L. A., Ambrose, N. C., Fisher, M. G., & Zobel, D. L. (1991). Comparative effects of sexual assault on sexual functioning of child sexual abuse survivors and others. *Issues in Mental Health Nursing, 12,* 89-112.

Mahler, M. S., Pine, F., & Bergman, A. (1975). *The psychological birth of the human infant: Symbiosis and individuation.* New York: Basic Books.

Maletzky, B. M. (1991). *Treating the sexual offender.* Newbury Park, CA: Sage.

Maltz, W. (1988). Identifying and treating the sexual repercussions of incest: A couples therapy approach. *Journal of Sex and Marital Therapy, 14,* 142-170.

Maltz, W. (1991). *The sexual healing journey: A guide for survivors of sexual abuse.* New York: HarperCollins.

Maltz, W., & Holman, B. (1987). *Incest and sexuality: A guide to understanding and healing.* Lexington, MA: Lexington Books.

Marlatt, A. (1985). *Relapse prevention: Maintenance strategies in treatment of addictive behaviors.* New York: Guilford.

Masters, W. H., & Johnson, V. E. (1970). *Human sexual inadequacy.* Boston: Little, Brown.

Masters, W. H., & Johnson, V. E. (1976). *The pleasure bond.* New York: Bantam.

Masters, W. H., Johnson, V. E., & Kolodny, R. C. (1988). *Masters and Johnson on sex and human loving.* New York: Little, Brown.

Masterson, J. M. (1981). *The narcissistic and borderline disorders.* New York: Brunner/Mazel.

Mathews, R., Matthews, J., & Speltz, K. (1990). Female sexual offenders. In M. Hunter (Ed.), *The sexually abused male: Volume 1. Prevalence, impact, and treatment* (pp. 275-293). Lexington, MA: Lexington Books.

Mayer, R. S. (1988). *Through divided minds: Probing the mysteries of multiple personalities—A doctor's story.* New York: Doubleday.

Mayer, R. S. (1991). *Satan's children: Case studies in multiple personality.* New York: Putnam.

McCarthy, B. W. (1990). Treating sexual dysfunction associated with prior sexual trauma. *Journal of Sex and Marital Therapy, 16*(3), 142-146.

McCarthy, B. W. (1993, March). *Relapse prevention: Strategies and techniques in sex therapy.* Paper presented at the annual meeting of the Association of Sex Educators, Counselors, and Therapists, Denver.

McGuire, L. S., & Wagner, N. N. (1978). Sexual dysfunction in women who were molested as children: One response pattern and suggestions for treatment. *Journal of Sex and Marital Therapy, 4*(1), 11-16.

Meichenbaum, D. (1974). *Cognitive behavior modification.* Morristown, NJ: General Learning Press.

Meichenbaum, D. (1977). *Cognitive behavior modification: An integrative approach.* New York: Plenum.

Miller, A. (1983). *For your own good.* New York: Farrar, Straus & Giroux.

Miller, A. (1986). *Thou shalt not be aware.* New York: New York Library.

Minnesota Higher Education Coordinating Board. (1993). *Professional education about violence and abuse: Summary findings for psychologists.* St. Paul, MN: Author.

Money, J. (1986). *Love maps: Clinical concepts of sexual/erotic health and pathology, paraphilia, and gender transposition, childhood, adolescence and maturity.* New York: Irving.

Morris, L. A. (1990, November). *Beyond the path to recovery: A multi-remedial approach.* Workshop presented at the Third Annual National Conference on the Male Survivor, Tucson, AZ.

Morris, L. A. (1993, September). *Socialization of the male sex role and the male survivor: Clinical issues.* Workshop presented at the Fifth Annual National Conference on Male Survivors, Bethesda, MD.

Myers, M. F. (1989). Men sexually assaulted as adults and sexually abused as boys. *Archives of Sexual Behavior, 18,* 203-215.

Nasjleti, M. (1980). Suffering in silence: The male incest victim. *Child Welfare, 59,* 203-215.

Nielsen, T. (1983). Sexual abuse of boys: Current perspectives. *Personnel and Guidance Journal, 62,* 139-142.

Nichols, M. (1989). Sex therapy with lesbians, gay men, and bisexuals. In S. R. Leiblum & R. C. Rosen (Eds.), *Principles and practice of sex therapy: Update for the 1990s* (pp. 269-297). New York: Guilford.

Novaco, R. W. (1975). *Anger control: The development and evaluation of an experimental treatment.* Lexington, MA: Lexington Books.

O'Connell, M. A., Leberg, E., & Donaldson, C. R. (1990). *Working with sex offenders: Guidelines for therapist selection.* Newbury Park, CA: Sage.

Olson, P. E. (1990). The sexual abuse of boys: A study of the long-term psychological effects. In M. Hunter (Ed.), *The sexually abused male: Volume 1. Prevalence, impact, and treatment* (pp. 137-152). Lexington, MA: Lexington Books.

Otani, A. (1993, September). *Psychotherapeutic approaches to male trauma survivors: Clinical models and techniques.* Workshop presented at the Fifth Annual National Conference on Male Survivors, Bethesda, MD.

Paul, G. L. (1969a). Outcome of systematic desensitization I: Background, procedures, and uncontrolled reports of individual treatment. In C. M. Franks (Ed.), *Behavior therapy: Appraisal and status* (pp. 63-104). New York: McGraw-Hill.

Paul, G. L. (1969b). Outcome of systematic desensitization II: Controlled investigations of individual treatment, technique variations, and current status. In C. M. Franks (Ed.), *Behavior therapy: Appraisal and status* (pp. 105-159). New York: McGraw-Hill.

Perry, A. P. (1993). *The disclosure experience of the male victim of sexual abuse: Findings from a phenomenological study.* Paper presented at the Fifth Annual National Conference on Male Survivors, Bethesda, MD.

Petrovich, M., & Templer, D. (1984). Heterosexual molestation of children who later become rapists. *Psychological Reports, 54,* 810.

Pierce, L. H., & Pierce, R. L. (1985). The sexually abused child: A comparison of male and female victims. *Child Abuse & Neglect, 9,* 191-199.

Pollock, V. E., Schneider, L. S., Gabrielli, W. F., & Goodwin, D. W. (1987). Sex of parent and offspring in the transmission of alcoholism: A meta-analysis. *Journal of Nervous and Mental Disease, 175,* 668-673.

Porter, E. (1986). *Treating the young male victims of sexual assault: Issues and intervention strategies.* Syracuse, NY: Safer Society Press.

Prentky, P. (1984, August). *Childhood physical and sexual abuse in the lives of sexually aggressive offenders.* Paper presented at the Second National Conference for Family Violence Researchers, Durham, NH.

Putnam, F. W. (1989). *Diagnosis and treatment of multiple personality disorder.* New York: Guilford.

Ramsey-Klawsnik, H. (1990, November). *Sexually abused boys: Indicators, abusers and impact of trauma.* Paper presented at the Third National Conference on the Male Survivor, Tucson, AZ.

Reber, A. S. (1985). *Dictionary of psychology.* New York: Viking Penguin.

Rogers, C. M., & Terry, T. (1984). Clinical interventions with boy victims of sexual abuse. In I. Stewart & J. Greer (Eds.), *Victims of sexual aggression* (pp. 91-104). New York: Van Nostrand Reinhold.

Ross, C. A. (1989). *Multiple personality disorder: Diagnosis, clinical features, and treatment.* New York: John Wiley.

Sacks, R. (Speaker). (1988, October). *Hypnotic techniques for multiple personality disorder.* Workshop conducted at the Fifth International Conference on Multiple Personality / Dissociated States, Chicago.

Sacks, R. (Speaker). (1990, June). Hypnotic techniques in the treatment of MPD. Workshop conducted at the Second Annual Eastern Regional Conference on Multiple Personality and Dissociation, Alexandria, VA (Cassette Recording No. 37-569-90 a-b). Alexandria, VA: Audio Transcripts.

Salter, A. C. (1988). *Treating child sex offenders and victims: A practical guide.* Newbury Park, CA: Sage.

Sarrel, P. M., & Masters, W. H. (1982). Sexual molestation of men by women. *Archives of Sexual Behavior, 11,* 117-131.

Schreiber, F. R. (1973). *Sybil.* Chicago: Regnery.

Schwartz, M. (1992). Sexual compulsivity as post traumatic stress disorder: Treatment perspectives. *Psychiatric Annals, 22,* 6.

Sebold, J. (1987). Indicators of child sexual abuse in males. *Social Casework: The Journal of Contemporary Social Work, 68,* 75-80.

Selye, A. (1956). *The stress of life.* New York: McGraw-Hill.

Sepler, F. (1990). Victim advocacy and young male victims of sexual abuse: An evolutionary model. In M. Hunter (Ed.), *The sexually abused male: Volume 1. Prevalence, impact, and treatment* (pp. 73-85). Lexington, MA: Lexington Books.

Sgroi, S. M. (1975). Child sexual molestation: The last frontier in child abuse. *Children Today, 44,* 18-28.

Sgroi, S. (1989). Stages of recovery for adult survivors of child sexual abuse. In S. Sgroi (Ed.), *Vulnerable populations* (Vol. 2, pp. 111-130). Lexington, MA: D. C. Heath.

Showers, J., Farber, E. D., Joseph, J. A., Oshins, L., & Johnson, C. F. (1983). The sexual victimization of boys: A three-year survey. *Health Values, 7,* 15-18.

Shukitt, M., Goodwin, D. W., & Winoker, G. (1972). A study of alcoholism in half-siblings. *American Journal of Psychiatry, 128,* 1132-1136.

Spencer, J. J., & Dunklee, P. (1986). Sexual abuse of boys. *Pediatrics, 78,* 133-137.

Spiegel, D. (Speaker). (1987, October). *Use of hypnosis with dissociative disorders.* Workshop conducted at the Fourth International Conference on Multiple Personality / Dissociated States, Chicago (Cassette Recording No. Ve-383-87). Alexandria, VA: Audio Transcripts.

Spotnitz, H., & Meadow, P. W. (1976). *Treatment of the narcissitic neuroses.* New York: Manhattan Center for Advanced Psychoanalytic Studies.

Steele, B. (1989). A model for abreaction with multiple personality and other dissociative disorders. *Dissociation, 2*(3), 151-159.

Steele, B., & Alexander, H. (1981). Long-term effects of sexual abuse in childhood. In P. B. Mrazek & C. H. Kempe (Eds.), *Sexually abused children and their families* (pp. 223-234). Oxford, UK: Pergamon.

Steele, K., & Colrain, J. (1990). Abreactive work with sexual abuse survivors: Concepts and techniques. In M. Hunter (Ed.), *The sexually abused male: Volume 2. Application of treatment strategies* (pp. 1-56). Lexington, MA: Lexington Books.

Stein, J. A., Golding, J. M., Siegel, J. M., Burnam, M. A., & Sorenson, S. B. (1988). Long-term psychological sequelae of child sexual abuse: The Los Angeles Epidemiologic Catchment Area Study. In G. E. Wyatt & G. J. Powell (Eds.), *Lasting effects of child sexual abuse* (pp. 135-154). Newbury Park, CA: Sage.

Steinberg, M. (1991). Detection of dissociative disorders in psychiatric patients by a screening instrument and a structured diagnostic interview. *American Journal of Psychiatry, 148,* 1050-1054.

Stewart, B. D., Hughes, C., Frank, E., Anderson, B., Kendall, K., & West, D. (1987). *Journal of Nervous and Mental Disorders, 175*(2), 90-94.

Stoller, R. (1975). *Perversion: The erotic form of hatred.* New Haven, CT: Yale University Press.

Stroebel, C. G. (1978). *Biofeedback procedures.* New York: Grune & Stratton.

Struve, J. (1990). Dancing with the patriarchy: The politics of sexual abuse. In M. Hunter (Ed.), *The sexually abused male: Volume 1. Prevalence, impact, and treatment* (pp. 3-46). Lexington, MA: Lexington Books.

Suedfeld, P. (1990). *Psychology torture.* New York: Hemisphere.

Summit, R. (1983). The child sexual abuse accommodation syndrome. *Child Abuse & Neglect, 7,* 177-193.

Summit, R. (1993, September). *Take it like a man.* Keynote address presented at the Fifth Annual National Conference on Male Survivors, Bethesda, MD.

Swift, C. (1979). Sexual victimization of children: An urban mental health survey. In L. Schultz (Ed.), *The sexual victimology of youth* (pp. 18-24). Springfield, IL: Charles C Thomas.

Talmadge, L. D., & Wallace, S. C. (1991). Reclaiming sexuality in female incest survivors. *Journal of Sex and Marital Therapy, 17*(3), 163-181.

Thomas, T. (1989). *Men surviving incest.* Walnut Creek, CA: Launch Press.

Timms, R. J. (1992, September). *Treatment of self-destructive behavior in survivors.* Workshop presented at the Fourth International Conference on Male Survivors, Portland, OR.

Trivelpiece, J. W. (1990). Adjusting the frame: Cinematic treatment of sexual abuse and rape of men and boys. In M. Hunter (Ed.), *The sexually abused male: Volume 1. Prevalence, impact, and treatment* (pp. 47-72). Lexington, MA: Lexington Books.

Urquiza, A. J. (1993, August). Adult male survivors of child sexual abuse: Issues in intimacy. In L. A. Morris (Chair), *Wounded warriors: Male survivors of childhood sexual abuse.* Symposium conducted at the 101st Annual Convention of the American Psychological Association, Toronto, Ontario, Canada.

Urquiza, A. J., & Capra, M. (1990). The impact of sexual abuse: Initial and long-term effects. In M. Hunter (Ed.), *The sexually abused male: Volume 1. Prevalence, impact, and treatment* (pp. 105-136). Lexington, MA: Lexington Books.

Urquiza, A. J., & Crowley, C. (1986, May). *Sex differences in the long-term adjustment of child sexual abuse victims.* Paper presented at the Third National Conference on the Sexual Victimization of Children, New Orleans, LA.

van der Har, O., Brown, P., & van der Kolk, B. A. (1989). Pierre Janet's treatment of post-traumatic stress. *Journal of Traumatic Stress, 2,* 379-395.

van der Kolk, B. A. (1988). The biological response to psychic trauma. In F. M. Ochberg (Ed.), *Post-traumatic therapy and victims of violence* (pp. 25-39). New York: Brunner/Mazel.

van der Kolk, B. (1989). The compulsion to repeat the trauma: Reenactment, revictimization, and masochism. *Psychiatric Clinics of North America, 12,* 389-411.

van der Kolk, B. (1993). *Desnos and DSM-IV.* Paper presented at the Conference of International Society of Traumatic Stress Studies, San Antonio, TX.

Vander Mey, B. J. (1988). The sexual victimization of male children: A review of previous research. *Child Abuse & Neglect, 12,* 61-72.

Watkins, H. (1993). Ego-states therapy; An overview. *American Journal of Clinical Hypnosis*, *40*(4), 389-413.

Watkins, N. G. (1978). *The therapeutic self*. New York: Harold Science Press.

Watkins, N. G. (1989). The affect bridge: A hypnoanalytic technique. *International Journal of Clinical and Experimental Hypnosis, 36*, 21-27.

Westerlund, E. (1992). *Women's sexuality after childhood incest*. New York: W. W. Norton.

Winoker, G., Cadoret, F., Dorzab, J., & Baker, M. (1971). Depressive disease: A genetic study. *Archives of General Psychiatry, 24*, 135-144.

Wolpe, J. (1958). *Psychotherapy by reciprocal inhibition*. Stanford, CA: Stanford University Press.

Wolpe, J., & Lazarus, A. A. (1966). *Behavior therapy techniques*. New York: Pergamon.

Woods, S. C., & Dean, K. S. (1984). *Final report: Sexual abuse of males research project* (NCCAN Report No. 90-CA-812). Washington, DC: National Center on Child Abuse and Neglect.

Yolenson, S., & Samenow, J. (1977). *The criminal personality: Volume 2*. New York: Jason Aronson.

Zaphiris, A. (1986). The sexually abused boy. *Preventing Sexual Abuse, 1*, 1-4.

Zilbergeld, B. (1992). *The new male sexuality*. New York: Bantam Books.

Index

Abandonment, 101
    avoiding, 84
    fear of, 35, 90
    partner's feelings of, 38
    threats of, 7
Abel, G., 22, 23, 26, 27, 28, 30, 52, 53
Abreaction, 52
    attempting too early, 91-92
    building alliance for, 90
    mastery and, 17
    readiness, 95
    spontaneous, 85
    with ego states, 46-49
Abstinence, 51, 60
Abuse:
    adult compulsive sexual behavior
        and, 56-79
    age of, 23, 87-88
    assessing elements of, 23-25
    attribution of responsibility for, 13
    cyclical, 15, 157-158, 172
    disclosure of, 103, 104, 167-169
    frequency of, 23
    natural responses to, 5-6
    negative effects of, 156
    partner's experiences of, 141
    reenacting, 11, 60, 63, 131-132
    repetitions of, 9-13
    source of, 23-24, 25

    See also Sexual abuse
Abusers:
    abused as children, 15, 157-158, 172
    access to children, 125
    adolescence and, 53
    assigning responsibility to, 118
    bond with, 13
    changing moods of, 4
    confrontations with, 50, 129, 173
    death of, 129
    dependency on, 3, 4
    expressing emotions toward, 50
    female, 155, 168 169
    forgiveness of, 122-123
    health care professionals as, 25
    identification with, 16
    identifying in assessment, 23-24
    internalizing, 15
    introjecting voices of, 15-16
    siblings as, 23
Abuse survivors:
    career choices of, 85
    dysfunctional assumptions and, 27
    identity of, 111, 146, 147
    internal critic, 94
    male, 24, 37, 154-173
    treating sexual dysfunction in, 21-41
    treating very difficult, 83-97
    understanding concept of, 119

restructuring, 17, 46
Bender, L., 154
Bergman, A., 87, 89, 90
Berliner, L., 165
Bestiality, 73-74
Betrayal, 101
Beutler, L. E., 166
Binge eating, 10, 101, 110, 130
Bisexual clients, 37, 158
Blau, A., 154
Body image, 28, 32
Bolton, F., 156
Bondage/discipline, 74
Borderline personality disorder, 3, 84, 85,
    90, 94, 116, 131
Borderline triad, 94
Boredom, relief from, 44
Boundary issues:
    sexual dysfunction and, 40
    sexuality and, 124
    substance abusers and, 108, 131
    treatment and, 90, 92
    voyeurism and, 71
Bowlby, J., 5
Brain, changes in, 11
Braun, B., 8, 43, 47
Briere, J., 21, 22, 101, 103, 105, 118
Brown, J., 21-41
Brown, P., 107
Browne, A., 23, 25, 27, 156
Burgess, A. W., 26-27, 159
Button, B., 136-153

Cadoret, F., 100
Capra, M., 156
Caregivers, support from, 2
Caretaker role, 142
Caring, capacity for, 2
Carnes, Patrick, 56, 59, 61-62
Catecholamine depletion, 12
Catharsis, 17, 114
    abreaction and, 47
    hypnosis and, 50
Central nervous system, 12, 44
Character defects, 115, 119
Character disorders, 87-89
Chemical dependency. *See* Substance
    abuse

Child development, 7
Childhood:
    mourning lost, 170-171
    nondistorted memory of, 13
Child rearing, 5-6, 7
Children:
    angry, 5
    becoming abusers, 15, 157-158, 172
    growing up to be batterers, 10, 15
    natural defenses of, 2
    needs of, 6-7
    protecting next generation, 124-125
    scapegoated, 6
    sexual response in, 27
    society's attitude toward, 6
    See also Abuse survivors
Cichon, J., 22, 23, 26, 27, 28, 30
Classical conditioning, 27
Clonidine, 12
Cognitive reframing, 110
Cognitive restructuring, 17, 31-32, 114,
    166
Cognitive therapy, 86
Cognitive verbal articulation, 8
Coleman, E., 59
Colrain, J., 47, 114
Communication skills, 51, 143-144
Community education, 125
Compassion:
    capacity for, 2
    learning, 15
Compulsions, 2
    alleviating, 10
    defined, 59
Compulsive personality, 84
Compulsive sexuality. *See* Sexual
    compulsivity
Conditioned responses, 27
Conformity, 7
Consciousness:
    continuity of, 8
    levels of, 57-58
    reconstructing trauma experience
    and, 114
    state-dependent learning and, 66
Control:
    abreaction and, 48
    addiction and, 60

About the Editor

Mic Hunter is a Licensed Psychologist, Licensed Marriage & Family Therapist, and Certified Chemical Dependency Counselor—Reciprocal, and a Nationally Certified Alcohol and Drug Counselor. His educational background includes a bachelor's degree in psychology (Macalester College), a Master of Arts degree in human development (Saint Mary's College, Winona), and a Master of Science degree in education/psychological services (University of Wisconsin—Superior). He has completed the Alcohol/Drug Counseling Education Program (University of Minnesota), the Two-Year Intensive Post-Graduate Program (the Gestalt Institute of the Twin Cities), and the Chemical Dependency and Family Intimacy Training Project (University of Minnesota). He is currently studying for a doctoral degree in the Clinical Psychology Program (Minnesota School of Professional Psychology). He completed his class work in 1994.

Prior to opening his practice in St. Paul, Minnesota, he was employed in several chemical dependency treatment programs and mental health centers in Minnesota. He speaks throughout the country to both professional audiences and the general public. He has presented at the annual meetings of the American Association of Sex Educators, Counselors & Therapists; the Society for the Scientific Study of Sex; and the American Orthopsychiatric Association. He has presented at all five national conferences on male sexual abuse survivors and has given a keynote address at the conference in Tucson. He has been interviewed by the print and broadcast media more than 100 times. He serves on the editorial board of the *Journal of Child Sexual Abuse, Journal of Men's Studies,* and *Moving Forward.*

In addition to articles and chapters, Mr. Hunter is the author of *Abused Boys: The Neglected Victims of Sexual Abuse, The First Step for People in Relationships With Sex Addicts, Joyous Sexuality: Healing From the Effects of Family Sexual Dysfunction, The Twelve Steps & Shame,* and *Recovering From Shame Through the Twelve Steps.* He is the contributing editor of *The Sexually Abused Male: Volume 1. Prevalence, Impact and Treatment* and *The Sexually Abused Male: Volume 2. Application of Treatment Strategies,* as well as the editor of *Child Survivors and Perpetrators of Sexual Abuse: Treatment Innovations* (Sage, 1995). His most recent projects are coauthoring *The Use of Touch in Psychotherapy* with Peter Dimock and Jim Struve, which will be submitted for publication in early 1995, and seeking a publisher for his photographic documentary focusing on the disappearance of the traditional male barbershop, which is titled *The Barbershop: An American Classic.*

About the Contributors

Jeff Brown, MS, LP, is a Licensed Psychologist in private practice in St. Paul, Minnesota, specializing in the areas of sexuality, intimacy, and self-esteem. In addition to his practice, he serves as a consultant to the Pride Institute, an inpatient chemical dependency treatment program for gay men and lesbian women, as well as Project Solo. He is the author of "Shame, Sexuality and Intimacy" in the *Journal of Chemical Dependency* and "The Treatment of Male Victims With Mixed-Gender, Short-Term Group Psychotherapy" in *The Sexually Abused Male: Application of Treatment Strategies*. In the past 9 years, he has presented many workshops to the public and other professionals.

Betty Button is a healing survivor of childhood sexual abuse. As director for the Texas Senate Committee on Health and Human Services for 6 years, she helped bring legislative attention to family violence and disability rights issues. She was appointed by the Lieutenant Governor as Staff Advisor to the Human Resources Committee of the Southern Legislative Conference and received a gubernatorial appointment to the Texas Home Health Services Advisory Council. A former community college and university instructor and child welfare caseworker, she has a BA in English, French, and psychology from East Texas State University and holds a Texas teaching certification at the secondary level. She earned an MA in French with emphasis in Secondary and Higher Education from East Texas State, where she also pursued graduate studies in psychology. She did postgraduate work at the University of

Texas at Austin in French linguistics. Currently, Ms. Button is the Director of Programs for the Association for Retarded Citizens—Austin and serves on the Board of Directors of the Mental Health Association in Texas. Ms. Button and her husband, Allen Dietz, conduct workshops for therapists and for adult survivors of childhood sexual abuse and their partners on relationships and other survivor issues. They write a regular column on adult survivor relationship issues for a professional journal, *Treating Abuse Today*.

Allen Dietz is a Licensed Master Social Worker, with orders of recognition as an Advanced Clinical Practitioner. He was staff counselor for the Austin Police Department and the Austin Emergency Medical Services for 6 years, where he designed and implemented a program to provide counseling to police officers, paramedics, and civilian employees, and helped establish and train members of a civilian crisis intervention team and a police hostage negotiation team. He has been involved in a variety of community and legislative activities concerning sexual assault and family violence and has done extensive clinical work with children with autism and children with severe emotional disturbances. He has a BA in psychology from the State University of New York at Stony Brook and did extensive graduate work in clinical psychology at the University of Texas at Austin. Mr. Dietz and his wife, Betty Button, conduct workshops for therapists and for adult survivors of childhood sexual abuse and their partners on relationships and other survivor issues. They write a regular column on adult survivor relationship issues for a professional journal, *Treating Abuse Today*.

Lori D. Galperin, LCSW, is Clinical Co-Director of the Sexual Trauma Program at Two Rivers Hospital in Kansas City, Missouri, and at River Oaks Hospital in New Orleans, Louisiana. She received her degree in clinical social work from Tulane University. Previously, she was on staff at the Baylor College of Medicine, Department of Psychiatry in Houston, Texas. Ms. Galperin has taught as faculty at Tulane Graduate School of Social Work and the University of New Orleans Psychology Department and lectured at Tulane Medical School.

William H. Masters, MD, is Co-Chair of the Board of Masters and Johnson Institute. He began his study of reproductive biology at the University of Rochester School of Medicine, where he received his MD. Early in his career, Dr. Masters resolved to focus on the study of human sexual activity but was advised by an older colleague to first establish himself in a different field, gain the support of a respected university, and acquire a strong scientific reputation before entering the controversial area of human sexuality. Dr. Masters followed this advice by conducting extensive research on reproductive biology, focusing on hormone replacement, sexual function and aging, and solutions to the problems of infertility. In 1954, Dr. Masters began his preliminary studies into human sexuality. Three years later, he was joined by Virginia Johnson, who provided the needed female perspective, in observing and analyzing the physiology of sexual response. Together they wrote the landmark texts *Human Sexual Response* and *Human Sexual Inadequacy*. Although written in medical terminology, both books became popular bestsellers, emphasizing the paucity of information on sexuality available to the general public at that time. Their subsequent books include *The Pleasure Bond*, *Homosexuality in Perspective*, *Ethical Issues in Sex Therapy and Research*, Volumes I and II, *On Sex and Human Loving*, and *CRISIS: Heterosexual Behavior in the Age of AIDS*. Dr. Masters's scientific publications number more than 150. He is a Professor Emeritus of Clinical Obstetrics and Gynecology, as well as a Lecturer in Human Sexuality in Psychiatry on the faculty of Washington University School of Medicine in St. Louis, Missouri.

Robert S. Mayer, PhD, is an Associate Professor at Kean College of New Jersey and a practicing psychotherapist in New York City. He earned his doctoral degree from Rutgers University and has a postdoctorate degree in psychoanalysis from the American Institute for Psychoanalysis and Psychotherapy, where he became a professor, training analyst, and clinical supervisor. He has published numerous books and articles, including *Through Divided Minds: Probing the Mysteries of Multiple Personalities* and *Satan's Children: Case Studies in Multiple Personality*.

Larry A. Morris, PhD, is a clinical psychologist with a private practice in Tucson, Arizona. He has specialized in the evaluation and treatment of victims of childhood sexual abuse and sex offenders for two decades. He has served as a consultant to or evaluation project director of several federally funded social action programs designed to increase the information base and skills of prospective parents, to expand self-help programs for abusive parents, and to foster the cognitive and emotional growth of young children through family education programs. He has conducted training seminars for child protective services staff and has served as an expert witness in cases involving physical and sexual child abuse. Dr. Morris coauthored *Males at Risk: The Other Side of Child Sexual Abuse* (Sage, 1989) and is currently completing a book on the development of male sexuality to be published by Sage in 1995 or 1996. In 1990, he served as the Chair of the Third National Male Survivor Conference, "New Perspectives for a New Decade," and continues to be an important member of the Conference's Steering Committee. Active in the American Psychological Association, he organized the symposium "Wounded Warriors: Male Survivors of Childhood Sexual Abuse" at the Association's 1993 Convention and the symposium "Male Survivors of Child Sexual Abuse: Toward a Better Understanding" at the 1994 Convention. He spends as much of his time as possible hiking the Grand Canyon.

Mark F. Schwartz, ScD, is Clinical Director of the Sexual Trauma Program at Two Rivers Hospital in Kansas City, Missouri, and at River Oaks Hospital in New Orleans, Louisiana. He was previously a member of the staff of the Masters and Johnson Institute, where he was Director of Psychosocial Research, educational workshops, and the sexual abuse program. Considered one of the nation's prominent sex therapists, he continues to serve as a consultant to the Institute.

Caryl Trotter, MA, LPCC, is the founder and president of Sexual Assault Treatment Services, Inc., a private counseling practice specializing in the treatment of adult survivors of childhood sexual trauma. She is the cofounder and current president of the New Mexico chapter of the American Professional Society on the Abuse of Children (APSAC). She provides training for local and national companies, including the Cenaps Corporation, whose president is Terence T. Gorski, best known for his work in recovery and relapse prevention with the chemically dependent. As a sexual trauma treatment specialist since 1980, Ms. Trotter has vast knowledge of the unique needs of the adult survivor of trauma. Combined with her user-friendly techniques, compassionate approach, and much-needed humor, she is a widely sought-after speaker. She is the author of *Double Bind: A Guide to Recovery and Relapse Prevention for the Chemically Dependent Sexual Abuse Survivor* and an assessment packet for survivors of sexual trauma.